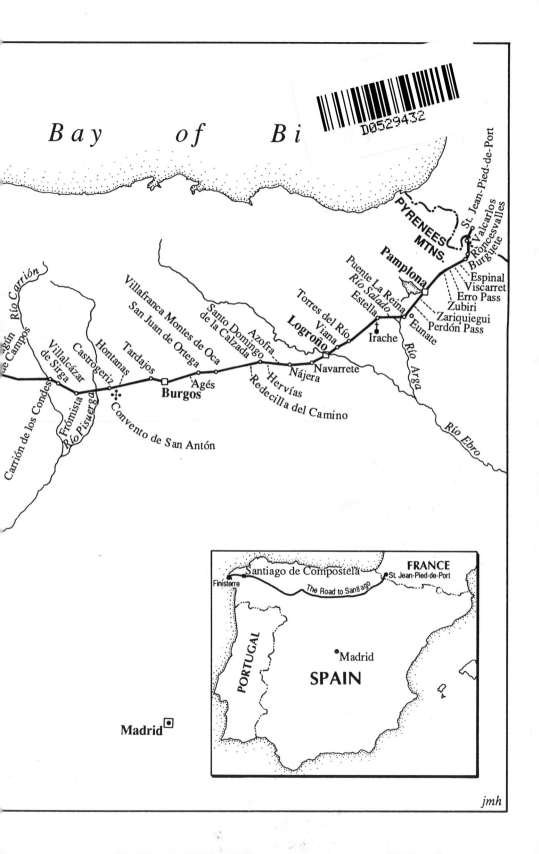

Road of Stars to Santiago

For Conrad,
  our accidental
      pilgrim —

    from
    Steven,
      &
    Nina

Road of Stars
to Santiago

EDWARD F. STANTON

THE UNIVERSITY PRESS OF KENTUCKY

Publication of this book was made possible by a grant from The Program for Cultural Cooperation between Spain's Ministry of Culture and the United States Universities.

Library of Congress Cataloging–in–Publication Data

Stanton, Edward F.

Road of stars to Santiago / Edward F. Stanton.

p.   cm.

ISBN 0–8131–1871–9 (alk. paper)

1. Spain, Northern—Description and travel. 2. Christian pilgrims and pilgrimages—Spain—Santiago de Compostela. 3. Stanton, Edward F.—Journeys—Spain, Northern. 4. Santiago de Compostela (Spain)—Description and travel. I. Title.
DP285.S73   1994
946'.11—dc20   93–39521

To the memory of
FREDERICK C.H. GARCIA

Contents

Illustrations

Introduction

> When a man's passions bewilder him, he should
> put on black clothes and travel to a place where
> he is not known.
>
> —*Talmud*

I walked west on the road traveled by men and women for a thousand years, following a path of stars to the city of Santiago de Compostela where the apostle James is said to be buried, and beyond to the end of the world.

If you ask why I walked the Road, the Camino de Santiago, there is no simple answer. Try as I do, I cannot remember how the idea was born in my head. Like many of our most important decisions, this one was slow and deep in its working: all I know is that one day I had to walk to Compostela. My life was a shambles, I felt exhausted by work, my marriage was foundering. When finally I had the time to make the journey, I prepared my backpack, found a walking staff, flew to Spain and took to the road. I knew what I was fleeing from, not what I was seeking. The Camino would teach me that and many other things.

In the Middle Ages when thousands teemed along the Road to Santiago, most pilgrims had a clear motivation—repentance, a vow, remission of sins that was the prize for reaching Compostela. But even then pilgrimage was often an excuse to travel, to search for adventure and the unknown. The trip itself was the thing. After all Chaucer never did have his pilgrims reach the tomb of St. Thomas à Becket in *The Canterbury Tales*. James Michener, who considers the apostle his patron saint, calls the route to Santiago the best in Spain and one of the finest anywhere. And Hemingway, who truly loved the cathedral of Compostela more than any building in the world, said that a serious book does not have to be a solemn one. So this is a book about travel too.

Santiago may be the last holy city in the West. Today Jerusalem is more a battleground than a shrine. Rome was an empire before it became Peter's house, forever tainted by power. Later it would be the whore of Babylon for Protestants, and for those who love her today she is still a whore, at best a mistress. Unlike Rome, Compostela was sacred from the start. It was founded on a site in the northwest of the Iberian peninsula about sixty miles from the sea, where St. James' body was supposedly transported after he was beheaded by Herod Agrippa in Judea. There it lay for a sleep of eight centuries when it is said that a hermit, guided by the light of stars, discovered the apostle's tomb. The city of Sant' Yago—St. Jacob or James in Spanish—was founded on the spot of the miracle; it would come to rival Rome and Jerusalem as one of the three great goals for Christian pilgrims in the Middle Ages. As in other holy cities the things of Caesar and God were not always separated. The story of the struggle to control Compostela reads like a chapter out of Machiavelli: bribes, intrigues, sackings, murders, uprisings, last-minute escapes over burning rooftops by princes of the church disguised as pilgrims or beggars. Yet the city's small size and remoteness in a wet, green corner of Europe kept her more intact than either Jerusalem or Rome.

Since the hermit saw those stars over a field around the year 814, uncountable millions have crossed land and sea, by foot, on horseback, in ships, later in cars, buses and airplanes to the apostle's tomb in Compostela. Along the Camino de Santiago have walked kings, queens, cripples, lepers, popes, cardinals, peasants, artisans, prostitutes, gypsies, monks, nuns, artists, builders, saints, thieves—pilgrims all. Most were Catholics but men and women of all faiths have made the journey from many parts of the world. Some think the Way goes back beyond Christianity to the Celts and prehistoric peoples; they believe the Church merely adapted a sacred route that had existed since the late Stone Age. Such diversity of opinion reveals that the Road to Santiago—like the Eleusinian mysteries in the ancient world, the hajj to Mecca and the march to the purifying waters of the Ganges—has surpassed the limits of a single creed, church or people to form one of the great religious traditions on earth.

St. James was beheaded in 44 A.D. In the forty-fourth year of my life I walked to Compostela. By chance, by luck, perhaps by another miracle of Santiago, I made the pilgrimage at the time of its modern rebirth. Between the Jubilees or "Great Pardons" of 1982 and 1993 the number of pilgrims who entered Galicia on foot, bicycle or horseback grew steadily; it now averages more than five thousand in a normal year. I'm not referring to the hundreds of thousands who travel annually to the apostle's tomb by car, rail, sea or air—a form of modern pilgrimage hard to distinguish from tourism: in 1993, the most recent Holy Year, more than three million people visited the apostle's tomb in Compostela. I mean the men, women and their children who walk the Camino de Santiago by following the ancient route, using only their feet as pilgrims did a thousand years ago. Most are young, some old; many are Catholics or Christians; some have different gods, others none. What are the reasons for the revival of this ancient custom at the end of the twentieth century?

For whatever causes, "Friends of the Camino de Santiago" began to spring up in Spain and abroad during the mid-1980s and early 1990s. The first international conferences on the Road have been celebrated with participation by Jacobean societies from Spain, Portugal, France, Italy, Belgium, Holland, Germany and England. An American association was formed in 1989, the same year the pope met some thirty thousand young people in Compostela. Meanwhile local, provincial and regional governments have moved to protect the Road from further encroachment by agriculture, industry and speculation, and to provide simple, free lodging for pilgrims who do not want or cannot afford to stay in hotels. When Spain was recently voted a member of the European Union, many saw the Camino becoming the spiritual axis of the Old World as it was in the days of its glory. Now the Council of Europe has named the Road the continent's "premier cultural route," and UNESCO has baptized it grandiloquently "the universal heritage of mankind." Eight, nine, ten centuries ago the Way brought together masses of people from many countries; can it do the same today? Can we imagine a rebirth of pilgrimage at the end of our century, tens of thousands following the footsteps of their ancestors toward the ancient tomb and the setting sun, another great hour of the Camino de Santiago come round at last?

Whatever we imagine or believe, there is something—on the road beneath the star-filled skies, in the shrine of Compostela or beyond by the sea—a memory, a presence, an intimation—that has called men and women for as long as we can remember and will continue to call after we have passed into the new millennium. This is the story of one man's journey on the Road to Santiago and beyond.

PART
ONE

1   Day of St. James

Allons, the road is before us!
—Whitman

"Saint Jean-Pied-de-Port." The conductor's voice wakes me from my sweaty, wrinkled sleep. I hitch up my backpack and walk off the old train.

"Bon voyage" says the conductor.

I mumble "Thank you, gracias, I mean merci."

"Bon voyage" I think to myself looking bleary-eyed at the station and the village; the French expression always makes me think of ocean cruises. So here I am ready to embark from St. Jean-Pied-de-Port, St. John-at-the-Foot-of-the-Port, imagining the smell of docks and salt-spray and pipe-smoking, tatooed sailors in a Mediterranean harbor. But there's nothing Mediterranean about the village on this clear, bracing day and the port is a mountain pass over the Pyrenees to Spain.

Like all French or Spanish towns at the hour of the midday meal, St. Jean looks as if it has been evacuated by war. It's a village of warm brown stone and white houses with red roofs and shutters in the Basque style. On the way through town toward the mountains, I pass the old church, push open the door and enter the cool darkness. There's nobody inside. I walk to the altar, kneel, pray for my family and a safe trip to Compostela.

My skin has goosebumps from the cool. I rise and walk out into the sun thinking what a paltry, private ceremony this has been, remembering the pilgrims in the Middle Ages who had a special Mass celebrated before their departure, who received a public blessing from the parish priest—even for their packs and staff! But this is not my parish, if I have one anywhere; I'm alone with an unhallowed pack and staff.

The sun feels good on my bare arms. I go under the arch of Notre Dame to the stone bridge over the River Nive. In the fast-running water a few trout work their fins to hold against the current, making shadows on the pebbly bottom. Everything seems to stand out in the light after the darkness of the church and my fitful sleep on the train: trout, ripples in the water, pebbles, houses with wooden balconies over the river. I leave the village by the old walls, walking through the Porte d'Espagne.

The road lies before me: I feel a rush of joy. For at least three years I've dreamed and imagined this moment and it's hard to believe I'm actually here on the open road, free. My pack feels lighter, with every third step the rubber tip of my staff pushes off the ground, my boots seem to spring up the gradual incline. It's a luminous day with a high blue sky, billowy clouds over the crestline above me.

Now that I'm finally on the Camino, I think of the hours spent to get here. Only this morning on TWA flight 903 from New York to Madrid, the pilot announced we were passing over Santiago de Compostela, just as dawn was breaking. I looked down at the city nestled in the fog and in the hills, its many windows reflecting the light of the new sun. Beyond to the west and south the Galician coast zigzagged all the way to Portugal, indented by the fjord-like arms of the rías. I was amazed that of all the places we could have entered the continent, it was over Santiago; of all the hours, at daybreak. Never had this happened to me in five trips by air from America to Spain. I took it as a sign and remembered that the new day was St. James', July 25, a national holiday in Spain, the most important of the year in Compostela. The king and queen were probably down there with the Archbishop of Santiago and throngs of pilgrims to witness the annual offering. To celebrate my happiness I imagined myself parachuting out of the window and becoming the first airborne pilgrim in history. With the crazy joy, I felt fear too. Looking ahead toward the sun in the east I saw the landscape fade into the white horizon: I would have to cross that expanse on foot, alone. How small, what a mote of dust I would be in that vast quilt of greens.

Walking now I don't feel the fear, surrounded by another green landscape on a human scale this time: road, trees, fields, orchards, a few country houses, farms, stables. I must be one of the few pilgrims ever to see his destination and his point of departure on the same day. How different from the medieval men and women who left home and found the shortest way to Santiago, where they would not arrive for days, weeks, months. I've had to travel more than three thousand miles just to reach this road and I enjoyed a foretaste of my goal in that vision from the sky. Not long afterwards we were approaching Madrid for landing; in little more than half an hour the plane had covered about the same distance it might take me a month or more to travel by foot. The rest was going through customs at the airport, changing planes, flying to Pamplona, snatching a meal before getting on the train to Irún and Bayonne, falling asleep on the local from there to St. Jean-Pied-de-Port. It's as if I've lived in two eras in less than half a day, each with its own sort of time: the twentieth century with its schedules, trains and jets, the Middle Ages with a village named after a saint, a landscape that has hardly changed in centuries, my two feet walking the Road as men and women have walked forever.

Most of all I notice the difference in sounds. After the roar of airplanes and the noise of cities, I hear birds singing in the trees, the crunch of gravel under my boots. Smells too: new-mown hay, a whiff of cow manure. Now I hear the chest-deep bark of a German shepherd. I see him running back and forth behind the fence of a country house on the right. Somebody is leaning over the low gate, beckoning to me. I walk up a few stone steps and see a man of about fifty-five with a ruddy face, a network of red capillaries on his nose and cheeks.

"Bonjour" he says with a smile.

"Bonjour."

"Pèlerin?" I don't understand until he adds "Saint Jacques? A Saint Jacques de Compostelle?"

"Ah, oui, oui." It's hard to believe someone has recognized me as a pilgrim so soon, only a few hundred yards from St. Jean-Pied-de-Port, a full five hundred miles from Compostela.

The man calls his wife, who is picking apples in the orchard behind him. She has rosy cheeks too and a white handkerchief over her head.

Carrying a wicker basket full of green apples, she comes smiling to the gate and offers them to me, beads of perspiration on her forehead: "Pour le chemin."

My first reaction—as a city-dweller—is to say no. But I remember that generosity toward pilgrims is an ancient custom, once a legal and religious obligation. By giving food, hearth and lodging, the offerer hoped to participate in the blessings reaped by the traveler at the end of his journey. I don't know what blessings I'll reap but it's my duty to accept what they proffer.

"Merci." I take several apples, unhitching my pack and putting them in one of the outside compartments.

"Plus" they insist, "plus" until the compartment is stretched full.

"Encore" they say. I don't know how to say "Enough" in French so I fill both front pockets of my pants until my thighs are bulging like a fullback's.

"Merci, merci" I repeat feeling stupid, angry at myself for not knowing more French, smiling and waving goodbye before they can offer more apples.

On the road again, I realize that I have nothing to eat except this new fruit. There are no stores or shelters between here and the monastery of Roncevaux, the Spanish Roncesvalles, and it's twenty miles of mostly uphill climbing. It must be a good omen that these first inhabitants along the Camino have given without being asked.

After a steep incline I come to a fork in the road dominated by an enormous, ancient chestnut tree. Never have I seen such a tree: gnarled and gashed, two lengths of my walking staff in diameter—a good eight feet. I've driven a car through an arch cut in a giant redwood, far older and more majestic than this tree but less human, less venerable with the knots of time. I take the pilgrim's map from my waist-belt and see the spot marked "Castaño de S. Luis," the Chestnut Tree of St. Louis. I can't help remembering the city on the Mississippi, Charles Lindbergh and his solo flight—that was a kind of pilgrimage too, another American in Europe. I remember also that the giant redwoods of California are not named after saints: how far from the mentality of my country and our century! This is a different place and time with a village, a road and a tree all named after saints—Jean, Jacques, Louis. The old chestnut stands like a guardian at the entrance to an enchanted wood.

The road becomes a path shaded by mossy beeches and chestnuts, softened by layers of fallen leaves. There's nothing that could not have been the same two hundred, five hundred, eight hundred years ago. I seem to be going back in time as I move forward in space.

Beyond the forest the land becomes too steep for cultivation. I see mountain sheep and goats with curled horns on the slopes ahead. Some graze, some sleep on the green hillsides. As I approach they startle, those that were sleeping jerk to their feet, then all frisk away. I turn around and see a vast panorama of lower Navarre extending toward the coast, Biarritz and Bayonne where I took the train to St. Jean this afternoon.

As I climb, my pack feels heavier, sweat soaking my T-shirt where the straps come over the shoulders. Almost out of breath I stop on a ridge overlooking a valley to the left. Here shepherds have erected a statue of the Virgin surrounded by rocks. The map shows that I'm directly across from another valley to the north where the Spanish town of Valcarlos lies—Valley of Charles. Charles the Great of course, for like every main character in early French and Spanish history, Charlemagne played a part in the story of the Road to Santiago. One legend holds that the emperor was the first pilgrim to Compostela but this would have been too great a miracle even for St. James: his tomb had not yet been discovered. Later it was said that Charlemagne merely had a vision of Santiago pointing at the Milky Way, telling him: "The starry route you see in the sky means that you will lead a great army to Galicia, and after you all the peoples on earth will go there on pilgrimage until the consummation of time."

Like so many legends of St. James and the Camino, this one is no doubt spurious yet the prophecy has been fulfilled, at least so far. Even if he had known about the rediscovery of Santiago's body, the white-bearded emperor would rather have returned to any place in the world before Spain, where he had received the soundest drubbing of his life. Not far from where I'm sitting now, Charlemagne's rear guard was ambushed and destroyed by the Basques. Thus says history but poetry has its own version: in the great *Chanson de Roland* the French fight against Muslims in the dark woods of Roncevaux, where the emperor's beseiged nephew Roland calls for help with a mighty blast of his ivory horn.

Back on the road I see peaks with unpronounceable Basque names—Monte Hostateguy, Pico Urdasbure, Pico Urdenarri—vultures whirling around them. I'm at about three thousand feet. Some people believe the old nursery rhyme may come from this part of the pilgrimage: "Over the hills and into Spain / Over the hills and back again." Remembering the French couple, I stop to munch a few of the bittersweet apples, feeling grateful for their bounty. Thank you, friends!

The road levels off in a canyon with loose slate. I've reached the Spanish border, marked only by a wire fence and a small stone marker. It seems strange to be entering Spain for the second time in one day. How nice to cross an international line without surly customs officers! I'm always glad to be in the country I love less only than my own, sometimes more.

The sun drops behind the high peaks to the west. This is the famous Pass of Cize where the twelfth-century *Codex Calixtinus*, or *Book of St. James* says you can almost touch the sky with your hands. The night is falling so fast I can hardly see the sky, never mind touching it. I feel cold for the first time today.

Now I'm on the old Roman road that descends into the valley of Roncesvalles, entering a forest even more ancient than the one in France. Suddenly it's another world, the sky covered by beech and oak trees out of a fairy tale—spreading, twisted, moss-barked—white mist swirling in and out of the thick trunks around me as drizzle falls, the wind howling. I cannot believe it's the middle of summer; I take the

1   The forest of Roncevaux (Roncesvalles). [Photo Gonzalo de la Serna]

rain jacket from my pack and pull up the hood. The air breathes moisture, trees groan in the wind, the forest is alive. In winter when the
wind moans and snow falls heavy at the pass, they say you can still
hear the mournful call of Oliphant, the horn of Sicilian ivory that
cracked when Roland winded it so loud and long. In the old days some
pilgrims perished here in the cold, others were devoured by wolves.
This place has what Spaniards call duende—spirit, demon, power—
something you feel but cannot explain. If you ever get caught alone in
the forest of Roncesvalles, friend, you will deny none of the legends
that are told about it.

I wander lost in the woods, beginning to feel afraid of not arriving,
when the sound of running water leads me to a stream, beech-roots
bulking above the shore. Crossing it on mossy stones, I follow its
course down the valley. A dull gong strikes—is this Tibet or Spain, the
Himalayas or the Pyrenees? Out of the rolling mist the grey stone of
the monastery rises, then a few warm lights in the tiny, fortress-like
windows. It's the same bell that has sounded for centuries to guide
lost pilgrims to shelter.

2 Roncesvalles

The door lies open to all, to sick and strong,
Not alone to Catholics but to pagans too,
Jews, heretics, idlers, vagabonds,
In short to good and bad, sacred and profane.
—Twelfth-century poem in praise of Roncesvalles

When I approach the entrance to the massive building, my watch says almost 9:30. I ring the doorbell and look up toward the roof—concealed in the mist. A young woman in an apron opens the thick wooden door. I'm surprised to see her; her face is so friendly that I don't know what to say.

"Peregrino?" she asks. It's the first human voice I've heard since the French couple more than eight hours ago.

"Sí" I answer glad to speak the language.

"Come in out of the rain. One moment please" she says and goes away. I stand in the threshold dripping, a puddle at my feet.

A small wiry man in dark glasses appears in the doorway, laughing: "You pilgrims don't leave me time for anything, not even supper." He has sideburns and wears a cleric's collar with informal clothes, not the monk's habit I expected.

He asks me to follow him down a dark hall. This is Spain, I think to myself: in any other country the brothers would have eaten long ago and would be ready to sleep by this hour.

"Where are you from?" he asks using the familiar second-person as he opens a door.

"The United States" I answer.

"Truly? About 750 pilgrims have passed through here this summer and you're the first North American. Come in."

We enter an office with modern furniture. Nobody would guess that it is part of a monastery more than seven hundred years old. It feels much warmer than in the hall.

Sitting behind a desk, he gestures for me to have a seat. "You are making the pilgrimage backwards" he laughs. "Most pilgrims try to arrive today, not depart—the twenty-fifth of July, day of St. James."

"It just happens I couldn't start before today." It's so warm that I unsnap my rain jacket.

Opening a large leather-bound notebook, he says: "My name is Javier Navarro, canónigo hospitalero in charge of receiving pilgrims. We register only authentic peregrinos, not hikers or excursionists. I'd say you're a pilgrim because no hiker in his right mind would arrive at this hour."

"Then the doors of Roncesvalles are no longer open to nonbelievers as well as believers, as in the old days?"

He laughs. "The Church could afford it then. Dozens of canons, almoners and hospitallers used to be in charge of attending to the pilgrims. Now I must do it alone."

"I don't know if I'm an authentic pilgrim" I tell him, "but I do know that I'm not a hiker. If I were, my feet wouldn't be so sore."

He laughs again. I notice he's looking carefully at my sweat-soaked T-shirt. "Is that some sort of symbol for a pilgrim's feet?" he asks.

Now it's my turn to laugh: my shirt has a pair of footprints over one breast, the logo of "Hang Ten" sportswear—slang for some kind of maneuver on a surfboard.

"Not quite" I say, tempted to make up a wild story. From the medieval monastery of Roncesvalles to Hang Ten: light years.

Feeling a warmth rising from the floor, I look beneath the desk and see a large brazier of shiny brass filled with glowing red coals, its legs shaped like a lions's paws.

"To keep the feet warm" he says. "It's always cold here in Roncesvalles. It would be a sin to turn on the electric heat in the month of July."

Picking up a fountain pen he asks "Name please?"

"Edward Stanton." I spell it for him.

"Estanton" he tries to repeat, prefixing the extra vowel like most Spanish speakers.

"Stanton" I say again.

"Estanton" he insists. "Nationality, North American . . . Age?"

"Forty-three."

"Profession?"

"Teacher."

"Motivation for pilgrimage?"

I think for a moment before answering: "Not sure."

"Don't worry about it Estanton. I've walked the Camino myself and neither was I very sure the first time."

The frankness of his remark surprises me; I no longer feel defensive. Under the glass on his desktop I notice several reproductions of paintings—Renoir, Modigliani, Velázquez.

"This is your pilgrim's certificate" he says, handing me an ivory-colored folio. On the front it has an icon-like figure of St. James in an attitude of blessing, a seal of the Royal Collegiate Church of Roncesvalles with the stamped signature of the Abbot-Prior, and a cross in two corners: one the emblem of the monastery and the other that of the Knights of Santiago—both with the upper quadrant in the shape of a sword's hilt. The text of the folio says "Don Edward Estanton, who is departing for Santiago de Compostela, has received today the pilgrim's blessing."

I've never thought of myself as a Don. "Why does it say I've received a blessing?" I ask.

"Because normally pilgrims arrive much earlier in the day when the church is open. You'll have to wait until tomorrow morning. And if you don't mind one peregrino giving advice to another, try to set out early each morning and find refuge before it's too late in the afternoon. When you attempt to go a little farther, the way often becomes tedious and you may have to rush in order to reach the next village before nightfall. All haste comes from the devil."

He's certainly not in haste as he takes a pack of cigarettes from his shirt pocket and offers me one. I'm not a smoker but learned long ago to accept a cigarette or cigar from Spaniards as a first token of friendship. The two rules for a foreign man to get along with Spanish males: accept or offer tobacco and leave the women alone.

He lights our cigarettes.

"Is there any other advice you can give me?" I ask.

"Above all watch for the arrows. A pilgrim could walk the entire road to Compostela by simply following the yellow arrows."

"I saw a few on the French side today, none in Spain."

"You must have been lost. I marked the whole thirty kilometers from St. Jean-Pied-de-Port to Roncesvalles with these very hands. I'm responsible for the yellow arrows all the way to Pamplona."

"How did you know where to place the arrows?" I ask him.

"Either I attempted to mark the traditional route or one that captures the medieval experience: narrow paths off the highways, through towns or woods that might have been on one of the historical pilgrims' roads."

"Might have been?"

"Yes."

"Do you mean to say you've marked some places that conceivably were not on the historical road to Santiago?"

He laughs again. "How one notices this is your first pilgrimage, Estanton. Often the old route is covered with the asphalt of a modern highway or even a turnpike. Isn't it better for the pilgrim to enjoy the ambience of a medieval path? And remember that in the end all roads lead to Santiago."

It bothers me that the road I'm walking may not be the authentic Camino I've dreamed of.

Before I can tell him, he asks "Have you read the newspaper about the theft of Spanish monasteries by your compatriots?"

"No."

"A professor of architecture has just published a doctoral thesis exposing the stone-by-stone removal of two complete monasteries— Sacramenia and Ovila. It's in all the papers. The stones were packed in boxes and marked, sent by truck to the nearest station, carried by train to the port of Valencia then shipped to the United States with an export permit stating that they were construction materials."

Vaguely I remember the story about William Randolph Hearst transporting Spanish monuments to his gaudy San Simeon palace in California. "You mean Hearst, the newspaperman?" I ask.

"Of course, we knew that. What has come to light now is the shameless bribery of Spaniards by Hearst's men—from the lowliest night watchmen to baggage-masters of train stations, highway policemen, customs officials and some of the most preeminent figures in the Spanish military and government. All of them silenced by money. And I'm sorry to say that some administrators of the Church sold the properties illegally to middlemen who in turn sold them to Hearst's henchmen."

The story fascinates me, and his lively way of telling it. We're both enveloped in the heady smell of dark Spanish tobacco.

"If you give me a place to sleep tonight" I tell him, "I promise not to steal the monastery of Roncesvalles."

Once more he laughs, reminding me of the monk who said he always laughed because God was tickling him. "I'll accept the offer" he says, "even though it smacks of more North American bribery."

We put out the cigarettes in an ashtray on the desk. Again I follow him through the hall, up a wide stone stairway that must be very old, past construction debris to some drafty rooms on the second floor. He shows me an eating area with a large wooden table and benches, a bathroom with sink, shower stall and toilet, rooms with triple bunk beds of unvarnished wood.

"This is where pilgrims stay" he tells me. "You'll almost be alone tonight."

I sling my pack on one of the lower bunks; they have mattresses but no sheets. A thick woolen blanket is folded at the foot of each bed.

2 Father Javier Navarro, in charge of pilgrims at the Royal Collegiate Church, Roncevaux.

"Good night, may you rest well" he says in the Spanish fashion. "Hasta mañana."

"Until tomorrow and thank you."

I sit on the edge of the bed thinking what a good word mañana is— probably means heaven said old Jack Kerouac. He knew something about the road alright. I take off jacket, boots and socks. My feet have some red spots that will probably turn into blisters. I put on my moccasins, find a towel and go to the bathroom.

The tap water is so cold that it makes my face hurt. A small water heater hangs on the wall but the butane tank below it is empty: no shower tonight.

On the way back to the bedroom I meet a tall, awkward man with crew-cut white hair and glasses.

"Bon soir" he says, probably as surprised as I am to see somebody else.

"Buenas noches" I answer and walk to my bunk thinking this is still a Camino francés, a French road as they called it in the Middle Ages.

I turn out the light, grope my way through the dark and crawl into my sleeping bag. The bell that reminded me of a Tibetan monastery dins a hollow gong, less welcome this time. It booms every quarter-hour. It, thunder and lightning and the cramps in my legs keep me awake for hours. The last bell I remember is 3 A.M.

Sunlight filters through the shutters. I get up to look out the window and see Roncesvalles without rain and mist: a pile of grey conventual buildings with strange pyramidal roofs of slate or zinc against a back-drop of green hills and a cloudless sky. After washing in the icy water and packing my things, I go downstairs, my feet already sore. I walk to the posada, or inn down the hill where I order coffee and a roll.

Walking back up the hill, I have a good view of the buildings grouped around the long, fortress-like monastery, all of them dominated by the square, ribbed tower of the main church. It's not hard to tell that Roncesvalles used to be one of the most important hospices on the road to Compostela. Thousands of pilgrims arrived over the mountain pass all year long and the canons of St. Augustine washed their feet, shaved their beards, cut their hair. A manuscript of the time says that if travelers were treated so well everywhere, many regions would have been depopulated by their inhabitants going on pilgrimage.

What spoils the appearance of Roncesvalles today is the incongruous metal roofing. It must be practical in the harsh, mountain climate but it's as if the pope, wearing his pontifical robes, had donned a baseball cap.

I enter the main church. An old lady is sweeping the floor with one of those Spanish brooms that haven't changed for centuries: a bunch of dried straw tied to a stick.

"Padre Javier?" I ask.

"In the sacristy."

I knock and he comes to the door wearing his dark glasses despite the dimness of the light.

"Ah, the blessing" he says smiling. "Wait for me here."

Within a few seconds he returns wearing a cassock with a surplice on his shoulders, suddenly transformed from a humble man of middle age into a dignified celebrant of the divine offices.

"Follow me" he whispers as he walks up the steps in front of the main altar. Under a canopy of chased silver stands an image of the Virgen de Roncesvalles, patroness of Spanish and French Navarre.

The canon turns his back to the altar, holding a book in both hands. I take off my pack and place it with my staff on the steps, kneeling.

He begins: "May the Lord guide your steps and be your inseparable companion on the way."

He looks up at me from the text. I guess that I'm supposed to respond: "Amen."

"May the Virgin, Santa María, grant you her maternal protection, defend you from dangers to body and soul, and beneath her mantle may you deserve to reach the end of your pilgrimage without harm."

He looks at me again. "Amen" I say.

Raising his right hand in prayer he recites: "Oh God, who brought forth your servant Abraham out of the city of Ur in Chaldea, watching over him in all his wanderings, and who guided the Hebrews across the wilderness, we ask you to watch over this servant of yours who for love of your name goes as a pilgrim to Compostela. Be for him a companion in walking, a guide at the crossroads, a relief in his weariness, a defense against dangers, shelter on the road, shade in the heat, light in the darkness, courage in his dismay and firmness in his uncertainty so that following you, he may arrive safely at the end of his journey, and blessed with grace and strength, he may return uninjured to his home, where his family now suffers from his absence, full of wholesome and unending joy. In the name of Our Lord Jesus Christ. May the blessing of the all-powerful Father and the Son and the Holy Spirit descend upon you." He makes the sign of the cross slowly over me.

"Amen" I say.

"Herru Sanctiagu, Got Sanctiagu!" he exclaims the old Flemish invocation of the apostle.

Then looking at me and raising his right hand he pronounces in a resonant voice the traditional closing words: "Ultreya e suseia! Deus adiuva nos, onwards and upwards! God help us."

Canon Navarro steps down toward me, holds me by one arm and says in Spanish, smiling: "Ánimo, coraje y seguir adelante, courage, forward and never fear!"

After picking up my pack and staff I walk with him to the door of the sacristy. "Can you tell me something about the ceremony?" I ask.

"It's from a missal of the year 1038 in the cathedral of Vich, in Catalonia, with a few changes. Did you like it?"

"Very, very much."

"You promise not to steal the monastery then?" he asks, laughing as he did last night.

"Prometido. Thank you for everything."

"May you preserve the pilgrim's spirit all your life Estanton."

3 Sacred and Profane

> Take the Disciples, for instance. They annoy the
> hell out of me, if you want to know the truth.
> They were all right after Jesus was dead and all,
> but while He was alive, they were about as much
> use to Him as a hole in the head. All they did was
> keep letting Him down.
> —Holden Caulfield in *The Catcher in the Rye*

From Roncesvalles the road follows the main highway between St.
Jean-Pied-de-Port and Pamplona. A few clouds cross the sky. In the
west over the beech and oak forest a waning moon sets. The blisters on
my feet are very sore. Remembering the main altar of the church, Padre
Javier and the ceremony, I pass a pilgrims' cross with a relief of the Virgin on a stone column. In St. Jean yesterday my solitary prayer seemed
inadequate but the official blessing has been too much. The ritual has
moved me—the aura of the place, the rhythm of the language, the dignity of the words, the weight of tradition. During those moments, for
the first time since taking to the road I almost forgot about myself. Yet
something was missing—in me, in the ceremony, in both? I haven't
paid my creditors, drawn up a will or made a confession of my sins as
pilgrims did in the Middle Ages; I'm not going to Compostela for love
of Christ's name but for complex reasons I don't understand. I'm not
capable of releasing myself to the sort of childlike confidence in the
protection of Jesus, the Virgin Mary or the God of Abraham invoked in
the blessing. Somehow they all seem remote to me.

As for Santiago he was only mentioned in the Flemish words stuck
onto the end of the ceremony: "Lord Santiago, God Santiago!" I'm
probably not the first to notice the heresy of these words in their elevation of the apostle to the status of a divinity. Maybe this is part of
the problem with St. James: he's too far away, too much like a God on
high. I search for the man of flesh and blood in him as I would in St.
Francis of Assisi, for example (who made the pilgrimage to Compostela
according to one legend). I cannot find him, we know too little about
Santiago—his humanity lost over time, sacrificed on the altar of his
godliness. I try to evoke the fisherman, son of Zebedee, mending his
nets on the Sea of Galilee with his brother John, later the Evangelist.
Even his family makes him special, a possible blood-relation to Christ.
The Golden Legend says that Mary Salome, mother of James the Elder—our Santiago—was half-sister to Mary Virgin, making the saint
no less than a cousin to Jesus. Whether or not this is true, there can be

no doubt that James, with his brother John and Simon Peter formed part of the innermost circle of Christ's disciples in whom he confided, to whom he revealed his secrets: privileged eyewitnesses of the transfiguration on the mountain and the agony in the garden as well as the death and resurrection. For this very reason they let him down more than the others, falling asleep at Gethsemane when he had only asked them to watch with him for an hour.

Christ called James and John "Boanerges," Sons of Thunder, presumably because of their excessive zeal. Like two little boys, the brothers asked him to seat them at his right and left hand in glory; when their messengers to a Samaritan village were poorly received, the two wanted Jesus to consume the offenders with fire from heaven. Perhaps this impetuosity alone gave Santiago a unique character, an individuality among the apostles. In those sparse details from the New Testament lie the seeds of the metamorphosis of a Galilean fisherman, who never lifted a weapon in his life, into a sword-swinging Moorslayer, Santiago Matamoros, eight hundred years later. He became a kind of medieval Superman who cut down ranks of Muslims, mounted on a brilliant white charger, expelling the infidels from the Iberian peninsula to the battle cry of "Santiago y cierra España!" (Santiago and close ranks Spain!), becoming the country's patron saint and leading the banners of explorers and conquistadores to the New World. How can I feel close to this James, more a soldier than a saint?

In the first town after the monastery, Burguete, the water from last night's storm still flows down the channels on each side of the road. After the steady climb yesterday, it's good to be walking downhill to the sound of running water. Burguete is wholly Pyrenean like Roncesvalles, recalling the Tyrol more than Spain or France. Walking by immaculate stone houses with red shutters, I look through open doorways and see polished floors, some still wet from mopping on this Saturday morning, shiny copper kettles and flowerpots in the corners.

As I leave Burguete, I turn around and look once more at Roncesvalles, remembering Padre Javier and his laugh—the mountains hidden already by a great bank of rolling white fog as if from another world. Something new begins there, or ends, something different from all of Spain, from Gibraltar to the Bay of Biscay. Perhaps the French are right, Africa does begin in the Pyrenees. How foreign, Nordic and cold Roncevaux and its mountains must have looked to the Arabs, far from their deserts, oases and Mediterranean ports. No wonder they didn't pass beyond here; in their legendary defeat by Charlemagne there is a poetic truth more convincing than history.

After cutting across a field, I follow yellow arrows to the highway again. It leads me to Espinal—clean, immaculate, like a scale model of a Basque town in the Pyrenees. The arrows direct me off the highway once more, the sky overcast, up a hill across fields of wheat, through a barbed-wire fence into a dark, dripping forest where the undergrowth soaks my shirt, pants, socks.

I take my rain jacket and pants from my pack and slip them on, smiling to myself, recalling Padre Javier and his arrows. As he would say, I must be lost. But how did I get lost unless it was by following his arrows? Still I feel grateful when I see more yellow paint on a stone fence where a line of poplars marks the fertile course of the Erro River. To err is only human, brother Javier.

On the other side of the river, the town of Viscarret is in fiesta, hung with flags and banners, the people gathered around a long table set in the main square facing the church. The carafes of wine on the table and the smells of cooking make me hungry. Feeling out of place, a stranger, I continue walking.

The road crosses the highway, beginning to rise toward the Erro pass. Yesterday with the euphoria of starting, with fresh feet I didn't mind the climbing. Now my feet are blistered, my muscles ache, every part of my body hurts except my hands.

Soon I come upon some huge stones marked with Padre Javier's yellow paint. These must be the legendary Pasos de Roldán, or Roland's Steps, the ruins of a fallen menhir that was supposed to mark the length of the hero's stride. The longest stone measures more than six feet; a shorter one is supposed to show his wife's step and the smallest his children's.

The path goes through a thicket that becomes an oak grove. Hearing animal sounds, I stop to listen—bleating of sheep. I walk around a curve and there they are, nudging and close-stomping on the narrow path. Moving left to allow the herd to pass, I see what I cannot believe: on the slope rising from the opposite side between the moss and ivy-covered oaks, a girl or young woman is squatting, her dress pulled up to the waist, her back to me. I stand still, feeling awkward, too fascinated to move. Since the sheep have passed, I can hear the stream of her urine striking the forest-floor of leaves. She takes the loose folds of the dress in her right hand and wipes herself between the legs, rising to her feet so that I see her white, pear-shaped buttocks until the dress, catching for a second on her hip, falls to her knees. She stands there leaning slightly forward, arranging the dress around her waist in a posture stolen from some painting of a lady at her toilette, only more real. She shakes out her thick black hair, spins and comes gamboling down the slope with a shepherd's staff in one hand, walks by me smiling without embarrassment as if she knows I've been here all along, not speaking to me, the features of a sixteen-year-old girl with the hardness around the mouth of a woman who has labored all her life. I stop to watch her and she disappears around the curve.

I feel as if my senses have been invaded by the vision and the aroma of the shepherdess—grass, fruit, animal-smell and earth. She appeared like a familiar spirit of the place, out of another age: the way she came from nowhere, seemed a part of the scenery, blending with the oaks and sheep, then vanished.

I hear nothing now, not even the bleating. Buñuel's film *The Milky Way* comes into my mind, the part when two pilgrims are seduced by a blond prostitute before reaching the end of their journey. Would I be able to reach Compostela if this shepherdess, this girl-woman offered herself to me, or would I jump into the bushes after her like the pilgrims in the movie? And what gives me the right to think she would even bother to offer herself to me? There was nothing deliberately seductive in her behavior yet how could I fail to feel her sexuality when I surprised her in the act of peeing on the ground? I remember the bittersweet smell when she walked by me and I know it was stronger than my will. Perhaps it has always been this way: in the Middle Ages prostitutes worked the route to Compostela, human and divine love all parts of the Camino and the creation. Here on the Road the old divisions between man and god, body and soul, good and evil, sacred and profane are not so clear. Doesn't my language, Spanish too, have only one word to say love, from the holiest to the most erotic? That's what makes it such a living, human word and emotion. For me the appearance of the girl-woman has been as sacred in its own way as the pilgrims' blessing in Roncesvalles. I'm thankful for it, for her, feeling myself unworthy of both: an abundance, an overflow of life.

When the path comes out of the woods and crosses the highway at the peak of the Erro pass, I have to wait for the cars and trucks with their diesel fumes. My first reaction is to turn around and go right back into the forest, so strange does this world seem to me already—my world until one day ago. How foreign it is to the place I've just been, to the girl-woman and her flock of sheep, the fallen menhir, Roland's Steps.

Instead of turning back I cross the highway and plunge into the thicket on the other side, leaving the sound of straining engines and gearshifts behind. Sheep droppings on the ground remind me of the shepherdess. Thinking of the beautiful Spanish name for the Way to Compostela—Camino de las Estrellas—I can't help repeating aloud as the droppings crunch beneath my boots,

> Camino de las Estrellas,
> Camino de la Mierda.
>
> Road of Stars,
> Road of Shit.

"As it is above so it is below": the old Biblical expression often applied to the Way and its reflection in the sky. For centuries the Spanish people have referred to the Milky Way as the Camino de Santiago, since both have an east-west axis and pilgrims used the galaxy to guide themselves to Compostela. Yet I haven't seen a single star in the sky after more than twenty-four hours on the route to Santiago. With the clouds threatening now, holding back an energy you can almost smell in the air, neither will I see the stars tonight.

When you approach Zubiri at the foot of Mount Erro, the only landmark is a monolithic electrical transformer where the town's residents have chosen to dump their garbage. I'd rather spend the night in a more attractive place but I've already covered twenty-eight kilometers with blistered feet, I'm fatigued and hungry and I remember Padre Javier's advice about finding refuge before it gets late in the afternoon.

Zubiri is too small to have hotels or pensions. Nor do I know of a pilgrims' refuge. I ask for a room in a casa de huéspedes, a kind of bed-and-breakfast without the breakfast or any sign to indicate that guests are welcome. It's a three-story, eighteenth-century stone house with green shutters and a noble, creaking door that opens on top and bottom: it probably used to be the entrance for the animals when the people lived on the upper floors. A middle-aged lady shows me a clean room upstairs for eight hundred pesetas, about six dollars. I can share the bathroom and shower at the end of the hall with other guests.

I take off my shoes and boots—hot on the inside—get my towel from the pack and walk on tender feet to the bathroom where I take my first shower since leaving New York. After drying and putting on fresh clothes and moccasins, I limp downstairs to ask the lady where to go for dinner. When she tells me that the nearest restaurant is back on the highway to France, about a kilometer away, I almost collapse.

I feel every one of the thousand meters to the "Txori" bar and restaurant. But my first hot meal on the road, the Basque cooking and a bottle of rosado wine make it worthwhile. Eating the fresh, steaming white beans, the sautéed trout wrapped in cured mountain ham, I remember the advice of my old professor Walter Starkie, himself a traveler to Compostela: a pilgrim should know when to be austere and when to accept the good things of life.

I return to the house, in pain but content. Walking in the big un-locked door, I meet the white-haired man I saw last night at the monastery. An attractive blond woman with metal-framed glasses is speaking to him in French.

"Bon soir" we all say.

Slowly I climb the stairs, undress and get into the bed with its cool, clean sheets and oversoft mattress, wondering about the French man and woman, remembering the shepherdess and fragments of the blessing in Roncesvalles.

4　Bread, Meerschaum
and Pamplona

It's still dark when I leave the house. The town smells of fresh-baked bread. Following the aroma, I find a large bakery on the Pamplona-St. Jean highway. The store is shut so I enter through the service door on the side, feeling the heat of the ovens.

The bread is being sorted in huge wicker baskets. I ask one of the bakers, a large man coated with flour, if I can have part of a baguette. A whole one would be too much for me to eat and wouldn't fit in my pack.

"Toma" he says, breaking a crusty baguette with his big hands, giving me half of it. "Cuatro duros" he adds in the old way of calculating in five-peseta pieces.

I pay, thank him and say "Adiós."

"Adiós, adiós" he replies. One goodbye is rarely enough for Spaniards.

Looking for a bar and a cup of coffee to accompany the warm, fragrant piece of bread—it feels almost alive in my hand—I remember the legend of the pilgrim on his way to Compostela who was denied bread by a woman in a French town. "May it turn to stone" he cursed her, continuing on his way. When the woman opened her oven to take a loaf from the hot ashes, guess what! Santiago had turned it to stone.

Thinking that no American baker would break a whole baguette in two for a stranger, I say out loud over my shoulder, "May your loaves multiply and never turn to stone, brother!"

Bells begin to peal for Mass. I've already had a kind of communion on this Sunday morning: breaking bread with the good baker.

A woman is still mopping the floor of a café by the highway. I have to wait a few minutes for the stainless-steel expresso machine to warm up. A short, slick-haired man comes in the door. When he hears me order coffee from the bartender, he asks if I'm from Peru, no less.

"No, from North America." You have to specify North or South when talking to Spaniards since many of them don't believe the United States should have a monopoly on the word America.

"I asked because of your soft accent" he says. "Reminded me of a Peruvian I used to know in the factory."

He takes out a pack of cigarettes, offering me one.

I don't feel like smoking so early in the morning. "No thanks. Are there factories around here? I haven't seen any."

"You must not be coming from Pamplona because you would have seen the magnesita plant on the highway. You can't miss it."

I don't understand the word. "What do they make there?" I ask him.

"Magnesita, espuma de mar."

Translating "sea-foam" into English, I finally realize that he means meerschaum, magnesium silicate.

The expresso machine is making a loud sucking noise to prepare the hot, frothy milk for the coffee. The bartender serves my café con leche. The short man orders an anisette, the early-morning starter for many Spanish laborers.

When I break the half-baguette into smaller pieces, covering the counter with crumbs, both the man and the bartender look at me askance. Of course I know that Spaniards, always aware of decorum, would never eat store-bought bread in a café. But I'm not a Spaniard, I'm on the road and the bread tastes so good—crisp on the outside, tender in the middle, still warm.

The short man goes on talking: "Around here the factory is controversial. People from outside criticize it because of the pollution, but for those who live here it's been like manna from heaven." The bartender adds a grunt of approval.

"Obviously you work in the factory" I tell the short man.

"Thirty-one out of its thirty-five years. Before it was built we lived in the misery of the Gran Puta, the Great Whore, a man's wealth was counted by the number of cows he owned. Now some workers earn twenty thousand duros and still keep a few cows on the side." He gulps down the shot-glass of anisette. I calculate in my head: around eight hundred dollars, probably per month.

"Is meerschaum used for anything other than pipes?" I ask him, putting the rest of the baguette in my pack.

He laughs, stamps out one cigarette, lights another. He says something about stoves or furnaces but I don't understand him.

Suddenly I want to be on the road. I pay the bartender and say goodbye, hearing the multiple adioses as I walk out.

The first hundred yards or so are the worst, when sore feet are still cold. The pain becomes more bearable after they warm up. By the time my feet stop hurting, I see the factory ahead of me, a smokestack spewing yellow-brown clouds into the air. Manna from heaven. At least the wind is blowing the smoke away from me. The land turns from green to brown as I approach, trees stunted or dead. I'm upwind but I can smell the stench of the smoke. I take out my bandanna and tie it over my nose and mouth, a masked pilgrim now. Soon I realize the road runs directly through the property of Magnesitas de Navarra, S.A. I cannot believe the millennial Camino de Santiago has been expropriated by a factory only thirty-five years old! Or that this is the best route for a pilgrim between Zubiri and Pamplona. Taking out my map, I find this section of the road has a marginal note in bureaucratic doubletalk: "in need of restructuring for greater viability."

When I'm almost even with the enormous smokestack, I see a single yellow arrow painted on an electrical post against the background of the main plant covered by a white-brown scoria. Never has the Camino seemed so small to me, so fragile, so irrelevant, in such need of protection and care. That arrow is absurd and glorious amid this wilderness of humming engines, poisoned air, cracked-earth basins, slag-heaps. Bravo, Padre Javier! Salud, camarada!

The blight and stink continue for more than a mile. I remember my smooth, creamy-white meerschaum pipe, its bowl almost brown with age, sitting on top of the desk in my study. Could it have come from a place like this? When the road draws near the banks of the Arga River, I see a whitish scum on its surface, knowing it's been contaminated upstream.

The landscape becomes less Pyrenean, the greens turn to yellows, the road leaves the river and crosses wheat fields golden in the sun. Yesterday I heard quail and other birds singing; now I hear cicadas in the brush. The air feels drier, I perspire more, drinking often from my canteen, finishing off the baguette.

I see Pamplona ahead. Thinking of my friends there, for the first time since leaving St. Jean-Pied-de-Port I don't feel alone. The city looks ugly and modern from the outside, surrounded by signs, factories and high-rise apartment buildings. Who would guess it's the old Iruña lusted after by Visigoths, Moors, Aragonese, French, the capital of the ancient kingdom of Navarre? This has always been a land besieged, forced to defend itself by holding fiercely to its traditions.

Following the medieval pilgrims' route, I cross the Arga once more, walk around the city walls, through the Gate of France with its drawbridge. Then I deviate from the road to find the street of Santo Domingo where the famous encierro, or running of the fighting bulls begins each morning during the fiesta of San Fermín. It's a good thing I don't have to run the bulls now with the blisters burning inside my boots.

The fiesta seems far away with the street and the city so empty during the Sunday lunch-hour. Only two weeks ago the men of Pamplona and the bulls were galloping over these cobblestones, surrounded by screaming crowds. Now a few passersby stare at me with my pack and pilgrim's staff as if I were some kind of rarity—maybe a climber of skyscrapers? I realize how accustomed I've become to walking outside of cities, feeling even more a misfit here than in the countryside.

When I reach José Mari's house on the far side of town, I don't want to walk another step. I've covered only eighteen kilometers from Zubiri to Pamplona, far less than the first two days yet I feel more fatigued than ever. The marble of the stairway in this modern building makes my feet hurt.

José Mari opens the door, smiling from cheek to cheek, his pale blue eyes laughing too, a napkin tucked into his open collar. It's one of the best smiles I know and it always makes me happy.

"Peregrino!" he cries out. We give each other an embrace in the Spanish fashion.

"Look what the wind has blown into the house!" he shouts as he leads me by the arm to the kitchen.

The whole family is seated at the table in the midst of the Sunday meal. Now I'm hugging Pili and the kids, all five of them, getting used to the kisses on both cheeks again amid How are you, Eduardo, It's been a long time, We've never seen you so sunburned, How are María and the children, while a dog I've never seen before jumps on my legs. The boys fondle my backpack and walking staff, ignoring their mother's entreaties to finish their meal, José Mari sitting me down to eat the ajoarriero—codfish cooked in garlic, oil, tomatoes and eggs. His second son Alberto brings bottles of wine from the pantry since there is none on the table: this is one of the only Spanish families I know that doesn't imbibe with meals.

"I don't need alcohol" says José Mari. "I get drunk on people and happiness."

Eating the spicy ajoarriero, I try to answer everyone's questions about the pilgrimage; the hot food and the wine make me sweat more than on the road. I'm with friends, coddled, surrounded by the noisy warmth of a Spanish family.

After the dessert of cuajada, or sweet milk-curds, we're piling into the car, all eight of us on the way to the Club Amaya with its swimming pools, not far from where I entered town on the Camino.

3   José Mari Torrabadella

We change into our bathing trunks in the dressing room. Taking my portable locker-basket, the girl attendant breaks into laughter when I tell her not to smell my sweat-soaked clothes unless she wants to die of asphyxiation. We go outside in the bright sun, dive into the Olympic pool, my sore muscles and bleeding feet soothed in the cold, turquoise-colored water. We sit on chairs beneath shady poplars on the café terrace, sipping coffee and the Basque liqueur pacharán, watching the older men play their card game of mus while teenage girls in bikinis and their boyfriends listen to rock-and-roll and drink Coca-Cola. The girls are attractive with their tan, shiny limbs; every year the women in Spain seem to have longer legs. I feel attracted to them but I'm also aware of the contrast between this world, no longer completely mine, and my new life on the Camino alone, walking on aching feet but free, doing what I only dreamed of doing once, in touch with my own steps, close to the road, the land, the weather.

Yielding to the warm tiredness in my legs, the torpor of a summer day in Spain after lunch, wine and swimming, a soft breeze rustling through the poplars, I fall asleep . . .

Back at the house José Mari tells me I cannot continue walking the Road to Santiago with my feet in such condition. Seating me on a stool in the bathroom, my legs propped up on the bidet, he and Pili wash my feet with alcohol and cotton, then treat the blisters in the way they've learned on the annual pilgrimage to St. Francisco Xavier. First they thread a sewing needle, dip it in alcohol and sterilize the tip with the flame of a match, then pass the needle and thread through the blister, pressing gently to remove the pus, finally snipping off the needle and leaving the thread.

"The blister may not bleed itself dry if you take out the thread," Pili says. "By walking on it you force out the water or pus."

They swab the area with Mercurochrome then repeat the operation on eight more blisters, leaving an inch-long piece of white thread in each. When they finish, my feet look like two red and white ships in a regatta with banners flying. The pain has gone out of the blisters.

"How long should I leave the threads?" I ask them.

"As long as you wish" answers Pili. "They'll fall out by themselves. I'm going to give you a blister kit for your pack: needle, thread, alcohol, cotton, matches, scissors, Mercurochrome."

José Mari goes out of the bathroom and returns in less than a minute. "I'm giving you this" he says, holding out a large scallop shell about five inches across—for centuries the symbol of the pilgrimage to Compostela. "Pili's gift represents Science, mine Faith."

I fondle the shell, rough on the outside, pearly smooth inside. "I'll keep it in my pack" I tell him, "next to the little stone I brought with me for good luck."

The children come to kiss us good night. Pili leads me down the hall to a room and shows me the bed she has prepared—starched sheets neatly folded back. José Mari joins us.

"Alberto has just asked me if he can walk the road with you tomorrow" he says to me. "Do you mind?"

"On the contrary, I'll enjoy his company." Alberto is fourteen, the same age as my older son. Perhaps for that reason we've always gotten along together.

"If he hadn't flunked so many courses last semester" José Mari goes on, "he could accompany you farther; but he has a tutor who comes to the house a couple of days a week. I can pick him up in the car tomorrow after work wherever you decide to stop."

"Take good care of him Eduardo" says Pili, giving me kisses on both cheeks and saying "Buenas noches."

After she leaves, José Mari lowers his voice and asks "Did you hear about the English pilgrims who were robbed the other day?"

"No."

"It happened between Zubiri and Pamplona in a wheat field, where you must have passed today. Two men pulled knives on a pair of elderly women who had separated from their group. Stole their money but returned their passports and papers."

"Thieves with honor."

"I don't want Pili to know about it" he says, "because she'll worry too much about Alberto tomorrow. He needs to get out of the house for at least a day. Come on, it's bedtime, you need to rest."

Walking out he points to my feet: "How far you planning to go tomorrow on those two pieces of hamburger?"

"Only twenty kilometers to Puente la Reina."

5 Travels with Alberto and Yako

Every expedition presupposes that in some way
Marco Polo, Columbus and Shackleton had not
completely lost the child inside themselves.
— Carol Dunlop and Julio Cortázar

After a Spanish breakfast of coffee and bread, José Mari announces:
"Base camp Pamplona prepared for ascent to Alto del Perdón." The
Perdón is the mountain we must cross to reach Puente la Reina.

Pili has already washed and dried my dirty shirts, underwear and
socks. I put them in my pack with the blister kit and scallop shell. Now
she wraps foot-long bocadillos, or Spanish sandwiches for our lunch
while Alberto asks her endless questions about what he should pack,
arguing with every answer. He wears a T-shirt with the logo of the 1992
Olympic Games in Barcelona on the front, a pair of shorts and tennis
shoes. With his tousled blond hair and turned-up nose, Alberto could
pass for an American teenager, even a German or Scandinavian.

"Surprise number two" José Mari declares, bringing the dog on a
leash to the kitchen. "Today we're going to get rid of Yako also—the
perro peregrino, the pilgrim dog." The animal looks like a cross between a spaniel and a terrier, with a white body, brown spots and a
mat of hair over its eyes.

"In fact there's an old legend that Santiago was accompanied by a
dog when he preached the gospel" I tell José Mari. "Your dog's name
even sounds Jacobean: Saint Jacob, Sant' Yago in old Spanish, Yako."

When I pronounce his name the dog looks up at me and barks,
yanking on the leash.

"That's a protest, Eduardo" says José Mari as we all laugh. "He
knows his name is pagan. I named him after a Greek spirit or demon."

We say goodbye to Pili, take the elevator to the underground garage
and get in the Austin station wagon. It seems strange to be in a car with
my pilgrim's clothes, my pack and staff. As we drive through the elec-
tronic door to the street, I realize it would be almost as strange to begin walking in this modern neighborhood with its high-rise
apartments, boutiques, cinemas, video clubs, discotheques.

José Mari says "It would be ridiculous for you to go back to the old pilgrims' road downtown, Eduardo. You've been there so many times, not to mention Alberto. I think Santiago will pardon you if you begin walking outside of town."

"Even before starting the pilgrimage" I say, "I decided not to cheat—or at least not very much."

He laughs, "I don't think that avoiding a traffic jam on a Monday morning could be called cheating. Here we are at the University of Navarre."

I look at the modern buildings constructed under General Franco in the American style: all the schools or colleges on a central campus, separated by lawns and trees.

"Is it true that the Opus Dei has a lot of influence here?" I ask, referring to the worldwide Catholic organization founded and dominated by Spaniards.

"Influence!" José Mari shouts. "They own the place! It's no secret. I wouldn't be surprised if they were responsible for the Camino de Santiago running through their property. The Road starts where the workers are repairing that nice old bridge."

José Mari parks. As soon as we get out of the car, the dog pulls at the leash in my hand, straining, ready to run. José Mari takes a couple of photographs of Alberto, Yako and me under the shade of the trees on the bridge over a small stream.

He embraces us and says goodbye: "Call me from Puente la Reina."

When we leave the shade of the trees, the sun strikes us on the head. It's very late to be departing—almost noon. How fast the mornings fly in Spain! It doesn't dawn until nearly eight o'clock, many people sleep in and have a late breakfast, some stores don't open until ten. Everything seems to be delayed by an hour or so compared to other countries in Europe, almost two hours compared to the U.S. There are many theories about Spain's historical backwardness; I wonder if it doesn't begin with the time-lag in daily life.

Yako doesn't believe in time-lags as he strains on the leash, always keeping ahead of Alberto and me. Soon we leave the paved road, remove the dog's chain and watch him run with his new freedom. Feeling the softer earth under my boots, I realize with amazement that my feet don't hurt for the first time since the Pyrenees; José Mari's and Pili's surgery has been successful.

I have to put on my French Army bush hat to protect my head from the brilliant sun. It shines in a pure blue sky such as I've seen only in Castile and Navarre.

Alberto seems to be in as much a hurry as Yako. His pace is faster than mine: he's fourteen not forty-three, I tell myself. His overnight bag contains only our lunch and a canteen, unlike my pack with its sleeping bag, inflatable mattress and other equipment for a month or more on the road. But it feels good to have company after three days alone. I'm more relaxed as I watch Yako's tail wagging in front of us, Alberto walking with the long tree-branch he's found for a walking stick.

The first six or seven kilometers after Pamplona are marked better than any stretch of the Camino so far. In addition to the arrows painted on asphalt, rocks, fences, walls and lightposts, somebody has tied long strips of yellow cloth or plastic to bushes and trees to show the way across the open country. The Road is riddled, sewn, stitched with markers and arrows like a martyred St. Sebastian. I appreciate the good intentions but wonder if there might not be some way of guiding pilgrims without cluttering the landscape with these yellow flags. Father Javier was discreet compared to this zealot, this fanatic who has terrorized the countryside with his weapons of paintbrush and scissors.

We climb steadily toward Perdón. The sun shines in our faces. The mountain is more a barrier than a peak, like a ridge that never seems to get closer. A pale moon is sinking below it now. I wonder if there could be something symbolic about its name, since most pilgrims have gone to Compostela through the centuries in order to obtain pardon for their sins.

Entering the unpronounceable village of Zariquiegui about halfway up the mountain, we stop to drink water from our canteens. As in so many communities, the Camino de Santiago forms the main street, paved here with stone, traversing the town from one end to the other. Half the street is in the shade, half in the sun—almost blinding. It's lunchtime and not a soul appears. We can't find a public fountain. Deciding to ask for water, we choose a gabled house with a weathered coat-of-arms emblazoned on the façade. Two large brass flowerpots flank the door. The knocker, also of brass and shaped like a hand, echoes on the silent street. I have the feeling that old women are scurrying to the windows of every house to see the strangers in this dying village.

An elderly lady in black opens the door; she smiles at us without the mistrust of a city-dweller. When we ask her for water, she hands us a large botijo, or round earthen jug with a spout like a cherub's penis. I look through the doorway at the flagstoned entrance, feeling its cave-like coolness as Alberto pours water on his head and drinks. I see a carved chest standing against one wall, a wood-framed mirror above it, an old brass bed-warmer hung on another wall: a still-life of a Spanish interior that could be from another age.

As I lift the botijo and tilt back my head to drink, I see an open window and an exposed oak beam where this noble house has a hayloft on the second floor. The water from the jug goes down well, cooled by the clay. The woman invites us to fill our canteens from another botijo, this one white, since we've drunk off the first. Yako has discovered our oasis; he laps the water we've spilled on the street. I take the scallop shell from my pack, fill it and hold it out for the dog.

"Are you going to Santiago?" the woman asks. She must have recognized the scallop shell.

"Sí señora" answers Alberto enjoying the half-lie.

"Remember me when you arrive" she says. Nothing more.

We thank her and wave goodbye. Alberto goes on talking as we leave town. I don't listen, thinking of the inhabitants along the Camino and the pilgrims who pass through their towns, cities, villages. While we depend on their generosity, we give something in return. Not only remembering or praying for them in Santiago—that's remote and abstract because they can never be sure if we'll comply. I mean something now, tangible: the surprise of an unexpected knocking; a face never seen before, never to be seen again; a stranger's smile, a greeting or farewell; a break in the boredom of everyday's routine; the ability to give something that's urgent and appreciated deeply, like the cool water of the botijos which we wouldn't have exchanged for the gods' nectar.

The road ascends steeply through fields of wheat and rye. We know we're lost when we have to cross several barbed wire fences, both of us cursing the arrow-fanatic who must have squandered all his yellow paint and banners by the time he got this far. A farmer in a huge John Deere combine points the way to a pine-grove on the mountain's flank.

Just before the trees, we top up our canteens at a trickling natural spring called the Fuente de Reniega, or Fountain of the Denial from the legend of a thirsty pilgrim who refused to deny God, the Virgin or Santiago in exchange for water offered by the devil. The man kept his faith, conquered the temptation and was succoured by the apostle disguised as another pilgrim; carrying him to the secret spring, St. James gave him to drink from a scallop shell. Alberto doesn't show much interest in the story but he agrees that the old woman in black has been our Santiago today. If nothing else the legend is accurate in choosing water as the most important element in the steep, lonely ascent to the Alto del Perdón.

On top of the ridge we look for a shady spot to rest and eat our lunch. We find none but we don't suffer too much from the heat because the wind is blowing stiffly from both sides of the mountain. The plastic thermometer attached to a zipper on my pack, no bigger than a keychain, registers 88 degrees Fahrenheit. Yako is glad to stop too; he lies panting in the small shadows cast by our bodies.

Eating Pili's bocadillos of tortilla, or Spanish omelette made with potatoes and onions, we look at the panorama of upper Navarre through the transparent air: the blue-gray Pyrenees on the horizon, Pamplona at the foothills, an undulating sea of grain fields on the hills rising toward us. The cereals have already been harvested on the plains but waves of mature wheat and rye still bend in the wind on the higher, cooler slopes. The view is so vast that we can see distant trains puffing and tiny cars driving in every direction, as though we had the valley of the world before us. The mythic, magical realm of Charlemagne, Roland, menhirs and the shepherdess lies far away now, lost somewhere in the deep, ancient woods of the Pyrenees. Here on the edge of lower Navarre everything is clear, open, exposed by the light. Pamplona itself looks small, smaller than an American city of the same population because it has grown in density as well as sprawling over the countryside in suburbs. Seeing the agglomeration of multistoried buildings surrounded by open fields, the wide plain of the river Arga where the city might have expanded even more, I think how gregarious are the Spaniards by nature and how isolated are Americans in their suburbs, their single-family dwellings bordered by plots of grass.

Alberto devours his two bocadillos, gives the scraps to Yako and begins to carve our names on a rock with a pocket knife. I remember all the tree trunks and sidewalks with wet cement where I used to write names, initials and dates as a teenager, driven by some futile, obscure need for permanence. Alberto shows me his inscription proudly:

EDUARDO, ALBERTO Y YAKO ESTUVIERON AQUÍ

"I'd like to carve my girlfriend's name here too" he says.

"Do you think she'll ever see it?" I ask.

"No, she's spending the summer with her family at the beach. That's not the point."

"How long have you known her?"

"Only a week" he says blushing. "No sooner do I meet her and she has to go away on vacation." He scrapes the dry ground with his knife. I remember the Spanish-American proverb *"Amor de lejos, amor de pendejos"* (Faraway love, fools' love), but decide that Alberto is not ready for it.

We talk about girls, his school, the sports he plays, the music he likes. His favorite songs, singers and groups are almost identical to those of my older son Daniel. Today Alberto seems almost to be a son of mine.

When we get up to continue walking, my body creaks like the hull and rigging of an old ship. My feet ache until they warm up again on the gradual descent down the other side of the mountain. The old blisters don't hurt but I can feel new ones forming inside my hot boots.

Mount Perdón is one of the main watersheds on the road; by passing it you enter a different realm. As soon as the Pyrenees drop out of sight, the air becomes warmer and drier; encinas, or evergreen oaks and chaparral replace pines, poplars, deciduous oaks and beech trees. There are fewer grains, more truck gardens. The peaks of Arnotegui and Montejurra lie ahead but the mountain influence of the Pyrenees is gone. In a clump of dwarf oaks and thick brush, I stop to do what nobody else can do for me. Alberto and Yako go blithely ahead, soon they're out of earshot, I'm surrounded by the buzzing sounds of summer. Back on the path I'm glad to walk alone for a while, more alert to sights, sounds, smells.

Without warning I come upon a field of sunflowers in a curve of the path on my right. Suddenly I'm at the center of a semicircle formed by the plants—as tall as I am, their great yellow flowers with dark centers ripe for harvest, motionless on their green stems, like heads of living creatures. Since the sun is behind me, the sunflowers are trained on me eerily: I feel as though I'm being observed by thousands of golden faces, the field shimmering in the light, pulsating to the rhythm of cicadas, wholly alive. I begin to walk again, almost expecting the plants to turn their heads and follow me.

The vision of the sunflowers has surprised me almost as much as the shepherdess two days ago. Only two days? So much has happened since then, my feet have walked so many miles, my eyes have seen so many people, things, landscapes, it's hard to believe not more than forty-eight hours have passed since the girl-woman and her flock appeared in the woods. I wonder how many pilgrims have been blessed to see her or this many-eyed field of flowers. In order to see it like this, one would have to be here in midsummer when the plants are fully grown, in the afternoon of a brilliant day like this when the sun has fallen behind the walker's back, making him the focus of those thousands of golden, unblinking eyes.

The road comes out on three villages in close succession, each with a mouthful of Basque syllables for a name—Aquiturrain, Uterga, Muruzábal. After the larger town of Obanos, the two major pilgrims' routes from France come together: the one I've taken through St. Jean-Pied-de-Port and Roncesvalles, and the other, even older way through the mountain pass of Somport and Spanish Aragón. An ugly metal statue has been built on the historic spot; already rusting, it looks like a rickety Don Quixote disguised as a pilgrim. The expensive Mesón del Peregrino, or Pilgrim's Inn has also been built here to take advantage of the famous crossroads. Alberto and I look yearningly at its swimming pool as we plod toward Puente la Reina, sweating, covered with dust. Even Yako is unhappy: the traffic forces us to put on his leash.

After several hundred yards of breathing fumes from cars and trucks, we leave the highway. Soon we reach a monastery and a church flanking the road, connected by a vaulted arch. Here the Knights Templar used to run a large hospice; my guidebook says the Padres Reparadores still offer refuge to pilgrims.

We ring the doorbell. Finally a young priest opens the door to the cloister, looking as if he's just awakened from a nap. We ask if pilgrims can spend the night here. He points to a pile of backpacks on the ground behind him—each with a scallop shell sewn on it—and says there is no more room. He tells us we're welcome to rest here, wishes us luck and walks away.

We leave the cloister, cross the road beneath the arch and enter the Iglesia del Crucifijo, named after a famous wooden carving of Christ on the cross. We sit on a pew while Yako lies on the cool stone floor. The crucifix is unlike any I've seen in Spain or elsewhere, strangely primitive and modern at the same time. The bony, bloody, larger-than-life Jesus is nailed with thick spikes to a Y-shaped tree; his abnormally long arms follow the 45-degree angle of the branches, making him resemble a hovering, stylized, tragic-faced bird.

We leave the church and walk toward the town. Puente la Reina is celebrating its annual fiesta, a kind of miniature San Fermín. As we walk down the streets we have to dodge cattle dung from the encierro. Yako stops to sniff every one of the bovine monuments. Meanwhile the bars and cafés are spilling over with people, music blares from loudspeakers, fireworks explode. I realize that there's nothing less Jacobean than a Spanish town in fiesta: a pilgrim arrives too tired to dance, drink and carouse, desiring only to rest his weary body.

Knitting and chatting on balconies, some old ladies give us directions for lodging. We find a room at the noisy Bar-Hostal Puente, located on a modern avenue lined with horse-chestnut trees. It has replaced the old Rúa Mayor or Street of the Pilgrims as the town's thoroughfare.

While Alberto calls his father on the public telephone—shouting into the mouthpiece to make himself heard over the din of the fiesta—I order a beer at one of the outside tables. Before the harried waiter can serve me, the tall, awkward Frenchman, his blond companion and another, older woman come out of the bar. Again we've ended up at the same place, as on those first two nights in Roncesvalles and Zubiri. The coincidence is too much for us to believe; we greet each other in macaronic French and English. Alberto arrives speaking Spanish, making the conversation even more confusing.

Luckily the younger of the two woman speaks both French and Spanish; she becomes our interpreter. As far as I can understand, her name is Bernadette, she's French but lives in the Spanish city of Logroño, a little more than sixty kilometers west of here on the Camino de Santiago. She looks about thirty-five, already well-tanned by the road, attractive in her white walking shorts, T-shirt and socks, with suede hiking boots. Her companions are René, an engineer with a constant, kindly smile, and his wife Guillemette, a small, pixy-like woman in her fifties who works as a nurse at the Pasteur Institute in Paris.

I say goodbye to them when José Mari pulls up in front of the bar. It's only about twenty kilometers from Pamplona to Puente la Reina yet I find it unbelievable that he has arrived so soon. He's covered in fifteen minutes the same distance it has taken us a whole summer afternoon to cross on foot.

José Mari cannot stop laughing when he sees us, sunburnt, dusty and sweat-soaked, Yako lying in a panting heap on the ground: so different from the way we looked this morning. We enjoy telling him about our walk. Alberto exaggerates every detail as if we've climbed and descended Mount Everest.

José Mari says he must return to Pamplona on business but he would like me to stay in Puente tomorrow so that we can spend some time together in the afternoon. "I must show you Eunate" he says. "It's one of the wonders on the other Camino de Santiago."

My feet and body are so sore that I agree at once: "Maybe I can catch some of the fiesta" I tell him as an excuse, beginning to feel embarrassed by my ailments. At home I get plenty of exercise but like most Americans who depend on a car, I don't walk enough to be prepared for a five-hundred-mile trek.

Alberto and I give each other a wet and odorous abrazo, a Spanish embrace. I look into his blue eyes and thank him for coming with me. "You're a good pilgrim—someday you'll walk all the way to Santiago" I tell him, wondering whether I'll get that far myself.

6 Fiesta, the Black
Santiago, Eunate

When rockets awake me in the morning, I realize this has been another dreamless sleep. Perhaps my days have been so full that I don't have enough energy left for dreaming.

The fiesta is already warming up. After a café con leche at the bar, I go into the street, strewn with empty cans, bottles, papers. Following the crowds to the main square, I climb up the wooden slats to find a spot where I can observe without being crushed by people. The entire plaza has been closed off by the railings, covered with a few inches of sand to transform it into a makeshift bullring. Hundreds of spectators watch from ground level or above from windows and balconies.

An unshaven man tells me they've already run the encierro through the streets to the corral next to the main square. From here the animals will be released one at a time for the young men of Puente la Reina to prove their bravery. The crowd suddenly screams as a black creature shoots from the corral; it's a fighting cow, not a bull. The bravery is supposed to derive from the female and the estampa, or size and figure from the male. Last year in the town of Leyre, not far from here, a fighting cow killed a man in the local fiesta. You might think these animals were steers since they have no visible udder, no signs of cowhood or femininity, as Hemingway put it. This cow has come in as fast as a horse, charging, feinting, darting, tossing her horns at whatever moves. The young men watch from behind the wooden slats, letting her tire a little before jumping onto the sand from her blind side, dashing across the ring before she can turn enough to catch them. No elegance is involved, no use of cape, banderillas, muleta or sword that can make of the formal bullfight a ritual art. The purpose of the encierro is much more primitive: for young men to test themselves against the dangers of life and death embodied in the horns.

I'm beginning to feel bored and confined by the crowd pressing at my back. Spaniards under the new democracy are more courteous but they still may be the pushiest people in Europe—much as I love them. Maybe I'm getting too acustomed to the open spaces on the road.

After struggling through the crowd I come out on the Calle de los Romeros where the medieval road used to cross the town. On my left is a Romanesque portal, its capitals and archivolts almost obliterated by time, in front of a church with the usual additions from later periods. Inside I know this must be the Iglesia de Santiago: on the Baroque altar-piece there are two reliefs with scenes from the life of St. James. I see a wooden statue of the apostle dressed as a pilgrim, the famous carving known as El Beltza in Basque, "The Black One"—the painted wood was darkened by smoke from tapers and the grime of centuries until it was rediscovered, like Santiago's tomb, in a loft of the church. People say the figure was almost chopped up for firewood; you can still see the mark of an ax-stroke on one side of the head. Another miracle of St. James! Not only his life, even his images have their own history of wonders, narrow escapes, deaths and resurrections.

I draw closer to the statue: it's the first time I've seen Santiago represented as a pilgrim with cloak, walking staff and hat adorned by cockleshells. He also has a book under one arm, symbol of wisdom; the other version of the saint, the Moorkiller, never carries a book. This apostle stands upright, barefoot, while the Matamoros is always depicted on horseback. With his uncombed hair and the beard of a man who's slept many nights under the stars, the image has a dignified humility that is foreign to the Moorslayer. In spite of his shoeless feet and torn cloak, this Santiago projects a power, a presence, a serenity that are new to me.

Standing in front of the statue I ask myself how one historical figure could have become two such contrasting personalities in legend, such different icons in art. If only the apostle's impetuosity justified his metamorphosis into the scourge of infidels and a symbol of the Reconquest, how was he transformed into this proud yet humble image, model and patron of pilgrims who walked to the shrine built over his own tomb in Compostela? For only the flimsiest of reasons, based on legend rather than fact—like almost everything else that has to do with Santiago. St. James the Elder was the apostle who traveled farthest to spread the gospel, supposedly to Roman Hispania when it lay at the end of the known world. He anticipated the great westward movement of pilgrims to Compostela by crossing the Mediterranean, landing near the delta of the Ebro River, following its banks upstream, eventually making his way as far as Galicia. (Tradition offers nearly as many alternate itineraries as a good travel agent.) But the small number of years between the crucifixion of Jesus and Santiago's death hardly would have been sufficient for the apostle to preach in the Holy Land, go to Spain, spread the good news across the whole peninsula and return to Jerusalem in time for his own martyrdom. Unlike most of his life, St. James' death is based on reliable facts. His beheading by Herod Agrippa on the 8th of the calends of April (May 25) is the only Biblical record of an apostle's decease. He was the first disciple to drink Christ's cup of death and to receive the promised baptism of suffering.

We wouldn't expect a saint who performed so many wonders *after* death to have died without a miracle. The *Book of St. James* tells us that when the executioner decapitated Santiago with a stroke of his sword, the apostle caught his own falling noggin in his hands, holding it so tightly that nobody could take it from him until his followers spirited him away in the night—both body and head, one presumes—placed him in a deerskin with aromatic essences and set sail from Joppa in a sailless, rudderless ship of stone toward the same faraway land to which he had reputedly journeyed when alive. So even after his death Santiago continued to go on "pilgrimage," returning to Spain this time for burial, much later for battle. As the skeptical Richard Ford said in the heydey of travel by ocean liner, the apostle's voyage from the Holy Land to Galicia took only seven days, "which at once proves the miracle, since the modern Oriental Steam Company can do nothing like it." The doubting Englishman, who anticipated some of the current theories on the Jacobean cult by a century, also believed "there is no tittle of real evidence to prove that Santiago ever was in Spain, dead or alive." What all this means now is that St. James the pilgrim, who stands before me in this image of wood, is almost as much a creation of fantasy as the Moorkiller mounted on a white steed. At least he's closer to the Galilean fisherman who never rode anything in his life except a donkey, and who forsook his nets to become a fisher of men.

When I come out of the church, the crowd is dispersing from the main square. They're nearly all men and I have a sudden intuition that the encierro and the corrida, those masculine prerogatives for displaying valor, are somehow related to the violent, mythic world of Santiago Matamoros. The bullfight is known as the national spectacle of Spain; St. James—invariably seen as the Moorslayer rather than the pilgrim—is of course the national patron. Moving against the crowd on the old street, I notice that the men walk in groups, telling stories about the encierro, each teller trying to outdo the others. I feel my solitude again; there's nothing more lonely than being a stranger without

4 Eunate. (Photo Emilio Peláez)

friends at a Spanish fiesta. These young men have nothing to do with me. I feel much closer to Bernadette, René and his wife wherever they are now, walking ahead of me on the Road to Santiago. Will I ever catch up with them or will I have to walk the rest of the Camino alone?

On the sidewalk under the horse-chestnuts I have a long Spanish lunch. Food and a bottle of wine can be good company. When the afternoon begins to cool off, the noise of the fiesta already mounting again, José Mari appears in his station wagon. Míkel, his next-youngest son after Alberto, is sitting in back. He's nine or ten with the same playful look in his eyes.

"You're going to see something you'll never forget" says José Mari as I get in the front seat. He's wearing his old Robin Hood cap with a scraggly, fallen feather attached by a safety pin.

Míkel says "Hola" when I greet him, looking up from the Rubik's cube that he fidgets in his hands.

We pass the junction of the two French routes to Compostela, where Alberto and I put Yako on the leash yesterday. Not more than two miles from the Roncesvalles road I see it: a little chapel of golden stone in the middle of a wheat field.

5 Stone pavement around
the chapel of Eunate.
(Photo José Luis Herrera)

"I knew you wouldn't want to miss this one" says José Mari with
the air of someone about to reveal a portentous secret.

I feel impatient to get out of the car and see this chapel standing
alone, uncluttered by surrounding streets or people with only the
field, poplars and an old stone barn for neighbors. Before José Mari can
come to a stop, Míkel and I open our doors, the boy runs off crying
"I'm going to chase mice!" and I walk through the waist-high grain,
staring at the church.

It's unlike anything I've seen, at once intimate and imposing in its
solitude, octagonal in shape with an open cloister around it in simple,

pure Romanesque. I reach the gallery, noticing the old pavement with its thousands of small stones arranged in rows radiating from the walls of the church, little tufts of grass growing in the cracks. Feeling myself pulled inwards, I follow the gallery clockwise, touching the rough stone of the building with my right hand.

When I reach the wooden door of the entrance, José Mari is there waiting for me. "Me cago en diez!" he says angrily. "It's closed. There's supposed to be a woman in charge of the keys in that barn. A priest also has the keys but he lives in another town and only comes here when they celebrate Mass. Let's go see if the woman's in."

As we walk toward the barn, I steal looks back at the chapel: it's turning a russet color as the sun drops in the sky.

"What do you think?" asks José Mari.

"It's the first monument on the Camino that has moved me. Seems to be more a part of nature than the human world, in the middle of nowhere."

"Right. There's a polemic about this little jewel. Catholics hold that it was simply another shrine in honor of the Virgin—Santa María de Eunate is its official name. At the most they believe it may have been a funerary chapel since some bodies have been disinterred here, identified as Jacobean pilgrims from the scallop shells buried with them."

We come to the front of the stone barn, locked as securely as the church. "Me cago en Dios!" says José Mari, defecating on God in a curse that sounds scandalous in any language but Spanish. "I wanted you to see the inside, Eduardo" he says. "It's as beautiful as the exterior. It feels so sheltering and so protective when you stand in the very center under the dome with a milky light filtered through the windows."

We walk back toward the chapel. Seeing the alabaster windows—narrow slits framed by two columns and a round arch—I feel angry, deprived, unable to penetrate these thick walls to the source of the centripetal pull on me and everything around us.

"Look at those marks on the stones" says José Mari pointing to the sill beneath a window, whitened by pigeon-dung.

I have to strain my eyes to see them, only a few inches long, carved on the blocks like primitive glyphs—variants of arrows, crosses, T's, X's, backwards and forwards S's.

"Some believe they are the signatures of the stonecutters" José Mari says, "their way of collecting payment for each block they hewed. But if that were true why are so many blocks unmarked? Others believe the church wasn't used originally for Christian service. Unlike nearly all Catholic temples, the apse faces south instead of east." Orienting myself against the setting sun, I see that he's right.

José Mari goes on: "They think the marks on the blocks are initiatory symbols of the master stonemasons who might have formed a secret guild or society like the Freemasons. Since Puente la Reina, only a few kilometers away was given by the Crown to the Knights Templar, they've been invoked as the possible builders of the chapel, which may be an imitation of the Church of the Holy Sepulcher in Jerusalem. Or even the Temple of Solomon—the sacred place of perfect, magical proportions, the center, the mystic temple of the soul."

When José Mari's lively voice becomes silent, we can hear the twitter of swallows that are swooping around the far-off poplars, feeding on insects in the twilight.

"The oddest thing of all is this detached cloister" I say. Through its arches we can see the profile of the graceful trees.

"You're right, it puzzles all the experts" says José Mari. "It's not even found in the other rare octagonal churches in Spain. The name Eunate itself probably refers to this detached arcade; it means something like 'the house of a hundred doors' in Basque."

"All of them closed" I say. "What kind of purpose could the open cloister have?"

"Nobody knows. Those who think this was a Templar church believe the Knights practiced their secret rites here; the gallery would have been a lookout, a screen or shelter to keep uninitiated ears away from the walls." He pauses to call Míkel who comes running toward us from the line of poplars, black spears against the western sky now.

"Anyway" he goes on, "the fascinating thing about this gallery is that it's an anti-cloister, not shut upon itself like every other cloister we've seen. It's open in all of its 360 degrees to the fields, the mountains, the world."

Míkel arrives out of breath, crying "Papá!" He wants to tell his father something but José Mari pats him on the head, telling him to wait a moment.

"Now you can understand why I didn't want you to miss Eunate" he says. "It belongs to the 'other' Camino de Santiago—not the official one."

Míkel finally has his chance to talk: "I couldn't trap any field mice but I've been chewing wheat—it turns to gum." With the same hand that holds the Rubik's cube, he pulls a doughy white paste from his mouth. In the other hand he holds a sheaf of barbed, golden ears of wheat.

José Mari takes the cube gently from Míkel, holding it up toward the chapel: "This cube has six sides but you can count eight if you conceive of it as two overlapping, four-sided surfaces. The church is octagonal yet it gives the impression of roundness from both inside and out. Look at it: Eunate, the squaring of the circle. The gallery girding the temple is circular, and in the twelfth century when it was built, architects didn't design something like that without a purpose. This round, roofless cloister was constructed for people to walk around it just as we've done, under the open sky, the moon and stars. Could Eunate have been a kind of medieval observatory, a miniature Stonehenge for siting heavenly bodies at special times of the year? Another microcosm of Spain like the bullring, where a primitive rite of initiation was also celebrated? I could go on, Eduardo, because most of the questions remain unanswered or haven't even been asked. Eunate is the greatest enigma on the whole Camino and one of its most beautiful places. Of course I'm a little partial since it's almost in my backyard."

"Papi don't talk so much" complains Míkel.

"You're right, hijo" José Mari answers. "Let's go."

As we walk around the chapel toward the car, I notice some large, uneven letters of red spray-paint on the stone walls. The Middle Ages and the twentieth century, I think.

"Don't tell me these are more esoteric symbols" I tease José Mari.

He laughs. "I wish they were. Even Eunate's not free from this kind of desecration. Our beloved terrorists have blemished it too." Looking at the red paint in the dying light, he says "These graffiti denounce Fuerza Nueva, a group of disgruntled former Franco supporters who think the democratic government is too weak in combatting ETA, the Basque separatists. So they take matters into their own hands by assassinating Basques in retaliation for ETA's kidnappings, murders and bombings. If it weren't for these damned barbarians—on both sides—the Basque country and Navarre would be the best place in the world, at least for me."

I cannot help agreeing with José Mari as we get in the car, looking at the horizon—shades of purple and green where the sun has set.

The emotion of Eunate still with me, everything we do now passes like a film. We visit a friend of José Mari's in nearby Obanos, who serves us supper, chooses a good local wine from his cellar and urges me to visit a cousin of his in Torres del Río, a couple of days' walk on the Road from here. We return to Puente la Reina and find the town in full fiesta. After parking the car we walk to the plaza where people of all ages are performing the delicate baile de la era, or threshing-floor dance on the same animal-smelling sand where the young men tried their courage against the cows this morning and will do the same tomorrow. The public ceremonies end with the traditional toro de fuego, a mechanical bull with firecrackers and rockets shooting from its wooden horns as it chases the little boys of the town who will someday run the encierro on these streets as their older brothers did, their fathers and their grandfathers.

The crowd scatters once more to carry the revelry indoors—to houses, bars or peñas, the drinking and eating societies. José Mari, Míkel and I walk arm-in-arm like everyone else, feeling the camaraderie of the fiesta, to the end of the Street of Pilgrims where the town's famous bridge spans the river Arga. It's fit for a queen as its name proves, as the name of the town itself has declared ever since the bridge was erected some nine hundred years ago to ease the passage of pilgrims through the kingdom of Navarre.

We walk onto the Puente de la Reina; it slopes gently up from each bank to the elevated central arch. As we approach the highest point, the farther shore becomes invisible for a moment and it's as though we're walking on the air. We stop, our gazes drawn upward to the sky where the Milky Way embraces the firmament like a pale woman's arm.

José Mari explains to Míkel that the Milky Way is considered a heavenly reflection of the Road to Santiago. He's a good father and a good friend, I think, knowing we must say goodbye soon, remembering my own younger son. I miss Carlos suddenly: it seems I haven't seen him for weeks instead of some five days.

"Listen to the frogs!" Míkel shouts. "Can I catch some, Papi?"

José Mari says no, changing the subject: "See that other bridge over there, Míkel?" He points to a modern, metallic structure about a hundred yards downstream. "That's the one we cross when we drive to Logroño and Burgos. Listen to this, Eduardo. That bridge collapsed several years ago and there were some deaths; it was only a few years old at the time. And here we are on the old bridge—still standing after all these centuries. It hasn't collapsed once."

"Yes but, Papi, they don't allow cars to cross it. All the cars and trucks have to cross the other one."

"Sí, hijo" says José Mari patiently, "the old bridge is now for pedestrians only. By the way, Eduardo, how are your feet?"

"Today has been a relief but I'm afraid they're still sore."

"You know I've walked the pilgrimage to St. Xavier several times" he says. "Since it takes less than a full day and comes only once a year, your feet never get in condition for it. So I've learned simply to accept the blisters and to forget about them. 'To hell with blisters!'—that's what you must tell yourself."

The croaking of frogs rises from both shores. An owl hoots far away, some bats corner into the darkness. José Mari shows Míkel the Big Dipper and the North Star.

Something strikes across the sky: "Una estrella fugaz!" cries Míkel, "A shooting star!"

"That means a child has been born somewhere" says José Mari, "or a soul has been released on its long journey."

7   Pilgrimage and Picaresque

> Our most sacred narrations of pilgrimages are, in
> a sense, picaresque novels.
>
> —Anthony Burgess

There's nobody in sight but what a noisy morning! Dogs bark as I cross the Queen's Bridge where I cannot help remembering José Mari and Míkel; the bells of a church—probably Santiago's—toll seven o'clock; frogs are still croaking; the birds in the trees and shrubs by the river bank have started their morning riot. When the road meets the highway, I look back at the Arga, my companion for much of the way since Zubiri and the meerschaum factory more than forty kilometers upstream. No wonder its surface is covered with foamy scum here too. They can destroy the water in the river but not this bridge. I see it in full profile, the six arches rising in the center where we stood last night, separated from the river as if it were floating on the surface.

My feet are better after a day's rest. I'm going to keep José Mari's words in mind: "To hell with blisters!" That's also what a little black ant tells me at my first rest under a live-oak tree where he struggles along with a piece of straw many times his size.

After getting lost in a field crossed by lines of rushes, I reach the second famous bridge on the Camino de Santiago, over the Río Salado. Not majestic like the Puente de la Reina, it looks quaint with its two uneven arches, dwarfed by a modern aqueduct. Even armchair pilgrims know that this river and bridge are the scene of the most notorious passage in the *Book of St. James.* The probable author of that manuscript, the French priest Aymery Picaud tells how he and his companions on the pilgrimage asked two Navarrese, who were seated on the shore sharpening their knives, if the water was fit to drink. When the two men said yes, the French watered their mounts in the Salty River whose name should have put them on guard; the horses died almost at once and were quickly skinned by the Navarrese, who must have sold the meat and hide for a profit. But the final word belonged to Picaud. He revenged himself by describing the people of Navarre as "barbarous . . . full of evils, dark in color, wicked in appearance, depraved, perverse, treacherous, disloyal and false, lustful, drunken, steeped in all kinds of violence, ferocious, wild, vicious and corrupt, godless and savage, cruel and quarrelsome, lacking in any virtue and expert in sins and iniquities" The French priest even went so far as to accuse them of fornicating with their cattle, alleging that the men placed a kind of chastity belt on the crupper of their she-mules to keep away prospective rivals.

Today the trickle in the Río Salado—it can be called a river only by an act of the imagination—doesn't carry enough volume to kill a horse, even if the water were poisoned. Walter Starkie and several modern pilgrims have tasted the supposedly brackish water without keeling over dead. A doubting Thomas, I decide to confirm their reports, walking to the middle of the almost-dry riverbed, sticking one finger in the warm, gentle flow: not even a salty taste to justify the name.

Still thinking about the story of the horse-flayers, I stop at a bar in the first town to ask about the Río Salado. The unbashful owner introduces herself as Carmen. Middle-aged and nothing like the exotic femme fatale of novel and opera, she tells me a dam and aqueduct have drawn off the salt deposits that gave the Salado River its name. It has become just another semi-dry Spanish river bed; we can close that chapter in the history of the Camino.

Carmen asks me to send her a postcard from Compostela. Not to pray for her eternal soul to St. James, as people used to ask; not even to remember her when I reach Santiago, like the old woman who let Alberto and me drink from the water jug the other day.

Anyone who has walked the road to Compostela without getting lost many times cannot be considered a pilgrim. I lose sight of the yellow arrows again, wandering for a while before returning to the paved road in order to find my way to the town of Estella. Long famous as one of the major stations on the Road, it no longer has a single refuge for pilgrims. After walking around the narrow streets, bumping into pedestrians with my pack and breathing the fumes of cars during the lunchtime rush, I finally take a room in a cheap pensión.

Aymery Picaud says in his famous guidebook that Estella is "fertile in good bread, superb wine, meat, and fish and full of every happiness." I cannot vouch for the happiness but his appraisal of the food still holds: in the dining room of the pensión I have a three-course meal, more abundant than delicate, with a liter of Navarrese clarete for 620 pesetas, not quite four dollars.

After a nap on the sinking mattress in my tiny room—the bed occupies more than half the floor space—I go for a walk. Knowing the importance of the town as a landmark on the Camino, I'm anxious to explore it. "Estella la bella" says an old adage. James Michener, a veteran Spanish hand who made a pilgrimage to Compostela by car in order to thank his patron saint for recovering from a heart attack, even said he'd choose this town if he were to live in Spain.

I walk through the narrow streets that smell of food from the many small stores beneath the old soportales, porticos around the squares. I go in and out of churches and cloisters, some of them built on steep, rocky hills. These monuments don't move me as Eunate did yesterday when all my senses seemed open and porous, eager to be filled.

As the afternoon fades I find a hardware store whose owner is a friend of José Mari's. After I introduce myself to Benito Gómez, he decides to close the shop and invites me to have a drink which ends up being more than one. In Spain a toast is never the last but the "penúltimo," or next-to-last. We go from one bar to another ordering the special tapa in each—here mushrooms sautéed with garlic, there a variety of chistorra, or hot red sausage, somewhere else a local cheese—always washing it down with the wine of the country. Since Benito knows all the bartenders in this town of thirteen thousand, they form a conspiracy to prevent me, the foreigner from picking up the tab. My money is no good in Estella. The Spaniards, especially the Navarrese, are the most generous people I've ever known.

At the last stop, or rather the next-to-last, Benito asks if I'm comfortable at my pensión.

"The bed's too soft but I'll see worse on the road."

"Lift your elbow, Eduardo" he says, "and remember the proverb: 'A mala cama colchón de vino, for a bad bed a pillow of wine.'"

We laugh and drink two more rounds before saying goodbye. Benito wishes me "Buen viaje" and I walk back to my pensión, dizzy on the wine of the country.

I'm on the road by 7:30, a little hung over from last night. This is my seventh day of pilgrimage. My feet don't hurt but I have a pain in my left hip, maybe from the sagging mattress in the pensión. To pass the time, I calculate the kilometers I've walked—about 117—and how many remain—almost 600. This figure sounds so forbidding that I try to erase it from my mind and look for something more encouraging. I find it in the smile of a young woman in the outskirts: a good omen for the day like the ant under the tree yesterday.

Ahead on the left I can see the peak of Montejurra, the sacred mountain of the Navarrese traditionalists. At its foot lies the Benedictine monastery of Irache, founded in the tenth century, later a university, then a school for seminarians. Like so many convents and monasteries in Spain, it has been abandoned. As the path borders the wall around the buildings—grass grows out of the roof tiles—I smell the earth, moisture and decay.

At a fountain by the highway I stop for my first rest, taking off my pack, putting it on the ledge of a cement trough where cold water spills from a pipe. I drink and hear a tinkling of bells when suddenly a flock of sheep and goats comes around the corner from the town, heading straight for me and the fountain. Before I can get my pack and staff out of the way they're jumping with their front legs clumsily onto the edge of the trough, paying no attention to me, their hooves slipping on the wet cement as they climb on top of one another, bumping me with their warm, steaming snouts frantic to reach the water. All I can do is hold my ground by digging my boots into the wet soil, one arm outstretched on the backpack to keep it from falling into the water, I see the shepherd going by quickly with his dogs, smiling without offering help, I remember the flock of sheep that Don Quixote thought was a charging army and I know why. The worst is over now as the man and his dogs reach the highway; his animals don't want to be left behind, torn between thirst and the herd-instinct. A car stops to let them cross to the other side where they scamper around a hill and they're gone, the sound of bells fading away.

I've saved my pack but my staff has been trampled in the mire, my boots, pants and the front of my T-shirt smeared with mud. Taking out my one and only towel, laughing at myself I moisten it in the water that is still turbid from the stampede. I clean off the muck, rinse the towel and hang it to dry on the aluminum frame of my pack.

When I finally begin to walk again I notice sheep- and goat-dung on the road, remembering the shepherdess. The same words come back to mind, "Camino de las Estrellas, / Camino de la Mierda." There's something about the act of walking, its rhythm nudges the memory, brings words, phrases, verses, songs to consciousness. Road of Stars . . . On the one hand this dung, dirt, mud, dust, sweat, blisters, pain, aching muscles and bones, a polluted river, stinking factory, abandoned churches, decaying towns living from the glory of the past or from nothing. On the other hand that white galaxy stretching across the sky, the one I saw with Míkel and José Mari in Puente la Reina, the three of us standing on the bridge that seemed to float above the water, lifting us halfway to the stars; the places with duende like the forest of Roncesvalles and Eunate, recalling an age when men and women were somehow larger than today, closer to the center, the sources of life, a mystery that has been lost to us. Shit, why don't you go ahead and say it: God.

The road is drawing closer to La Rioja, the best region for table wine in the peninsula; there are more vineyards on both sides of the road, fewer wheat fields. I could use a couple of shots of Rioja wine now for the pain in my hip. Instead I take two aspirins with water from my canteen and stop to rest when the pain becomes too sharp.

On top of a rise I stop to ask a shepherd—frank smile and straight teeth—if he thinks it will rain. He looks at the sky, rubbing his chin: "El cielo se arruga, the sky's brow is wrinkled" he says, meaning it's overcast. Then: "I don't think it will rain."

I believe him more than all the meteorologists and experts who prattle about the weather on radio and television. The world's true weathermen, the shepherds who live under the sun, moon and stars and learn to predict rain, shine or snow with their eyes and all their senses . . . they're nearly gone.

The man is right: the sky lours but no rain has fallen when I reach an escarpment above a valley and the town of Torres del Río. A van selling fruit and vegetables is parked by the shoulder of the road, "AMOR Y PAZ" painted in large letters on its side.

I ask the driver for three peaches. He refuses to take my money: "Keep them for the road" he says. "Y que sea usted muy feliz, and may you be very happy."

I don't speak for a few seconds: how can I express my gratitude for such an unexpected gift, one I'll never be able to repay? I wouldn't know how to reply in my own language but I remember the Spanish phrase for the situation: "Que Dios se lo pague, may god reward you" I tell him.

Walking down the steep road to Torres del Río, I try the peaches, the first thing I've eaten all day. They taste sweet but the man's words have meant more to me, still echoing in my ears, a kind of blessing. The sun has come out and shines over the town that is nestled on a hill like a small Toledo, a church and a Romanesque tower dominating its profile. With the fruit vendor's blessing, the sun, the memory of Eunate and my curiosity about this new town before me, I'm happy.

My guidebook says a man named Ramón Sostres lodges pilgrims in his own house, "Casa Santa Bárbara" in Torres del Río—the only case of an individual who offers regular hospitality to strangers on the Camino de Santiago, it says. Recalling Santa Barbara, California where I spent time as a teenager surfing in the cool water of its beaches, I conjure up a well-appointed, clean bedroom with a firm feather bed where I can get a good sleep and rest my bum hip. As I walk up the hill of the main street, I see a two-story villa with a balcony covered by a climbing vine, a plaque of ceramic tiles on the façade saying "Casa Santa Bárbara". So far it has lived up to my imagination. The owner is probably at table for lunch; not to interrupt the most important meal of the day, I decide to look for a place to eat.

On the way to the center of town I pass a boy kicking a soccer ball. He stops to stare at me and asks if I'm going to Santiago. I tell him yes as I read the logo on his T-shirt: "California Windsurf Association / Newport Beach, California", framed by a picture of the ocean.

"Where are you from?" he asks.

"Do you know what that says on your shirt?"

"No."

"Well that's where I'm from—California."

"Ca-li-for-nia" he repeats slowly, making it sound as mythical as it must have sounded to the readers of the old chivalric novel in which the name appeared for the first time.

Climbing up the empty street I think how incongruous is the boy's shirt in landlocked Torres del Río; nobody in town has probably ever laid eyes on a windsurfer. As long as a jacket or shirt or pair of pants has words in English, the Spaniards will buy, thinking it must be in fashion. No matter that hardly anyone understands the words. I remember seeing pirated shirts in Madrid, blazoned with the colors and names of nonexistent institutions: Chicago College, University of Los Angeles, Harvard State. This is a sign of the new Spain, member of NATO, another consumer nation in the European Union.

The sound of a television leads me to the town bar. The American serial "Knight Rider," dubbed with melodramatic voices of Spanish actors, is playing at full blast on the "Sobremesa" or after-lunch feature—prime time in Spain where life comes to a halt for the sacred midday meal. Even in a tiny, one-bar village like Torres del Río on the medieval Camino de Santiago, I cannot escape my country.

Four or five clients, all men smoking cigarettes and drinking coffee, anise or brandy watch me shamelessly as I take off my pack and lean my staff against a chair. The smaller a town in Spain, the more brazenly its inhabitants stare at strangers.

When I ask the bartender what he has for lunch, he replies "Nada, nothing." A silence follows.

I tell him that I haven't eaten all day, stretching the truth a little. He scavenges for a tin of sardines and a crust of old bread, which he puts on a plate with a liter of red wine. Sitting as far from the blaring

TV as possible, I eat my lunch in solitude. Get drunk on the wine of the country, I tell myself, then stare right back at the locals.

At a time like this I yearn for the anonymity of a metropolis. Already I feel the boredom, the tedium of existence in this town, this backwater of history where people's lives are so empty that they have nothing better to do than ogle at foreigners. As the lunch-hour comes to an end, more men enter, the younger ones standing at the bar, the oldsters—dressed in the same jackets, sweaters and boinas, or berets all year round—sit at a table to play their afternoon game of mus. (So different from the card game at the elegant club in Pamplona!) How dull is a place without women, I think, no better than an army barracks.

When I walk outside in the heat I see a small crowd watching a tractor clear debris from a vacant lot. They comment, kibitz, analyze every move of the machine, wholly absorbed: this may be the most important event of the summer in Torres del Río. The Latin peoples, especially the Spaniards and Italians, have a way of transforming everyday happenings into momentous dramas complete with characters, plots and denouements. One could spend an entire life doing this—many do—while time marches on and the engagements of history are fought far away.

On my way back to the villa I pass the octagonal church, more graceful than Eunate because of its dome and lantern but less powerful, hemmed in by other buildings. An old woman in black is sweeping the entrance. I ask her if visitors are allowed. The top of her head reaches no higher than my chest. Without speaking she takes a bunch of old iron keys—each one about six inches long—and opens the main door.

I'm alone in here, the only sound the muffled sweeping of the woman's broom outside. I feel a peacefulness in this clean, simple building, almost bare of decoration. A sign on the wall says "Iglesia del Santo Sepulcro," with the hours of the Mass. I let my eyes run across the upper ranges of capitals where the stone has been carved to represent leaves, pine cones, honeysuckle vines, a centaur. The columns in the windows have masks with birds and snakes whispering in their ears, other birds with necks entwined. This chapel doesn't need the natural setting of Eunate, I think: it contains a vision of nature in stone, the animal and plant kingdoms expressed in images. I don't feel like a tourist here; I'm a participant, as if those birds and serpents were whispering their secrets to me, messengers of earth or sky . . . "Camino de las Estrellas . . . "

After giving the silent woman a tip, I walk to the Casa Santa Bárbara. By now the owner must have had time to finish his lunch and
even take the customary nap. When I knock, a man comes out on the
balcony; I look up, seeing him against the sun and a coffered wooden
ceiling. What a house, I think.

"I'm coming" he says.

The man opens the door and offers a flaccid Spanish handshake,
introducing himself: "Ramón Sostre, para servirle, to serve you." He's
about sixty, sallow, unshaven with only two front teeth intact,
dressed in a dark suit too large for him. I notice that his collar and
sleeves are frayed, the elbows worn shiny from use. The entrance hall
is so dark that I'm almost blind after the sun outside. He probably
keeps the house dark so that it will stay cool.

"Where are you from?" he asks in the formal third-person.

"The United States."

"How nice, that makes seventeen countries. Five hundred and
eighteen pilgrims from seventeen countries have stayed here now.
You are the first from the United States. It makes me happy when
someone from a new country arrives."

He speaks with a guttural Catalan accent uncommon in this part
of Spain. I want to ask him about it but there's something evasive in
his demeanor, a kind of adolescent shyness that makes me forbear.

He leads me to a large, cool room to the left of the stairway. As
my eyes get used to the dark, I see that it's bare except for a mattress
on the floor: empty walls, no chairs, bench, table—nothing.

"This is all I have to offer pilgrims" he says timidly, speaking with
his eyes turned away.

"It's enough to rest this tired body" I tell him, somehow feeling
that I'm the host and he the guest.

"If only I had the means I'd build the most magnificent refuge on
the whole Camino de Santiago" he says, "because pilgrimage is for la
cultura, culture." He says the word as though it were written with a
capital letter. "Make yourself comfortable" he adds. "Ésta es su casa,
this is your home."

When I take off my pack and drop it with relief on the mattress, a
cloud of dust rises, tickling my nostrils, almost making me sneeze.
"Let me show you where the water is" he says walking through a door
in the back of the room.

I follow him to the kitchen or what once might have been a
kitchen: there's nothing here now but a sink and two boxes full of
empty beer bottles.

He fills a bucket at the faucet. "They don't turn on the water in town until eleven o'clock in the morning. You may want to keep this bucket for tomorrow if you leave before then."

"And the servicio?" I ask using the Spanish euphemism for toilet. I don't want to say "bathroom" because a shower or bath is clearly out of the question here.

He makes an effort to laugh but it turns into a rasping cough. "Follow me" he manages to say with phlegm in his throat.

Ramón walks to a door at the back of the house. Opening it he points to a large, walled yard overgrown with bushes and weeds, a pile of empty cans in one corner. "There's the bathroom" he says smiling. "Dondequiera, wherever you wish." His eyes look far away.

"I'm used to that from the road" I answer trying to make him feel better.

"I will leave this door open now" he says, "so you will have more light." Finally I realize that the house is not dark because of the heat: there is no electricity.

We return to the room which I already think of reluctantly as mine. Feeling nervous, not knowing what to say I begin to unpack my sleeping bag, barely able to see in the dark.

Staying several yards away from me—Spaniards usually stand much closer when conversing—he asks me quietly if I've visited the church.

Relieved by the break in the silence, I answer "Yes, a few minutes ago. It's beautiful."

"Yes it is."

Just as I'm about to ask him a question regarding the church, he clears his throat, stands bolt-straight, makes a kind of reverence and says "Ramón Sostres a sus órdenes, at your service for whatever I can do to assist. If I do not see you in the morning, may you have a successful trip to Compostela. I always rise very early to take my constitutional."

"Can I offer to buy you a drink at the bar?" I ask him.

"No thank you" he returns, "I do not touch those things." I remember the empty beer bottles. "Adiós" he says bowing, then walks up the stairs.

What in hell have you gotten yourself into this time, I ask myself, after your dreams of a feather bed? What could you have hoped for in a town like Torres del Río, this pueblo de mala muerte, a bad place even for dying if there ever was one? Now that I can see a little better, I run my hand along the floor through a layer of dust and inspect the

mattress. It looks almost as old as the medieval church of the Sepulcher in town; will it be my tomb? I don't see any bedbugs but I'll need
more than a pillow of wine to make it through tonight. How about a
gas mask to begin? And what do I know about Ramón, this strange old
coot in a house with an exterior like a villa, an abandoned tenement
inside? Why not clear out, leave right now? What difference would it
make? I'll never see him again.

Something I don't understand very well—my stubbornness, a
fragility and childlike gentleness in Ramón—inclines me to stay, to
make the best of it. I should have learned by now that life offers itself
only to those who take risks.

I beat the mattress, creating a small dust storm that makes me
sneeze. After unrolling the sleeping bag, I go outside in the light, dazzling after the dark house. Luckily José Mari's friend from Obanos,
near Eunate and Puente la Reina, gave me his cousin's name so I have
a contact in this town where time seems to be standing still.

The rest of the afternoon and evening is asking for Joaquín Tartas,
walking to his house by the Logroño road, meeting him and his wife
Codés, going through large comfortable rooms decorated in the Castilian style, descending to his wine cellar where he selects two local vin-
tages and a 1964 red from La Rioja, the Spanish Bordeaux, to go with
our supper. The wine is the best I've tasted ever, anywhere, over-
whelming in aroma yet smooth going down, full and warming.

As we finish with cognac, the conversation turns to the enigmatic
Señor Sostres. My hosts tell me that he came to Torres del Río years
ago when a religious order in Catalonia bought the Casa Santa Bárbara
to use as a school for delinquent boys, sending Ramón as the resident
teacher. Malicious rumors about sexual inversion spread through the
town, fabricated by the boys, Codés believes, so they would be released from the school.

"I know for a fact he likes women" she says, "because he has written me the most florid love poems you can imagine—always prefaced
'con todo respeto a su señor y marido, with all due respect to your lord
and husband'—his very words." With her long blond hair and stately
figure, Codés must be the object of other men's affections too, the
town beauty of Torres del Río.

"Frankly I don't think he's ever touched a male or female in his
life" she adds. "Women can feel such things. He's an idealist who lives
in a world of dreams. His politics are also unreal, far to the right,
strongly Catholic."

Joaquín and Codés tell me that the school was eventually closed
by the religious order; the fathers left Ramón as guardian of the house

without a salary or even an allowance to maintain such a large building and grounds. Little by little he had to sell the furniture to make money for food—or drink, because he likes his beer. Those who bought the furniture were like vultures, says Codés, taking it for almost nothing, aware of how desperate he was.

"He sold everything" explains Joaquín. "I'm one of his only friends in town and one of the few who've been inside that house since the boys left. The ground floor is empty and the piano nobile where Ramón sleeps, if you can call it that, has only his bed, a table, a single dresser with mirror that has survived by a miracle, and a legless armchair where he must sit for hours every day. Bare as a monk's cell. No electricity in the house, no heat, no bathroom, nada! You can imagine the cold he suffers in the winter."

"He has nothing" Codés goes on, "yet he manages to give, as you know. Others have much and give nothing. The pilgrimage is his passion—'cultura' as he would say. It allows him to feel the only dignity that has not been robbed from him. Before the pilgrims, he took in anybody who needed a roof over his head. Not long after the school closed, a family of gypsies came to town and of course good old Ramón let them camp in the yard behind his house. The townspeople despised the strangers—they were the first gitanos to settle in Torres del Río—and they've never forgiven him because that family stayed. They condemn Ramón for not working but you know how it is in Spain: many are so proud that they would rather die than work. Anyway what kind of work could he find in a village like ours? Give private lessons to students? His reputation has been ruined. He has no family, no place to go. He's been half-starving for a long time and he's too weak to work anymore, too proud to beg. He's just un alma de Dios, one of God's poor souls. He couldn't harm a fly."

We say good night and agree to meet for drinks tomorrow in Logroño where Codés and Joaquín go each Friday for their weekly shopping; it's also my next station on the road. Walking back to the Casa Santa Bárbara, my head turning from the wine, I see the waning moon of this August eve as it rises above the houses. The door of Ramón's house is unlocked—of course, he has nothing that could be stolen. I enter and grope my way to the mattress like a shipwrecked man swimming to an island, take off my shoes and socks, crawl in the sleeping bag. The house is so dark that I can't even make out the ceiling or my own hand in front of me. My head is going around in circles; it's a good thing I have a pillow of wine tonight—wine of the country and estate-bottled Rioja. As I lie looking into the dark, Codés' words about Ramón's sexual inversion come back to me:

what do I really know about him, what if the old bird tries to assault me while I'm asleep? Surely they would have warned me if they thought he was dangerous but *they*'ve never had to spend a night in this house. How can they be so sure that the rumors about Ramón are only fabrications? I'm stuck with one hell of a host, an innkeeper spookier than Tony Perkins in *Psycho*. At least there's no bathroom for him to stab me in the shower.

All the wine I've drunk makes me get up to urinate. I should have used the bathroom at Joaquín's while there was a chance. I walk blindly toward the back of the house, bump into the sink and decide to go no farther; I can't see the door to the back yard anyhow. I feel the pleasure of relief as my urine splashes into the sink, remembering the shepherdess, for some reason I hear a dripping on the floor then a rush of water, my feet are getting warmly wet. Jesus the sink has no drain pipes, my pee is pouring straight through it onto the floor, what did you expect in a place like this, talk about fouling your own nest, no sense stopping now the damage is done, go ahead and finish man, standing here like a damn fool in a puddle. All I can do is take the bucket of water, rinse off the floor and my feet, go back to the mattress with my wet soles picking up all the dirt from the floor, too drunk to care now, forget about Ramón, this night is too ridiculous to end in tragedy, good night, fall asleep on a soft spinning pillow of wine.

8   La Rioja

There are walking and sitting forms of contemplation.

—*The Hidden West*

I've slept better on this dusty old mattress than anywhere else on the road, I think as I get out of my sleeping bag. The pain in my hip has disappeared. I cannot wash my face since there's no running water and I emptied the bucket last night. My fears of being molested by poor old Ramón seem silly now with the birds singing outside. "He couldn't hurt a fly" Codés said. I feel smaller than a fly for not trusting him.

Leaving the house I find a small wooden cross and a note on the doorsill. I pick them up and read the squiggly handwriting in the semi-dark: "Buena suerte que esto le proteja en el Camino, good luck may this protect you on the Road." Wondering why he has given me the cross, I place it in my pack next to the scallop shell and my little rock from home. If it makes Ramón happy, so what, nothing to lose. Now I'm protected by a Christian as well as pagan talismans.

I walk up the hill on the way out of town, speculating that Ramón has offered me this parting gift so that I'd leave him one in return. On the other hand he might be offended if I gave him anything, with his damn Spanish pride. Probably would spend it on beer anyhow.

By the time I reach Viana, the last town in Navarre, I regret not leaving something for Ramón. Why couldn't I simply have done it without second-guessing, without judging him? You miser, I tell myself, he needs it more than you. Tips from pilgrims may be his only income now. He has nothing yet he's made you a gift for the road, probably all he could give, not to mention his hospitality. You changed a travelers' check the other day and your pocket is full of pesetas, 135-to-the-dollar. Now it's too late. Drop him a postcard from Compostela, I tell myself, knowing it's not the same. What could I write on it—"Reached Santiago with the cross you gave me"? Old Ramón. One of God's poor souls alright. How many like him must be scattered all over Spain, nursing their honor in houses with decent façades, empty as boxes inside? Yes appearances deceive, don't judge a book by its cover, this is still the country where what is and what seems to be are worlds apart.

Codés and Joaquín pass me on the highway, honking and waving on the way to our rendezvous in Logroño. They must think I'm crazy to walk; they offered me a ride in their car last night. All of a sudden I feel sad leaving Navarre where I've spent the first week of my pilgrimage, where I've been many times before, where I can rely on friends like José Mari, Pili and all the people I've met through them. Not only have I never been in La Rioja; I don't know a single person in the whole province.

The boundary between Navarre and Castile is marked by the great Río Ebro, wide, brown and slow where I cross the stone bridge. This river has been so fundamental to Spanish life that it probably gave the whole Iberian peninsula and its ancient peoples their names. Born in the cool Cantabrian mountains to the north, the Ebro passes through market cities like Logroño and Saragossa, waters the country's best fruit and vegetable gardens with its irrigation canals begun by the Arabs, pours its silt into the largest delta in Spain and reaches the sea almost six hundred miles from its source, the only major Spanish river that empties into the Mediterranean.

In the middle of the bridge I stop to get a sense of the water's volume and flow. As when I crossed the graceful Puente de la Reina, I feel a change: I'm leaving something on the old shore and something new begins on the farther side.

Joaquín is waiting for me in his car at the end of the bridge. He says that Codés has gone shopping; she'll meet us later. I put my backpack and staff in the trunk and we walk downtown because it's so hard to find parking, as in every other Spanish city.

I show Joaquín the yellow arrows painted on walls and sidewalks.

"*Coño* I've been on this street a thousand times and never noticed the arrows," he says.

We stop to drink water at the Fuente de los Peregrinos, the Pilgrims' Fountain opposite the church of Santiago el Real.

"There's the old boy himself" says Joaquín pointing to the high portal.

I look up and see a monumental Santiago Matamoros on the Baroque façade, a raised saber in his right hand, a flowing banner in his left, mounted in battle on a wide-nostriled, well-endowed stallion who tramples the contorted bodies and severed heads of the fallen infidels beneath him.

Joaquín laughs and cups his hands in the typical Spanish gesture for indicating a pair of good-sized testicles: "What a stud Santiago is riding!"

His words remind me of that morning in the fiesta at Puente la Reina: the encierro, the church where I saw the statue of the other Santiago, the peaceful pilgrim. There I sensed the connection between the male ritual of the bullfight and St. James the Moorslayer. Here I sense the brotherhood between the fighting bull—emblem of the masculine principle with his swinging testicles, the animal that symbolizes the Iberian peninsula with its very shape of a bull's hide—and this fighting stallion of Santiago Matamoros with his oversized scrotum, engaged in that other privileged male rite of warfare. Yes Spain is the country that confounds both Freudians and feminists: here the penis is not exalted but rather the testicles. The cojones are considered the center of a man's or animal's physical being, the source of his courage and strength, figuratively called "huevos" or eggs to emphasize their generative power while "cojonudo," untranslatable but meaning bigballed, more or less, is a compliment for whatever is superlative be it male or female.

Joaquín is saying something about the Battle of Clavijo which supposedly took place near Logroño, commemorated by this immense statue of St. James.

"The famous battle that never took place" I say, "where Santiago is supposed to have made his debut on horseback."

"What do you mean never took place?"

"The historians I've read say there was not an actual combat at Clavijo in the ninth century."

"Were they Spanish or foreign?" he asks more irritated.

"Spanish and foreign."

"They must be those historians who try to take away all of our glories."

There's no use arguing with Joaquín because like many of his compatriots, he refuses to admit that a foreigner may know more about an aspect of his country's life than a Spaniard. Anyhow I don't wish to argue with a man who has shared his house, table and wine with me.

We reach a narrow, crowded street, almost an alley, lined with small bars, many with their own wine cellars in the subsoil by the river below, all with their characteristic tapas. Codés is waiting for us in the busiest place, clients three- and four-deep at the counter, eating an appetizer made of two champiñones, or mushrooms speared around a little shrimp with a toothpick, fried in olive oil and garlic then served sizzling on a small piece of bread. We eat them with the house rosé called claro in Logroño. Joaquín tells me this alley has an official name that appears on maps but is ignored by the people. They prefer to call it the "Street of the Elephants" because "to put on a trunk" in Spanish means to go on a binge; by a triple figure of speech, a spiral of metaphors, this means that we're on the Street of the Drunkards, far removed from the pedestrian name on the map which has been forgotten in the process. As we order more rounds, always the next-to-last, beginning to grow our own elephant trunks, I marvel at the Spaniards' ingenuity for making good food and wines, for knowing how to enjoy them, for creating a language poetic enough to explain them and all their nuances.

Codés and Joaquín have to return to Torres del Río before their groceries spoil. Since there's no refuge for pilgrims in Logroño, they recommend a pensión where they drop me off in the car. At 1,600 pesetas or under twelve dollars, the Residencia Numantina costs less than a sleazy hotel in many American cities but its clean floors, double bed and private bath seem like the soft lap of luxury compared to the bare, dusty room in Ramón's house last night. After a shower, I leave my dirty clothes in the pensión's laundry room: my short pants, a T-shirt and pair of socks are still soiled from the stampede at the water trough. Then I go to sleep and don't wake till a few hours before dawn.

Men in waist-high rubber boots are hosing down the streets when I leave Logroño, women sweeping out the bars with sawdust—stale odors of wine, olive oil and who knows what else coming from the kitchens, well-lit against the darkness. I'll miss this town that opens its doors so widely to strangers. It's one of the most hospitable I know and I've been here less than a day. Let Michener keep Estella; I'll take Logroño anytime.

Except for the industrial outskirts, that is: the watchdogs in every garage and factory bark as I cross their territory. Next I meet most of the stray mongrels in Logroño's canine population. This must be the day of the dogs. These poor mutts cringe when they see my four-foot walking stick. If only to ward off the dozens of dogs I've met so far, I'm glad to have brought it, although it was a bother on the flight to Spain. The airline didn't allow me to carry the staff on board, saying it looked "dangerous." I had to check it as luggage to Madrid where it failed to arrive with my backpack; apparently TWA's luggage-handlers are unaccustomed to pilgrims' staffs. In the end they found it with their patented "Acu-Trak" baggage retrieval system. Or was it simply another miracle of Santiago?

My walnut staff has a leather thong at the top, already blackened from the sweat pouring down my wrist. A rubber tip on the bottom absorbs the impact of the road and saves the wood from wear. The shaft has three lathed spirals like a corkscrew; they make it a joy to see and run your hand along it. Already I'm attached to my walking stick and I feel affection for its scratches, nicks and spots. If you had to walk five hundred miles, most of them by yourself, amigo, you'd also cherish your staff. At times it's your only friend to lean upon, a relief when you're weary, a companion for the road, a defense against the unknown. Not for nothing do pilgrims of every faith use walking sticks, not by coincidence did it become one of Santiago's main attributes along with the scallop shell and the broad-brimmed hat. In the old days pilgrims had to defend themselves against vipers and wolves as well as dogs—worst of all the human wolves who ambushed them in the remotest parts of the Camino. As far away as Japan, devotees of the revered Kobo Daishi have always carried a staff on their long journey. In the West the walking stick came to represent the cross and the hope for salvation. As a "third leg" it also stood for the Holy Trinity and the forces of good fighting against evil.

My trusty staff helps me push my weight off the front foot as I go up the steep hill beyond Logroño where road and highway join. Ahead I spot two small figures also walking against the traffic on the left-hand shoulder. They must be moving slowly because I'm gaining on them. Now I can see that one carries a backpack. Could they be pilgrims, the first I've actually seen walking? As I draw closer I see that the one with the load is a man, the other a woman who walks with a limp. Just before catching up with them I hear rock-and-roll music from a portable radio tied to the man's belt.

We say hello to each other in Spanish and walk three abreast. The man turns down the volume of the radio. Both he and his companion are in their twenties: she is pretty, so shy she keeps her eyes to the ground, wincing with every step; he wears a goatee, has broad shoulders, a barrel chest, spindly legs—a kind of bearded Babe Ruth with a rucksack. He does the talking and tells me they're Basques from a small town in Guipúzcoa. They departed Estella yesterday on the Camino de Santiago and made the mistake of walking all the way to Logroño—more than forty kilometers without rest. The woman's feet are covered with blisters, worn raw he says. In order for her to continue, they've put all their essential gear in one pack and sent the other home. (I wonder why the radio is considered essential.) Feeling sorry for her, I think of mentioning José Mari and Pili's magic blister cure but this couple is so uninterested in my company that I say nothing. Anyhow I'm having trouble walking at their slow pace.

"Hasta luego" I tell them and walk ahead, finding my own rhythm again.

So this is the great brotherhood among pilgrims that I've read about in the books? I'd also be in a rotten mood after walking more than forty k's the first day. Buen viaje I wish them silently.

After moving a few hundred yards ahead of the Basques, I glance at my left wrist for the time. My watch is gone. I take off my pack and search the pockets—no luck—remembering the drawer of the nightstand in the pensión where I must have left it. That's what luxury will do for you: when I had no place to put the watch, no table or drawers at the pilgrims' refuge in Roncesvalles or at Ramón's, I wore it all night.

I take out my map to see how far I've walked from Logroño—more than eight kilometers. Eight plus eight more, sixteen round trip, it would take me at least four hours just to retrieve my watch and return to this spot again. Unthinkable! Also I'd run into the Basques, have to explain, feel dumb. Forget it I tell myself as I hoist my pack, slip into the yoke and start walking again. I'll have to get along without a watch, live by the sun and stars as pilgrims used to do on the Camino de las Estrellas. Anyway I've used it much less than I expected; already I can calculate the hour from the height of the sun—right now it's about ten o'clock. My sense of time has changed since I took to the road, days no longer mean much, today is Saturday, I think but no different from any other day. As I remember the past week, the nights, mornings and afternoons blur, overlap, fuse. It's deceptive to say "yesterday," "three days ago," "last week" because my memory now depends on space as much as time: how many miles have I walked, how many kilometers to the next fountain, the next town, station for the night, Compostela. One week on the Camino has contained more experience, more change than a year of my normal life, maybe several years; one day can hold a little birth, death and rebirth; one hour, one minute, seconds may offer an abyss or a joy like the one I feel now, free, without the watch, moving with my staff at my own speed, absorbing the landscape, always looking ahead on the road where each curve holds a promise.

Before the town of Navarrete, the Camino crosses over the autopista, or turnpike that goes all the way to the French border and beyond. The cars speed under me and away like cruel bullets. Those heading northeast, to my right, in a few hours could reach Bayonne where I took the train to St. Jean-Pied-de-Port on the first day of my pilgrimage. How could I explain to them what they're missing—no less than everything? How would they understand my slow progress by foot, through fields, forests, towns, villages whose inhabitants are like characters in a drama of which I'm a privileged spectator? No, the lives, the time and space of those car-people have nothing to do with me, they might as well be in a different world. They move so fast I cannot see the tires of their Renaults, Seats, Mercedes; that rubber doesn't pass over the asphalt as my feet pass over the ground, feeling its smooth or rough surface, its moisture or dryness, hearing it crunch or smack against my soles as I leave my imprint on the dust, grass, mud. Hypnotized by that white line that devours them as it disappears beneath their hoods, those people are sealed in their vehicles, outside of the natural world while I am *outside, in* the world. Before you start feeling superior, I tell myself, remember that you also served your time in those glass, steel and plastic prisons. You'll probably be sentenced to another when you finish the pilgrimage.

In Navarrete I ask a man on the road if he can fill my canteen. He draws water from the faucet of an old sink that must have been a drinking trough for animals at one time. (I remember the stampede.) He tells me that he often gives water to pilgrims: his house is on the Road to Compostela, the weather is hot and dry in summer and there are no towns between here and Nájera, seventeen kilometers to the west.

He hands me the full canteen and asks if I've heard about the pilgrim killed by a car.

"No."

"It happened just a little way down the road from here about a month ago. A Belgian woman, no youngster, in fact the newspaper said her son promised to walk to Santiago in his mother's honor."

I feel so shocked by the news that all I can do is thank the man for the water and say goodbye. Crossing the town, I wonder where the death occurred. I pass a bar, remember I haven't eaten today, feel nausea and walk on. The accident could have taken place anywhere, I think, the cars are like weapons here as on the turnpike, it's a wonder more pilgrims are not run over on these narrow, shoulderless roads.

Leaving Navarrete I come to the impressive Romanesque portal of a ruined pilgrims' hospice that has been turned into the gate of the local cemetery. The practical townfathers must have wanted to take advantage of the portal after the hospice fell into disuse: most people have ceased going on pilgrimage but they haven't ceased dying. Since I crossed the turnpike everything seems to remind me of mortality. Death has taken its time in making its inevitable appearance on the Camino de Santiago—a road whose destination is a tomb, after all.

It's a journey from east to west with the sun, a reminder every day that what rises must fall, like that sickle moon ahead of me on its way to setting.

Beyond Navarrete where the road follows the highway, a late-model car, clean and white stops in front of me. A tall young priest gets out, greeting me with a smile and a handshake stronger than usual among Spanish men.

"You look like a pilgrim" he says using the familiar second-person. "I've walked the Camino de Santiago several times and always try to salute fellow pilgrims." He looks too handsome to be a priest, I think, almost like an actor playing the role in a movie.

"Yes I'm going to Compostela" I say.

"I live in a village just this side of Santo Domingo de la Calzada" he says. "You won't get that far today, will you? It's about thirty kilometers from here."

"No. I've already done ten or twelve this morning. Tomorrow."

"Then why don't you stop and have lunch with me?" he asks. "Tomorrow is Sunday so I'll be home after the noon Mass. The village is called Hervías, five kilometers before Santo Domingo on the right. Just ask anybody for José Ignacio."

He offers me his hand again. I take it saying "Eduardo. I'll be there."

As he drives off I wonder if this has been my good omen for the day. Everything seems better to me, the road leaves the highway and passes an almond grove. Even the ruins of a convent don't bother me. Anybody in his right mind would be crazy happy on a noon like this: a bright sun neither too hot nor too cold, a blue Castilian sky with a few puffy clouds, the peaks of the Sierra de la Demanda ahead to the southwest, its lower flanks covered with pale wheat fields, hundreds of small, darker vineyards on the foothills. I have to stop as I did in the field of sunflowers, struck by the color and luminosity of a swirl of rye, then advancing through other fields I see vines taller than a man, their gnarled trunks thicker than my legs, the grape clusters already hanging close to the ground. I taste them though they're still green, just beginning to color and lose their bitterness, if they were ripe I'd become glorious on the grape juice of the country, haven't eaten since the Street of the Elephants in Logroño, no wonder La Rioja has the best wines in Spain, these vines so luxuriant they climb across my path, their green leaves against the red earth, I have to step over them, my boots covered with a layer of ocher dust, by the way what happened to the yellow arrows, I think, I'm so lightheaded and drunk on the landscape that I've forgotten to look for them, I must be lost in the middle of these hills, nobody to ask for directions, who cares just keep on walking, I'm coming out on a rural road lined with more almond trees now, I walk on, landing after floating and flying through the vineyards, a few cars pass and bring me back to this other world, the sun hotter now. I stop to rest beneath an olive tree, cool off and drink most of the water from my canteen, remembering the man in Navarrete and the pilgrim's death. I get up and finally reach the National 130 from Logroño at the crossroads where I enter the bustling new quarter of Nájera and cross the bridge over a fast river to the old part of town under a bare, rust-colored cliff pocked with caves.

I'm back in the human realm with its streets, cars and pedestrians. In the monastery of Santa María la Real I find the pilgrims' refuge; the church overrides the roofline of Nájera, looking like a massive ship that has stuck its prow in the sandstone hills. A Franciscan friar opens and leads me to a large, modern room with a single mattress on the floor; it reminds me of Ramón's place. But here the floor is clean, light comes through the windows, there's even a bathroom across the hall, the monk says.

When he leaves I unharness my pack and sit on the mattress to take off my boots. On the far end of the room I notice a wide blackboard covered with writing and drawings. I savor the pleasure of bare feet after twenty miles on the road, then get up and walk to the board. Seeing its chalk sketches of scallop shells, staffs, squash gourds and bicycles, its messages in many languages, I realize that it's been placed here for the use of pilgrims. Since I've seen so few walkers on the road, I'm delighted by the abundance of inscriptions in Spanish, French, English, Basque, even an Oriental language between whose characters stands out the word "Santiago". "ERIC, PATRICK ET BERNARD, RENDEZ-VOUS À ST. JACQUES LE 24 AOÛT À 15 HEURES À LA PLAZA DE LA INMACULADA. CLARA—BONNE ROUTE!" "TO THE BRITISH EXPEDITIONARY FORCE FROM THE THREE FRENCH MUSQUETEERS [I copy exactly as I read]: 'IT'S A LONG WAY TO SANTIAGO, BUT A THIRSTY MAN ALWAYS FINDS A BAR!' (TO BE READ WITH A FRENCH ACCENT) SEE YOU SOON!" I cannot help smiling when I read a question written by three women pilgrims who sign their names—Marina, Maruja and Amparo: "¿Qué tal tus ampollas? How are your blisters?" I also see a few cryptic notes by pilgrim philosophers: "Lo que no ha hecho el silencio no lo va a conseguir la palabra, what has not been done by silence will not be achieved by the word"; "ESCUCHA LA LUNA DEL CAMINO / TE

LLAMA DESDE EL FIN DEL MUNDO, Listen to the moon on the Road / It calls you from the end of the world." Three messages in Spanish are strangely signed "Templars"—an order I thought was extinguished more than six centuries ago: "Know thyself and thou wilt know the universe and the GODS"; "Be Templars on the road"; "I am glad to sleep very close to the Queen's cave"—signed with the Templar cross. The "Queen" probably refers to the Virgin Mary, worshiped by the Knights and around whose image the entire church of Santa María la Real has been constructed. At the very bottom of the slate I find a message in Celtic figures with planetary conditions written in astrological symbols, signed "PANORÁMIX (CLAUDIO)".

What surprises me most is the lack of Christian references. After all, this is a Franciscan monastery on the Road to Santiago, no less. If you take away the vague Templar allusion to the Queen—adjacent to their invocation of the plural gods of the ancient religions—nothing especially Catholic remains. Nor does St. James himself appear except in the name of the city, Santiago/St. Jacques. Maybe José Mari was right about the esoteric and initiatory aspects of the Road, what he called the "other Camino," in the Middle Ages or today.

My stomach growls and I remember that I haven't eaten since yesterday. I put on a dry shirt, go out in the dusty heat, find a restaurant with fly-specked walls and have a meal spiced with the sauce of St. Bernard, as the Spaniards call it: hunger.

After lunch I walk along the fast-flowing Río Najerilla and go swimming in a new public pool by the shore. A wind blows across the river, so desert-like that I don't need a towel to dry off. Lying on the grass at poolside I ask myself a question never pondered by Aymery Picaud, Walter Starkie or Captain Cousteau: how does a pilgrim remain steadfast in his purpose when he sees young Spanish women in bikinis frolicking in the water? I recall the other swimming pool in Pamplona but somehow I'm more distant now, I don't feel the pull of desire as I did there and with the shepherdess, I look at these nubile women with wonder after such little contact with females on the road, newly amazed by the suppleness of wet bodies in the sun, thinking I'm as chaste as the Franciscan monk at the refuge, had no sexual life since I left the U.S. I miss María badly.

Returning to the old quarter of town I visit the interior of S. María la Real. Above all I'm impressed by the statue of a dark Virgin in a chapel hewed from a cave where you can still see white veins of rock in the reddish sandstone. This is the first place on the road from Roncesvalles where the feminine seems to prevail: you feel surrounded, protected by the womblike earth with its color of human flesh mixed with blood.

I enter the pilgrims' room in the monastery adjoining the church, undress and get in my sleeping bag. No sooner have I closed my eyes than I hear a loud noise, the door swings open and a crowd bursts in carrying sleeping bags, portable cots and backpacks. Since I've put my glasses inside my boots for the night, I see only vague shapes of young Spaniards, men and women, Navarrese from Estella they tell me, on the second day of their pilgrimage to Compostela. I'm the first pilgrim they've encountered on the Camino. As a matter of fact, I think to myself this is the first time I've slept in the same room with other pilgrims. Unless you've spent nine days on the road in a foreign country, most of them alone, you'll find it hard to imagine how good it feels.

9 Of Saints, Cocks and Hens

When I awake, the Navarrese have gone without leaving a sign. Did I dream them? Dream or not I'm alone; I hoped we might walk together. At least I'll have company at lunch with the priest from Hervías.

In the town of Azofra I see two pilgrims in the local bar, both seated at a table having breakfast, their walking sticks and packs leaning against the wall. We introduce each other. They're from the big city of Bilbao in the north, in their fifties, a banker and a businessman. As they finish their coffee and I order from the bartender, one of them shows me the conservative newspaper *ABC* with an article about a German camper who was knifed by a Spanish shepherd.

"Where did it happen?" I ask.

"Near Herrera de Pisuerga in the province of Palencia" says the banker. "Got him at night while he was in his sleeping bag. Seems the shepherd wanted to screw the German's girlfriend; she denounced him at the local police station. How much you want to bet he raped the shit out of her?" There goes your theory of the shepherds as the last noble savages, I say to myself.

"That's one reason we're staying in hotels—the best we can find" says the other. "The Camino de Santiago passes right through the province of Palencia after Burgos."

The two men don't wait for me to finish my coffee before leaving. Let them go ahead, I tell myself. Mejor solo que mal acompañado, better alone than in bad company . . .

When I see it I'm still feeling downcast from the encounter with the pilgrims from Bilbao and their story: a yellow arrow on top of a metal stake, pointing ahead with "PEREGRINO ¡ANIMO!" painted on it—the exhortation Padre Javier used after the blessing in Roncesvalles, almost impossible to translate, literally "courage" but with the sense of Come on, cheer up! Next to the words I see a drawing of a scallop shell traversed by a walking staff from which hangs a squash gourd, the canteen of the Middle Ages, another of the pilgrim's symbols.

Just as I was getting in the dumps this sign pops up in the tall, dry grass! Unlike the yellow marks splashed on fences, tree trunks and

6 Pilgrims' arrow near Azofra, La Rioja. (Photo by the author)

stones, this arrow seems like a secret message for me alone. Who else is here to read it? And if I weren't here what use would it be? These and other arrows are like friends during the long stretches of solitude, a comfort as well as guides at the crossroads, little yellow shafts of hope. They speak the language of humble service, thousands of silent, merciful deeds showing the pilgrim his way—acts of charity even more fundamental than offering shelter. This must be the most unique system of road signs on earth, the work of a new kind of saint, martyrs of the yellow arrow, St. Sebastians of the twentieth century. The Orders of Santiago and the Holy Sepulcher, the Knights Templar and the Hospitallers have disappeared; the anonymous order of the yellow arrow remains as the protector and guide of modern pilgrims. I feel like kissing the little sign. Instead I take a picture of it with my miniature camera, the first I've shot on the Road.

Still feeling happy, I'm bouncing, springing over the path when I see the second arrow: "ADiOS". Like the first (forgot to tell you) it's placed at a spot where a walker might doubt which way to go. I take out the camera again, shoot another photo and say goodbye to the sign as I would to a comrade. After my feelings of loneliness, the meeting

7 Second pilgrims' arrow near Azofra. (Photo by the author)

with the businessmen and the bad news about the Germans, I feel as if I've been reborn for the day.

When the path joins the National 120, I see a town on the horizon ahead of me, shimmering in the heat. Could it be Santo Domingo de la Calzada so soon? Quite a few Spaniards seem to be out for Sunday drives. For some reason the cars coming my way are all passing very close. When a speeding van almost shaves off my beard, making me jump into the trench below the shoulder of the road, I look back to pay him my respects when suddenly I understand: these vehicles are driving directly into the morning sun.

No wonder some have proposed that the Spanish government place markers on the highway reading "Watch for Pilgrims," similar to signs for deer and cattle but with the silhouette of a figure wearing a pack and wide-brimmed hat. (I would add a walking stick.) Since the Camino de Santiago goes from east to west, the early morning hours are the most dangerous, when walkers have the rising sun at their backs.

All the oncoming drivers are so blinded that I'm forced to walk in the trench littered with empty cigarette packages, paper cups, pieces of faded plastic, candy bar wrappers, detached limbs of toys. Most of the cigarette packages are American—Winston, Marlboro, Camels. This makes me feel guilty until I conclude that many people who are prosperous enough to drive a car in Spain must smoke the imported "blond" tobacco instead of the cheaper "black" product from the Canary Islands. In these old European countries they even have a social hierarchy for cigarettes.

There must not be strong laws against littering in Spain; the roadsides are filthy. More likely there are regulations but the citizens ignore them, Spanish style: Hecha la ley, hecha la trampa, the law is made to be broken. Pilgrims in the Middle Ages had to endure wild animals, robbers and plagues but they didn't have to slog through this ribbon of junk, this obstacle course for tired feet. The only good thing about the cars and trucks is the momentary breeze they create while passing, the sole relief from the heat on this straightaway to Santo Domingo.

As the sun mounts higher I sweat more—a clean sweat in the dry air, without the acrid smell you notice when you perspire in the city. You may not believe this but it's true, another daily miracle on the Road to Santiago. Already this is the sweat, the heat and light, the landscape of Castile. Everything is flatter, the road is straight instead of gently curving, grain fields become more common than vineyards, colors modulate from greens to browns to tans and yellows as the landscape draws your attention to the sky and the horizon rather than enveloping you in its soft, rounded forms.

The town of Santo Domingo de la Calzada still wavers ahead of me like a mirage, its belfries barely drawing closer as I walk in the bright sun and heat, short of breath as if I were climbing. And of course I am. Since leaving the Ebro basin, a depression in Spain's great central meseta, I've been gradually, imperceptibly ascending.

When I reach the turn for Hervías, it seems too early for lunch with the priest so I plug on, wishing I had my watch this once to be sure of the time. I'll take a bus or hitchhike back to the village after reaching Santo Domingo where I'll spend the night.

On the outskirts at last, I come to an old whitewashed building. A sign on the wall announces the miracle of Santiago that gives this place one of its claims to renown, the other being its namesake, St. Dominic of the Causeway:

SANTO DOMINGO DE LA CALZADA
"QUE CANTO LA GALLINA
DESPUÉS DE ASADA"

8   The old and new on the road to Santiago: wall announcing medieval miracle of hen and cock; in upper right corner, an advertisement; on bottom, whitewashed graffiti. Santo Domingo de la Calzada, La Rioja. (Photo by the author)

"Where the hen clucked after it was cooked"—with a drawing of a hen on one side and a rooster on the other. Above the sign is publicity for an asbestos and cement company; below are political graffiti barely legible beneath a coat of whitewash.

I would like to spare you, oh patient reader, the story of the hen that is one of the greatest stretchers ever concocted by the medieval mind. But I suppose I'll have to give in and relate to you the tale that has been told and retold by every pilgrim to Compostela for centuries, trying to make it digestible to your modern stomach.

Long ago a French couple and their son lodged for the night in old Calzada town on their way to Santiago. The maidservant at the inn fancied the son, who didn't wish to "medyll with her carnally" as one old English pilgrim put it. In revenge she placed a silver cup in his scrip or pouch and accused him of theft. The poor Frenchman was hanged according to the summary justice of the time; his mother and father continued their sad way to Compostela. On their return they found their son still hanging on the gallows, miraculously alive because Santiago had intervened to save him! When the parents ran to tell the mayor, who was about to sup on roasted hen and cock, the man said he would believe their story if the two fowl before him should stand up and sing, which of course they promptly did. In remembrance of the miracle, a white hen and rooster have been kept happily ever after in an honorary coop inside the cathedral of Santo Domingo.

Most modern pilgrims have had trouble accepting this tall tale. The British Hispanist Robert Southey poked fun at the legend in his *Pilgrim to Compostella*, having the famous birds take vows of chastity after the miracle:

> And if every Cock and Hen in Spain
> Had their example taken,
> Why, then—the Spaniards would have had
> No eggs to eat with bacon.

Staring at this white wall, I regret that the quaint hoax has naturally become more renowned than the twelfth-century saint who gave his name to the town by working real miracles—clearing primeval forests, building a bridge of twenty-four arches over the River Oja and laying some twenty miles of the Camino against great obstacles, establishing hospices where he cared personally for travelers, fed and clothed the poor, nursed the sick, buried pilgrims who died on the Way. This wall with its doggerel on the ancient legend, surrounded by advertising and graffiti, with its holes, cracks and dazzling brightness seems to embody so much of Spanish life, old and new:

> ¡Oh blanco muro de España!

cried García Lorca, Oh white wall of Spain!

On the way to the refuge I decide to go by the cathedral and the pilgrims' hospice. The church was begun by St. Dominic; it contains his tomb surmounted by a carved, painted, gilt shrine of alabaster. What attracts most visitors' attention stands on the opposite wall—a vaulted niche with a glass cage for the famous white hen and rooster. Only in Spain, I suppose could you find a saint's shrine with all the magnificence of the Roman Catholic Church, next to a scene from a county fair with chickens clucking and scratching on a bed of straw.

The old hospice, also begun by St. Dominic, has been turned into a Parador Nacional, one of the first-class inns run by the Spanish Ministry of Tourism. I notice a strange contrast between the medieval architecture and the modern appointments—leather armchairs, coffee tables, lamps, a colored skylight.

This place is too valuable to be wasted as a free refuge nowadays, so the Brotherhood of St. Dominic has restored a more humble building for pilgrims. A man welcomes me in the cobblestone patio and leads me up a wooden staircase. We pass a group of elderly women before reaching several rooms with whitewashed walls and ceilings, oak beams, cots for pilgrims, floors paved with cool, wine-colored tiles. There's even a kitchen and a bathroom.

The man gives me his calling card and another with St. Dominic's image, saying he's at my service. He returns to the women; through the doorway I hear him say "Acaban de ver la llegada de un peregrino, you've just witnessed the arrival of a pilgrim." I feel like crawling under one of the beds before the women come to stare at me, some relic in a museum.

I read the calling card: "ANTONIO ROJAS ABEYTUA / Cuidador del gallo y de la gallina de la Catedral," Caretaker of the cock and hen in the Cathedral. The other card has a prayer to the saint, portrayed as an old bearded man carrying a pilgrim's staff, the ever-present rooster and hen at his feet.

After washing and changing into dry clothes, I walk downstairs to the patio where the man asks for my passport.

"You can pick it up at the police station when you leave" he tells me.

I ask him about buses to Hervías and he says there are none. My feet are too sore to walk the five kilometers. After trying without luck to hitch a ride, I have no choice but to do what has never been recorded in the annals of pilgrimage—take a taxi backwards on the same road I've just walked.

The driver drops me in the dusty square of Hervías. I have to pay him double since he won't be able to pick up a return fare in this small village. Not a soul appears but I recognize José Ignacio's white, shiny car in front of a two-story building.

He answers the door, still dressed in his cassock, welcomes me and asks me to accompany him to a house a few doors away. Here he introduces me to a family with whom he takes his meals. There is a daughter and several sons, one of whom did the pilgrimage to Compostela with José Ignacio a few years ago, running the final miles to the Cathedral. I'll be lucky to make it walking, I say and we tell stories about the Camino as we eat a simple, hearty meal. These are good people of the earth like the couple who gave me the apples on the first day—how long ago, how far away it seems!

After lunch José Ignacio and I return to his house where we begin to talk about his passion, the Road to Santiago. He seems to know every inch of the Camino: he's walked it many times and is in charge of the yellow arrows in this area. Not only does he make new arrows and maintain the old, he tells me as he lights a cigarette; sometimes he has to remove other arrows placed by well-intentioned but inexperienced pilgrims. Vigilante arrow painters, I guess. I'd ask him about the two signs near Azofra but he talks so quickly that I don't have a chance. On my pilgrims' map he shows me places to find refuge, writing down the names of priests or laymen who've been helpful to him, marking the fountains with bad water.

When the conversation comes around to the miracle of the hen and rooster in Santo Domingo, I ask his opinion.

He smiles: "I know it's hard for an educated person to accept, especially a foreigner. But remember when Jesus said the kingdom of heaven is for those who become as little children. I envy those people their simple faith. We should respect it just as we do the Camino de Santiago, walking on it as though it were covered with eggs."

I smile: "I guess when you live near Santo Domingo you can't help but talk about chickens and eggs."

He laughs and looks more relaxed. "Even cynics admit that the story prefigures the symbolic death and rebirth that all pilgrims must undergo" he says pouring me a Spanish brandy. He lights another cigarette.

A few sips of the brandy warm my insides and I begin to feel confessional. "Frankly I find it hard to believe in miracles" I tell him. "Especially when they're as naive as the legend of the reborn hen and rooster."

"A little credulity helps one get through life" he says. "Sometimes the noblest people are the most ingenuous. The problem, as your Anglo-Saxon philosopher Hume said, is that the record of known fabrications is so black that it can blemish all other claims—even the great, central miracles of Christianity. As Christians we must separate the Incarnation and the Resurrection, for example, from a popular legend like the one of the cock and hen, or the pious gossip about how Sister Consolation found a suitor for her cross-eyed niece by the aid of St. Anthony."

"My problem is that I cannot even believe in those central miracles most of the time" I tell him. "If I cannot accept the Incarnation, that Christ is in fact God, then all his teachings seem to be the worst kind of megalomania."

Something seems to change in his eyes and demeanor; I may have overstepped the limits of my welcome. Nervously he gets up, offering me another glass of brandy.

"That's a problem, Eduardo" he says. He starts to speak again but the words don't come out, he stutters with his lips parted trying to pronounce a syllable struggling to free itself, caught in his vocal cords. Suddenly I sense whatever deep complex might have led a tall, strong adolescent, as José Ignacio must have been, to renounce a normal life by taking vows for the priesthood.

The words finally come after a delay that has seemed to last for minutes: "That's a problem" he repeats. I fear another silence but he goes on quickly "Because Christianity is the religion of miracles par excellence. If you subtracted all the marvels from Hinduism, the essentials would remain intact, and you could say almost the same of Islam. As for Buddha he taught that the world was an illusion from which he came to wake us as from a nightmare, so why should he add to the nightmare by breaking the rules of an illusory world to perform miracles? But in the case of Christianity and especially Catholicism, the central miracles of the Immaculate Conception, the Incarnation and the Resurrection form the very foundations of our theology. Without them you'd have nothing but a kind of naturalistic belief." He has spoken so fast that he's out of breath.

"The same is true of the Camino de Santiago" I say, trying to give him time to catch his wind. "If you took away the original miracles of St. James' seven-day voyage to the Iberian peninsula after his death, and the hermit's discovery of his tomb with tongues of fire and heavenly music, the whole business of the pilgrimage would lack a foundation."

"That's right" he answers, "not to mention the hundreds of minor miracles associated with the Camino—like the hen and the rooster, to go no farther than Santo Domingo itself."

"I'm afraid my problem is more than just the miracles" I tell him. "It has to do with my inability to believe. I try yet cannot believe except under extraordinary circumstances—for a few seconds while the priest gave me the pilgrims' blessing in Roncesvalles for example, or a minute or so of ecstasy while contemplating a field of sunflowers in Navarre or a vineyard in La Rioja."

He lights another cigarette. "Eduardo, you're a person who bears the hardest of all crosses, the cross of disbelief. That's what our Spanish philosopher Unamuno called the tragic sense of life. It recaptures the instant of the crucifixion when Christ asked God why He'd forsaken Him. The difference is that it was only an instant in Christ's earthly existence; from what you say it's almost your whole life." I nod. "When a monk enters a monastery" he goes on, "the brothers ask him 'Are you truly seeking God?' Not 'Have you found God?' The Road to Santiago is also a search."

I feel the kind of relief I used to experience after confession. I tell this to him.

"If you wish we can consider this a confessional" he says. "I'll pray for you and I urge you to pray for me when you reach Compostela. Would you like me to give you a blessing for the road?"

"Yes."

He stands and blesses me silently, for which I'm grateful.

"Before you leave I'd like you to have this" he says, holding out a card similar to the one given me by the man at the pilgrims' refuge. Everyone in Spain seems to have his calling card. "I don't know if you are familiar with the Opus Dei, the Work of God" he says. "It's an organization to which I belong and I always hope that what fills my life may fill others' too."

After the relief of confession and the warm company of José Ignacio and the family, I feel let down, as if most of what we've said and done has been a pretext for this moment, this act. I remember the Mormons and Seventh Day Adventists who proselytize from door to door in the U.S. They too have their little cards and pamphlets.

He must notice the change in me. "I'll give you a ride into town. Excuse me for a minute" he says leaving the room.

Perhaps José Mari's words in Pamplona have predisposed me against the Opus Dei, I think. When he drove Alberto and me to the outskirts of the city that day, he said it wouldn't surprise him if the Opus had arranged for the Road to pass through their domain at the University of Navarre. Religious orders have patrolled the way to Compostela in the past—Cluny, the Knights of Santiago and the Temple among others. Why not the Opus, the most powerful religious organization in Spain today, perhaps in the entire Catholic world? Don't speculate about something you cannot know, I tell myself.

I look at the buff-colored card with its dour photograph of the Opus Dei's founder, Monsignor José María Escrivá de Balaguer y Albás. (What a high-toned name compared to St. Dominic of the Causeway!) Below it is printed a prayer or petition in his name. All this has the musty smell of sacristies, incense and tapers. I want to get out of here, on the road again.

The conversation flags on the drive back to Santo Domingo. I have an odd sensation as the car speeds over the same road I walked earlier—the third time I've covered it today. To fill the silence, José Ignacio talks about his plans for the future. He loves being in his native Rioja and so close to the Camino de Santiago, he says, but he'd go obediently wherever his bishop commanded. There's even been talk of sending Spanish priests to Cuba because of the island's terrible lack of vocations; he would accept that difficult assignment gladly. As he speaks I imagine José Ignacio as one of those dauntless Spanish priests who carried the cross to the New World during the Discovery and Conquest, loyal to God, Church, King and St. James, convinced of his superior mission to convert pagans to the one and only true faith.

He drops me in front of the refuge, reminding me to pray for him in Compostela. I thank him and say goodbye.

10 St. Dominic of the Causeway to St. John of the Nettles

I laugh at the bigotry and prejudice of Spain; I abhor the cruelty and ferocity which have cast a stain of eternal infamy on her history; but I will say for the Spaniards, that in their social intercourse no people in the world exhibit a juster feeling of what is due to the dignity of human nature, or better understand the behavior which it behoves a man to adopt toward his fellow beings.
—George Borrow, *The Bible in Spain*

I don't need a watch to awake in the morning because the bells of the cathedral could wake a regiment. After picking up my passport at the police station, I leave town and cross the Oja River that gave its name to the region and province of La Rioja. It's so dark that I can't see the riverbed.

Remembering the story of the German killed in his sleeping bag, I feel lonely and afraid in the dark. I also recall José Mari's news about the two elderly pilgrims who were robbed near Pamplona. Cheer up, I tell myself, you're not old yet, you're almost a third of the way to Compostela, don't forget the exhortation of Padre Javier and the arrow-sign, "Ánimo!" Besides you have your staff, your pebble, scallop shell and the cross for good luck. But alone on the road beyond the last lights of town, it's as if the centuries haven't passed, I'm simply a man with the same fears as a medieval pilgrim groping for his amulet in the dark. In spite of all the talk about the Camino de las Estrellas, the Road of Stars, I'm beginning to realize that few pilgrims could ever have traveled at night. It's not practical; even in our times the darkness holds a primitive dread.

It begins to dawn on an overcast day with a misty drizzle, perfect for walking. I feel better now and open my stride. My fears go with the dawn as I remember the words I whisper in Carlos' ear to tuck him in bed—"Good night, see you in the morning light." For him, three years old, the night has the same terror as for his father on this lonely road, relieved only by the rising of the sun. Carlos in turn reminds me of María. How much I miss them both— as much as I wanted to get away from them before I started the pilgrimage. I believe it's easier to make a clean break by leaving behind the people who live with you every day. That's what old John Bunyan believed when he had his Christian pilgrim run away from his wife and babes, plugging his ears to their entreaties, not looking back as he fled the City of Destruction.

I pass a sign announcing the province of Burgos. Two down—Navarre, Rioja—four or five to go. I've undergone another small death and recovery with the dawn; the Camino may consist of that more than any kind of total resurrection . . . too remote at least for now.

Right away I'm entering the town of Redecilla del Camino, "Little Net of the Road." I decide to look at the church with its famous baptismal font.

The building is locked. A neighbor tells me I should go to the priest's house across the street, warning that the good man may still be in bed.

I knock, no answer, knock louder. Somebody opens the shutters upstairs, sticking out a disheveled, squint-eyed head.

"I'm a pilgrim" I say looking up at him. "Is it possible to visit the font in the church?"

"No, hombre" he answers, "I showed it to a bunch of Navarrese at 6:30 and I've already gone back to bed once."

"I'm an American and this may be the last . . . "

He slams the window.

"Forget about your baptismal font, I don't need it anyhow" I say aloud in English, thinking the old priest-baiter Bunyan would have liked this. Get out of here I tell myself, shake the dust of this town from your feet like St. Teresa. At least I've learned that the pilgrims from Estella aren't too far ahead; maybe I can catch up with them.

Beyond Redecilla del Camino the grain fields are so abundant that I imagine myself swimming in an ocean of wheat. This will have to be your baptism, I say to myself. The towns could be islands—reddish buildings grouped closely together, an occasional white wall, a spot of green where trees surround a plaza or garden. The sky is cloudy, I'm barely perspiring, my body feels stronger than ever. Knowing the Navarrese are out there spurs me on, makes me walk faster.

I stop for food and rest in Villafranca Montes de Oca. In a restaurant by the crossroads I spot the two men from Bilbao—the banker and businessman—seated at a corner table. They pretend not to see me but I say hello to them on my way out. I notice two empty wine bottles and brandy snifters on their table. Seeing that both men have taken off their shoes, I ask them how their feet are holding up. They frown and tell me they're having serious problems with blisters. One of them has just consulted a podiatrist who diagnosed an internal hemorrhage in one ankle, advising complete rest. They've telephoned their brujas, their "witches" to pick them up and drive them back to Bilbao; I've never heard the expression but I guess it refers to their wives, poor ladies.

Good riddance, I think climbing the path out of town, I'm glad that pair is off the road. The sores on their feet are merely symptoms of the disease in their hearts. But don't be too quick to judge, I tell myself, feeling the soreness in my own feet after the rest. I've already walked more than one of my normal stages this morning—over thirty kilometers. But the sun has burned off the mist leaving a blue sky with cottony clouds, the air is clear and breezy, I've eaten well and feel strong enough for an afternoon of hiking through the mountains ahead of me, the last barrier separating me from Old Castile and central Spain. I pick up the pace, walking with a lighter step, breathing from deep in my chest. I'm happy again.

Although my pilgrims' map shows a modern highway running parallel to this dirt path, it's out of sight and I see no signs of civilization beyond some fences and a fountain. The place is wilder than any other since the woods of Roncesvalles. These mountains also have duende. Even on a luminous afternoon like this, it's one of the most forbidding landscapes on the Road to Santiago. Imagine what an obstacle it would be in the rain or fog, not to mention a snowstorm! Covered by a thick forest of oaks and pines, far from any town, these Montes de Oca were long known as a lair of thieves. "Si quieres robar, vete a Montes de Oca" an old saying held, if you want to steal come here. Foreigners have considered Spain the land of robbers for centuries. Richard Ford called her the country of "bullfights, bandits, and black eyes." The only Englishman who could be compared to Ford in his knowledge of the peninsula, the great missionary and writer George Borrow, worried about being abducted by a gang of banditti. In this bracing air and sunlight, I don't have the fear of being assaulted as I did this morning in the dark.

The sickle moon sets and the sun sinks below the trees. Somehow I feel that I may be headed in the wrong direction. I turn around and begin to retrace my steps, remembering other travelers who've lost their way in these mountains. When the sky turns a glowing red on my right, I realize that I've been walking north instead of west, who knows for how long, how many miles I've added to what is already the lengthiest stage of my trip. I sit on the ground and loosen my boots, feeling the heat on my soles and toes where new blisters must have formed. As in the early days of the trip, my two feet seem to be the center of my body and the whole world. Remember what St. Teresa said, I tell myself, "Everything passes." José Mari's advice also, "To hell with blisters!" To hell with pain too because my hip hurts again. To hell with all of it, I say to myself, you're no better than the two men from Bilbao, maybe you're not strong enough to reach Compostela, the sores on your feet are also signs of the disease inside you. What will you tell your friends, your wife and sons . . . that you were too weak to finish? That you broke down, gave up in the Montes de Oca? To hell with blisters I say, tie your boots, get up, move. Ánimo. You could never live with yourself if you gave up now, less than halfway to Santiago. How easy it is to complain of your small discomforts while you forget the pain of others, the pain that does not go away like a blister but gnaws, lingering—poverty, hunger, disease. At last I reach the summit, the third mountain pass after the Pyrenees and the Mount of Pardon. The descent is worse than the climb, following a rocky ravine where every step makes me search for a spot to place my front foot without pain. In a few minutes I've gone from the evergreen forests of Oregon to a dry gulch in Arizona. The path comes out in open country with scrub oaks, the light fading now—California. No wonder the Spaniards felt at home in the American West.

I pass a primitive cross fashioned from the trunk and branch of a tree still covered with bark. My backpack feels like a cross by now, one I've been bearing for some fifty kilometers today, far too many for this tired body, this bag of bones. Wouldn't it be nice if Santiago repeated for me the miracle he once performed for a boy from Lorraine, whom he swept up on his white horse, whizzed by mountains, rivers and the sun itself, setting him down on the Mount of Joy within view of Compostela? You don't deserve it even if you did believe in miracles, I tell myself, you're paying the wages of pride, overconfidence in thinking you could walk so far. To forget about the fatigue, I begin to weave another fantasy, imagining myself as a medieval pilgrim approaching the refuge constructed by San Juan de Ortega—the second of the two great roadbuilding saints on the way to Santiago, after his teacher St. Dominic of the Causeway. Both had cement in their veins: cement but also blood and the milk of kindness . . . I see an old man, white-headed, his face tanned and shriveled from working half a century in the open air of this mountain climate, from laying out bridges and roads, erecting hospices and churches for pilgrims. He's waiting in the middle of the path where he greets me in Latin, asks for news of the road and the weather, helps me limp to the haven where he washes my feet with a mixture of tallow grease, brandy and olive oil, fills my squash gourd with spring water, serves a hot soup to me and his brother canons of St. Augustine, guides me to a clean bed where I sleep like a child . . .

The sight of San Juan de Ortega after miles of wilderness must be one of the most joyous on the road to Santiago. Besides it's one of the few Spanish towns that hasn't been exploited for tourism; the profile of the medieval hamlet is still intact against the day's last light. Now I know why the saint and the shrine he founded were named Juan de Ortega, John of the Nettles: the old church and monastery rise from an upland valley covered with brambles.

You made it, I tell myself stumbling into the sandy little courtyard by the church where I see the Navarrese pilgrims sitting on a low brick wall. St. John of the Nettles himself is not here but I'll take these young pilgrims anytime: they welcome me, help me take off the pack with How are you, Eduardo, We've been wondering if you'd catch up with us, Let me give you a hand there, Estás hecho polvo, You look bushed, Come on we'll show you the refuge, Wait till you see it, mattresses, showers and all. They lead me inside through a large dining hall and kitchen, upstairs to a furnished commons room and dormitory with bunk beds for pilgrims, all of it constructed around a medieval cloister adorned with modern decoration—the shirts, pants and socks the Navarrese have hung out to dry. They help me unpack, shaking the dust out of a mattress on a lower bunk, unrolling my sleeping bag, saying We'll give you a few minutes to clean up but don't take too long, The priest's going to give us a tour of the chapel, Meet you downstairs.

The bed seems to beckon me but these kids are irresistible in their camaraderie, they've already made me feel like one of them. I wash my face with cold water and put on my moccasins, afraid to take off my socks to survey the damage on my feet. I hobble downstairs to join the others.

They're waiting for me in the courtyard next to a friendly man around sixty with a soiled white collar and frayed cassock: a provincial priest if I've ever seen one. He takes us into the church, dark by now. When he turns on the lights, we see a clean, well-restored Romanesque interior of soft white stone obstructed only by a florid, late Gothic shrine to St. John of the Nettles. It reminds me of a wedding cake.

The priest leads us down to a crypt where we see the austere tomb of the saint, who built the chapel and hospice for the service of the

poor on the Road to Santiago. As we walk back upstairs he explains
that Juan de Ortega wanted to be buried in the most spare surround-
ings. The ornate tabernacle above was added by Queen Isabella centuries later, in thanksgiving for her firstborn child. St. John of the
Nettles had long been worshiped by women seeking children. When
Isabella visited the church to implore his aid, the priest tells us, a fragrant swarm of white bees flew out of the tomb. They symbolized the
souls of unborn babies destined to the women who would ask the
saint for offspring.

The chapel and these legends would be interesting if my feet and
body didn't hurt so much; I'm hoping the priest will finish soon. He's
enjoying himself in the company of so many enthusiastic young visitors, especially the female pilgrims to whom he addresses most of
his lecture.

On a column to the left of the main altar, the priest points to a
carved capital representing the Annunciation. He tells us that on the
equinoxes, March 22 and September 22 at precisely 5 P.M. solar time,
a ray of light from the setting sun traverses a window in the church's
west façade, falls on the figure of the angel Gabriel, then moves onto
the Virgin Mary with her serenely joyous face looking at the source of
the light, receiving it on the palms of her upraised hands and on her
swollen belly wrapped in the folds of her dress. The peaceful, large-
headed, dignified Romanesque figures stand out in relief from the capital; how much more alive must they appear illuminated by a ray of
sunlight on those two unique moments of the year: the marriage of
sun and stone, heaven and earth, woman and nature.

Opening and closing doors with a set of heavy old keys, the priest
guides us from the church to the monastery, now in ruins. He complains that the Ministry of Culture ignores his endless petitions for
funds to restore it. Showing us where some thieves broke in to steal
religious art, he tells us that they didn't find the precious ivory coffer
they were seeking; by chance he'd taken it to his bedroom that day.
They were professionals because the only way they could have entered was by having a small child climb through a tiny window in one
wall, then having him open the door from inside. The sign they left at
the scene of the crime was that found in other burgled churches: a pile
of fresh excrement on the floor. Spain, land of thieves, I think, remembering my fears of this morning.

After showing us the rest of the old monastery, the priest invites
us all to dinner. The pilgrims from Estella tell him they've eaten. So
the good man asks me to accompany him to the kitchen.

While he begins to prepare our meal, I collapse in a chair, reading the large red letters on the white tiles of the wall in front of me:

TAMBIÉN EN LOS PUCHEROS SE ENCUENTRA A DIOS

"You can even find God in the pots and pans." The sentence seems familiar; I ask him who said it.

"A very astute woman" he replies. "Teresa of Avila."

This is St. Teresa's day, I say to myself, recalling the other times she's cropped up in my mind. More than anyone I can think of right now, she combined the sort of pragmatism and spirituality I've found on the Road to Santiago.

The priest serves a soup of onions and garbanzos followed by eggs fried in tomato sauce, talking all the while. He tells me that he uses up a good portion of his modest income to feed pilgrims. He's starved for company in this remote parish, above all in winter when the weather makes the Montes de Oca almost impassable. When he begins to talk politics, assuring me that there's more tyranny under the freely elected Socialist government than there was under Franco, I remember old George Borrow's advice: always have the same politics as your host, no matter how outrageous his opinions.

The priest hasn't ceased talking since we came to the kitchen. Now he discourses on the last elections, won by the perverse Socialists. The hot food has restored me; I'm profoundly grateful to this man who keeps alive the spirit of San Juan de Ortega, yet I cannot help thinking this meal has had its price.

When I return to the dormitory, the Navarrese pilgrims are already in bed. I crawl into my sleeping bag and hear several voices out of the darkness: "Buenas noches, Eduardo."

11 Through Burgos

Camerado, I give you my hand!
—Whitman

I awake with my bed rocking back and forth like a boat. Propping myself on one elbow, I realize that it's me, not the bed that's moving: my body and brain are still walking those fifty-some kilometers.

After eating breakfast I leave in the half-light with the pilgrims from Estella. Since the van carries all their equipment, they don't have to wear backpacks on the road. The leader of the group walks ahead of us through a brush-covered field surrounded by oaks and pines. Older than the others, in his thirties, intense, square-jawed, he's the Columbus or Cortés of this expedition, followed by his tall, graceful wife; they're the only married members of the nine. Next comes a big, strong young man with the reddish-brown beard of a conquistador, followed by a brown-skinned, smiling, white-toothed lad. Then three women: one tiny with short-cropped hair, always joking; another terribly young, wistful, wearing a T-shirt with "CHOOSE LIFE" across the front in English; another with thick black hair and a coquettish smile, asking me questions like "Have you traveled *all* around the world?", "Do they have cowboys in California?", "Are there bald men in America?" A tall, thin, unshaven boy is also curious to know about me and *"América,"* a word that even today rings with adventure for many Spaniards. Bringing up the rear with me (my feet still ache) is a priest in his late forties or early fifties with a salt-and-pepper beard; normally he accompanies the driver of the van but today he wants to travel with the walkers in order to get a sense of the road.

Each one of the troupe carries a five- or six-foot wooden staff, some with a scallop shell tied near the top. When we reach the town of Agés, they tap their walking sticks on the road in unison, making a noise like the muffled sound of cowbells, then sing a song they've composed in the style of Gregorian chant, "Vamos camino de Compostela / para ver a Dios . . . " (We're on the road to Compostela / To go and see God . . .) Some of the locals are roused from bed; they project frowning, sleepy faces from doors and windows, disturbed but also amused by this irrepressible group of youngsters who move like a forest of staffs down their street, saluting them with "Muy buenos días,"

"Cómo va eso, how is life treating you?", "Que tenga usted un buen día, Señora, may you have a fine day, Señora," answering proudly "Navarros from Estella" when the citizens ask where they are from. At first I'm a little embarrassed to be part of this invasion but soon they get me into the spirit; their vitality sweeps me away too.

We walk across fields of grass in the dawning light, fog swirling around a few stout, solitary oaks. Leaving the road, we climb up the flank of a mountain with rock-rose and broom flowering between granite outcroppings, dewy herbs releasing their sharp odors when we happen to step on them—wild marjoram and thyme, odors of Castile.

As we walk at different paces and change our groupings, I talk to each one of the Navarrese, getting to know them little by little. They tell me their names but I can't learn all of them at once. These pilgrims met each other at the parish church in Estella where some of them are catechists for children. The leader is an employee at the Adidas factory; his wife works at City Hall; one of the conquistadores has a job in a sawmill; the young man with the flashing smile teaches at an elementary school; one of the women is a lab technician; the rest, younger, are students. The priest is no sedentary urban cleric: he spent fifteen years in the Andes of Ecuador where he was jailed for championing the Indians' rights against the government. For the trip to Santiago he's purser, cook and spiritual advisor; he celebrates Mass each Sunday on the road. With the driver of the van, he forms the support team that travels ahead to find lodgings and a place to park the vehicle, where they prepare a three-course, hot lunch for the pilgrims' arrival each day.

A pair of big, black and white urracas, or magpies fly out of the brush and we spot two walkers ahead.

"The Basques" says a woman who is walking at my side. "They stayed at the refuge in San Juan de Ortega last night but slept in a separate room. They're a little standoffish; I think they enjoy being alone. They must have left before us this morning."

As we gain on the two figures, I recognize the Basques I met outside Logroño: Babe Ruth with the portable radio and his limping girlfriend.

"She was almost crippled when they arrived last night" the woman goes on, "a couple of hours before you. We soaked her feet in saltwater, lanced her blisters, fixed two insoles for her boots and gave her a long massage. Looks like she's doing much better today."

When we overtake the man and woman, I feel glad to see them, the first pilgrims I met while walking on the Road. We greet each other like old friends, with none of the reserve of our first encounter.

They tell me their names—Josemi and Sagrario—and we continue on the road.

The pace of the Navarrese, who have the freedom of walking without the burden of a pack, is too quick for me. Josemi also lags behind carrying his backpack-for-two. As much as I love the company of these young pilgrims from Estella, I won't be able to continue with them for long.

Now a group of twelve counting the Basques, we stop at a bar in the outskirts of Burgos for a merienda, the late-morning or afternoon snack for tiding over hunger until the next meal. The bartender refuses to let us use his table to eat bocadillos already prepared by the Navarrese, even if we buy drinks: we're in the city once more. In the countryside the tradition of hospitality toward pilgrims has survived more or less, while in the cities it has flown to heaven. There we were a part of the landscape with our wide-brimmed hats and walking sticks; here we're oddballs, objects of stares and chuckles. A hamlet like San Juan de Ortega manages to maintain a large, clean refuge for pilgrims, yet Burgos, capital of the province and one of the most important cities on the Road to Santiago, offers nothing. To think that in the heyday of the Camino it had some thirty hospices, many with priests to hear confession from thousands of pilgrims in all the major languages.

Two more bartenders refuse to serve us on the way into town. We have no choice but to eat our bocadillos outside. We end up at the fountain in front of the cathedral, without a tree or a building to shade us from the hot noon sun. The two jagged towers of the florid Gothic church look almost as tall as football fields, thrusting toward the sky.

After our snack we walk up the stairs to enter the cathedral. An old man at the door, one of those shriveled denizens of Spanish churches, sees our short pants and forbids us to pass—"by order of el señor Obispo, his excellency the Bishop." One of the Navarrese men tells him we've walked over 250 kilometers as peregrinos on the Road to Santiago; surely we have a right to enter?

"Peregrinos o pepinillos, pilgrims or pickles, go complain at the Episcopal Palace across the way" replies Quasimodo. "My instructions are not to allow anyone with short pants inside the cathedral. Hay que tener respeto en la casa de Dios, one must show respect in God's house."

The Navarrese are disappointed; they've never been in Burgos, the capital of Old Castile and city of the national hero, Cid Campeador. I toured this church on my first trip to Spain years ago and my feet are too tender for me to enjoy a visit anyhow. In fact I'm

9 Burgos, cathedral. (Photo José Luis Herrera)

amused: in this new Spain where women go naked or topless at the beach, pilgrims cannot enter a cathedral if they are wearing short pants. I guess you could say there's been progress since Franco's time when women were arrested for wearing bikinis and had to cover their heads in churches.

The pilgrims from Estella decide to make a rendezvous with their van, where they can change into long pants and return to the cathedral.

"We're supposed to spend the night at the Paulist Fathers' refuge in Tardajos," their leader tells me, "ten kilometers beyond Burgos. Why don't you join us there? We'll fix up those feet of yours."

"Thanks, it's been great walking with you" I answer. They pat me on the back and we tell each other Hasta luego, See you later, in the doorway of the cathedral as the Hunchback of Burgos looks on, glowering.

Another church you won't see on the inside, I think walking down the stairs, recalling Redecilla del Camino and Eunate. From my first and only visit to this cathedral I remember the famous Santo Cristo, a crucifix worshiped for centuries by the Burgalese and by pilgrims: the most terrifying Christ I've seen anywhere, his body bruised and festering with wounds, so lifelike that he's said to have human hair, fingernails, skin, and even to sweat, bleed and grow a beard. Spain.

I cross the milky-green Arlanzón River by a turreted gate with niches of statues for the Cid, Count Fernán González and other Spanish heroes. Standing here on a winter morning some twenty years ago, I saw a girl's face framed by the frosted window of a bus stopping at the corner; I grinned at her and she broke out in a glorious smile I'll never forget. Perhaps one of these portly ladies bustling home to lunch is the young woman who exchanged smiles with me on that faraway morning. Of course she's no longer young, must be middle-aged by now, marked by more than twenty years of living, working, her share of suffering.

There's no mail for me at the Lista de Correos window of the main post office. I've been looking forward to receiving news from María, Daniel and my parents, here at one of my two mail stops on the Camino. Yet I don't need to rely on letters, I no longer feel lonely, my contact with other travelers has given me a new confidence and sense of belonging to a community.

I mail my letters and cross the city to get back on the Road. When I see the sign for the turnoff to Las Huelgas, I remember my plans to visit this, the most celebrated of all convents on the way to Compostela. It's only about a mile from here but my feet reject the idea of a detour. Of course I visited the place on my first trip to Burgos but I knew nothing about it then, nor about its importance for the pilgrimage. If my feet would allow it, I'd go there not so much to see the royal abbey's Romanesque cloister again, its flower garden and wide meadow, its polychrome statue of St. James with movable arms that was used to knight the kings of Castile and León . . . No, I'd go there to pay homage to the American pilgrim whose memory is associated inseparably with Las Huelgas for me, a woman who knew the Camino as well as anyone, who wrote a book that's my lifetime favorite on the Road to Santiago—Georgiana Goddard King.

A professor of art history at Bryn Mawr in the early part of the century, when not many of her sex held chairs even at women's colleges, she wandered for three years across Spain on foot and donkey, in train, bus and coach carrying out the research for her greatest work, *The Way of St. James.* If there weren't many female professors at the time, there were even fewer women who traveled alone. Among her 1,600 pages on the history, architecture, sculpture and painting of the Camino, King interspersed anecdotes on the scandal she caused among Spaniards: she was hooted and called "Alemana! German!" by children, told that only a worthless woman would travel on foot or donkeyback. The most revealing passage, written in her discreet style, is a confession of the difficulties suffered by a foreign woman in Spain around 1915: "Those long hours in a Spanish winter. . . . For a woman alone, they are hard. . . . She cannot walk up and down the pavement, in the light of shop windows, as men are doing. She goes back to her room at the hotel. There she cannot go to bed to keep warm, for dinner is still three hours away; she makes her tea, then fills a rubber hot-water-bottle, and wrapping it and herself in a rug lies down under a faint electric bulb to read and shiver and dare not to doze."

King's descriptions of churches, convents and other buildings, sometimes too long, are still the final word on the subject in many cases. Although she wasn't a Catholic, she never showed the Protestant bias of Ford, Borrow and most Anglo-Saxon writers on Spain. Her work has contributed to the reinterpretation of the cult of St. James in our time: she shows Santiago to be a product of pagan syncretism and Christian myth, a sun, fertility and war god all in one; with more precision than Richard Ford, she depicts the legend of the Moorslayer as an urgent response to the holy war waged by Islam.

I'll always connect King with Las Huelgas because of her unforgettable evocation of the abbey and its nuns. By the time she visited the Cistercian convent during World War I, its period of greatness had long passed but the nuns were "still ladies, with the air and gentleness of the great." Some spoke to her in French, all in "the language of soft tones and benign regard." Inquiring the date of her imminent sailing across the Atlantic, the nuns promised their prayers for her safety from German submarines. "Those white prayers are a debt never to be discharged" wrote King after her safe arrival.

There's something so different in her story on this Road to Santiago where the masculine predominates. I know all about the various figures of the Madonna worshiped along the route—Virgins of the Road, the Bridge, the River, the Rock, the Fountain, the Snows; there's even a Pilgrim Virgin, believe it or not. But none is a saint of my particular devotion; for me Georgiana King will always be the main female presence on the Way of St. James.

Beyond the detour for Las Huelgas, just off the road is another landmark in the history of the pilgrimage—the ruined Hospital del Rey, probably the first hospice for travelers to Compostela, once directed by the powerful abbess of the neighboring convent. A sign says "EN OBRAS" ("under repair"). Half the country's monuments seem to be in this state; Spain is in a permanent state of reconstruction.

The only part of the King's Hospital not in ruins are the beautiful Renaissance doors to the former church, with their dark panels of carved walnut. One of them shows a family of pilgrims led by a father who looks back tenderly at his wife as she gives suck to a swaddled infant, followed by a fatigued older son who reaches to his father for support. A swirl of heads, bodies and feet, walking sticks, squash gourds, scrips, cockleshell hats—Jacobean images in rhythmic, overlapping waves of wood. The carving moves me more than most of the greater monuments I've seen so far on the Road; I wouldn't trade it for the whole cathedral of Burgos. In these sculpted figures I see my own family . . . María, who nursed Carlos for two years; Daniel, probably about the same age as the adolescent boy; me, the father. Yet I know a pilgrimage with them would be difficult: María has fragile health, Carlos is too small to walk five hundred miles, Daniel probably wouldn't want to go far without his Walkman.

The province of Burgos must be a sort of bottleneck on the Camino de Santiago, I think, seeing a pair of walkers ahead of me. They're adjusting gear as I approach them: a short young woman with an ankle-length, flower-patterned dress and dusty sandals, a canvas rucksack supporting an incongruous parasol on her back; a very tall man also in his twenties, must be six-feet-six, short blond hair, carrying enough cameras, lenses and light meters for a photojournalist. They look German or Dutch as surely as I've ever been in Europe. With their contrast in height, they also remind me of a male/female Don Quixote and Sancho Panza.

We say hello to each other in English. They present themselves as Marilyn and Wim ("Vim"), who are walking all the way from Amsterdam to Compostela. As we take to the road she tells me about their lives and their trip, without the initial wariness of so many Spaniards. She was studying humanities when a strike by students closed the university; she decided to make the pilgrimage to Santiago but didn't want to walk alone. When she placed an advertisement for a traveling companion in a newspaper and a bookstore, Wim was the only person to reply. They left Amsterdam last month.

This strange couple is moving so fast that I have to strain to keep up. Wim walks yards ahead of us. His stride must measure nearly five feet—I can see the zigzag prints of his boots in the dust of the roadside. (I remember the fallen menhir after Roncesvalles that supposedly measures Roland's step, not much longer than this flying Dutchman's.) Marilyn has to take about two strides for one of his, walking doggedly with head down, so quickly that the parasol bobs up and down on her back, bringing stares from the passing cars. She tells me they were sleeping on the riverbank in Burgos until an hour ago and are planning to travel all night by the full moon.

I cannot believe they could be so dead wrong about the phase of the moon, after weeks of walking from Holland to Spain: "To the best of my knowledge there's no moon tonight," I tell her. "I'm pretty certain because I've been watching it carefully ever since I started walking."

"We saw the full moon for August 5 on a calendar in Burgos," she answers.

"You may have seen the *new*, not the full moon" I suggest, imagining this Dutch couple wandering lost in the darkness. If it's clear again tonight, at least they'll be able to follow the Milky Way. No use trying to change their mind.

We say goodbye in the ugly highway town of Tardajos where I hope to spend the night with the Navarrese. I watch the couple as they go off to the west, raising the road-dust, Wim loping like a camel, Marilyn struggling to follow him, her parasol swinging like a metronome, allegretto. Old Vim and Vigor, I baptize them a second time, Don Quixote and Sancho on the quest of the missing moon.

At the large, modern school of the Paulist Fathers I discover that they no longer give refuge to pilgrims. A foul-breathed man says my friends from Estella passed through here more than an hour ago.

Too tired to walk further, I stop at a fonda, or inn on the main highway. The Basque couple, Sagrario and Josemi are checking in at the desk; they also separated from the Navarrese in Burgos. We agree to rent a pair of rooms with a common bath.

As we walk upstairs the Basques notice that I'm limping. They ask me to go to their room after we bathe so they can show me the foot treatment the Navarrese gave to Sagrario.

I collapse on the bed as I hear the couple in the bathroom. How strange that these Basques, so unfriendly when I met them coming out of Logroño, have ended up practically being my roommates. They travel and sleep together—taboo for an unmarried couple in Spain until a few years ago. I'm learning more about the changes in the country on the ancient Road to Santiago than in all the books and trips that have brought me to my second homeland.

After showering I go to the Basques' room. They soak my feet in a bucket of cold water mixed with unrefined salt. "It cleans and toughens the skin" Josemi tells me. Then Sagrario takes my feet in her lap: she dries them softly with a towel, massages my soles, insteps, ankles and toes, lances the blisters with the needle-and-thread operation taught her by the Navarrese, rubs the callouses with a piece of pumice stone. She's wearing short pants; my feet revive in contact with her golden thighs and warm hands. First time a woman has touched me in days, I think. When she finishes, my feet and ankles feel tired but healed, tingling with energy.

Now it's Sagrario's turn: she soaks her feet and I give her the treatment, Josemi handing me the instruments like a surgeon's assistant in an operating room: needle, thread, scissors, alcohol, cotton, matches, Mercurochrome, pumice. Then she and I share in giving her boyfriend a short massage instead of the full therapy; he hasn't suffered from blisters since they walked those forty kilometers on their first day.

When we go downstairs for dinner we're laughing and joking about our feet. "Let's hope the foot-washing doesn't mean this is our Last Supper" says Sagrario. I remember the episode in the New Testament and it occurs to me that this Basque woman's name is religious too, Spanish for "sanctuary." Imagine a name like that in English—impossible.

At the bar the Basques stand me to a chato, a short glass of the house's red wine. I return the favor, they treat me again, we lose track of the rounds as the barman scribbles the tally on the counter with white chalk. In the dining room we order a liter of red to wash down the menestra, a dish of fresh vegetables followed by the main course of morcilla, or blood sausage seasoned with herbs and rice, a specialty of Burgos. By the time we go upstairs we're all happy from the wine of the country.

I fall on the mattress, too tired to take off my clothes, thinking this is the first night I've slept in a bed since the pensión in Logroño. With my head spinning I try to review the events of the day—so full: the Navarrese, Josemi, Sagrario and I being turned away at three bars this morning, at the cathedral in Burgos, then at the Paulist Fathers'; not a single letter waiting for me at the post office; blisters worse than ever. Yet none of this matters: for the first time since leaving St. Jean Pied-de-Port, I've spent most of the day walking with other pilgrims. Whatever happens tomorrow, the next day and the day after, I know there are other travelers out there like the Navarrese, like Sagrario and Josemi, Marilyn and Wim who are willing to accept me as a companion on the road. Slowly I've become a tiny piece in a growing network of contacts and friendships weaved from walking and living together, part of a community, the community of pilgrims.

It's taken me more than a third of the way to Compostela to break out of my solitude. As I undress and climb into the sheets, I sense that another stage of the pilgrimage is beginning for me. They say that the first phase of initiation on the Camino ends in San Juan de Ortega, whose equinoctial rite makes it a privileged place for becoming receptive to cosmic rhythms. The second stage would correspond to the great expanse of the Castilian plain before me, whose austerity is supposed to allow a pilgrim to cleanse himself and die to the physical world. The final phase of transformation would begin after the mountains of León, the last barrier between the pilgrim and Galicia, land of St. James, Finisterre and the sea. These theoretical stages seem a little arbitrary to me; each traveler must follow his own rhythm on the road. Mine tells me that a change is growing in me as surely as I can feel my skin, warmed by sun and wine, against the cool sheets of this bed. Let the new moon be the start of a new cycle for me too, in my body and heart. (I remember poor old Vim and Vigor and I wish them luck out there in the night.)

Sleep quickly covers me with the cloak she offers to weary pilgrims.

PART
TWO

12 Water

You road I enter upon and look around, I believe
you are not all that is here,
I believe that much unseen is also here.

—Whitman

As we leave town the sun is rising on ancient human chores. Men walk toward the fields for the harvest, women carry winnowing forks to the threshing floors. A curved slice of new moon has risen only a few hours ahead of the sun; it too hangs in the east. I wonder how far Vim and Vigor walked last night.

We're off the paved road and it feels good to be in the country again after Burgos. Tractors are already chugging between the furrows of ripe grain. I'm glad to be with Josemi and Sagrario but their pace is brisker than mine. What a contrast with the first time we saw each other, when I overtook them on the hill outside Logroño! They're almost twenty years younger than you, I tell myself. It doesn't matter: in normal life we might not have much in common but here on the Camino, age, profession, status mean nothing. We're all pilgrims. Yet they are walking faster now and soon or late they will outstrip me.

We stop for Josemi to fill our canteens at a well off the road. It's the first time I've been alone with Sagrario. I sense she may be a little embarrassed, as I am.

Partly to put her at ease, also out of curiosity I tell her "You know, we've washed each other's feet but I don't have any idea what you and Josemi do when you're not on the Road to Santiago."

She smiles revealing two rows of small, immaculate teeth: "He works in a metallurgical factory and I teach in an ikastola, a private Basque school."

Like many Spanish women, she's too discreet to ask a direct question of a man, especially a foreigner. I have to take the initiative by describing my own work as a teacher, my family, my home.

She surprises me by asking if I've heard about the stabbing of the German. "A man told us about it in Burgos yesterday" she says, "also about the girlfriend. He advised Josemi and me not to travel as a couple. Said we should walk with at least one other man."

"I guess that's me."

"We feel less worried with you along."

I'm not the only one who's been afraid on the road, I think, a little consoled. It astounds me that a husky Basque like Josemi could have fears similar to those of an older, scrawnier, solitary foreigner like me.

We sit down in the prickly stubble of the wheatfield to rest while we wait for Josemi. The cicadas have already begun to sing. It's going to be another hot day.

Josemi returns holding proudly a damp, water-beaded canteen in each hand.

"What took you so long?" asks Sagrario.

"I had to relieve myself" he answers smiling. "For the first time in my life I understand the old proverb, 'Pasarlo peor que una puta en abrojos,' to be more uncomfortable than a whore in the stubble. Jesus, is that stuff hard on the old rear end" he says with a laugh, rubbing one of his boot soles on the stiff, freshly-cut stalks of wheat.

We laugh and get up. Ascending gradually, we cross a paved road, traverse more tawny fields of grain, see the tower of a church ahead.

"Hontanas" says Josemi with relief. We've walked more than ten kilometers without seeing a single town.

Unlike other settlements that appear first on the horizon, on a plain or hilltop, Hontanas lies in a depression below the meseta, with only its bell tower visible from the road. In a few minutes the whole village sits at our feet, almost as it might have looked in the Middle Ages except for an automobile junkyard at the entrance.

"Those cars look about as befitting here as Christ with a pistol" says Josemi.

We go down a winding dirt road between high stone walls and onto the main street of the town. Odors of barnyard and baked bread mingle in the air. On chairs made of rush-mats, several women are sitting in the middle of the street. All are old, dressed in black, knitting and chatting.

Without the normal shyness of people in a small Spanish town, they greet us "Buenos días, peregrinos." They must be used to receiving pilgrims here on the eastern end of the village.

"This pueblo is famous for its water" says one of them. "Don't miss the fountain on your left."

"We even have a swimming pool" adds another, smiling. The three of us exchange looks: a pool would be even more unlikely than the junkyard in this village of adobe, dust and stone.

"Thank you, señoras" says Josemi as we walk on. Then under his breath to us: "How sly are these old Castilian women." I have the impression that for my Basque companions, the people of central Spain are like residents of the Third World.

In a sunny little plaza we see water gushing from a stone well. Each of us drinks from it and looks at the others with wide-open eyes; it's the coldest, cleanest-tasting water I've ever tasted. We let it spill over our hair, our sweaty, dust-lined faces, necks and shoulders.

"Qué agua, what water!" exclaims Josemi. "Almost beats the red last night"—a supreme compliment coming from this Basque who loves his wine.

After refreshing myself at the well, I understand how water sometimes used to be valued more than wine in the arid Spanish and Arabic worlds. No wonder this town is called Hontanas, from fontanas, fountains, springs: in its water we've tasted what can live in a word or name—musical, liquid, true. We've tasted the deep salts in the earth and the pure rain from the skies. Where but in the middle of the Camino de Santiago, on the dry Castilian plain can something as elemental as water make you glad to have been born, happy as a child?

Approaching the church we see two bodies reclining on stone benches in the shade, fast asleep. I recognize Vim and Vigor. They must have walked in the dark until they realized the full moon was not going to rise after all.

"A Dutch couple I met yesterday" I tell Sagrario and Josemi as we walk on.

By the time we reach the end of town, our faces and hair have already dried in the hot sun. Then we see it as we go around a curve: the turquoise water surrounded by grass, like a mirage in the desert.

"Me cago en Dios" says Josemi. "The old crones were telling the truth."

"What are we waiting for?" I ask.

"Let's go!" he cries and we run through the gate, our packs bouncing on our shoulders.

In less than two minutes we've all raced to peel off our clothes in the bathrooms, put on our swimsuits and jumped into the water, laughing like three kids, still unable to believe it's true: a big blue-green swimming pool in an ancient town with only a few hundred inhabitants, miles from the nearest city, smack on the road to Compostela.

The water feels almost as icy as the well and suddenly I understand the mystery. Underground water must be so abundant in Hontanas that they've taken advantage of it to construct a swimming pool. When we get out to dry off, an old attendant in charge of tickets confirms my suspicion; he tells us that people come here to swim from all the neighboring villages.

We lie down on the grass: here they don't ruin their pools with concrete decks. How soothing to feel the cool, green blades of grass between our toes, after walking twenty kilometers in sweaty boots through the heat and dust!

A few more swimmers begin to arrive with the usual time lag in Spain. The old man who sells them tickets also waits on the inevitable bar, the only one in Hontanas, less than ten yards from the pool. Josemi, Sagrario and I sit down at one of the tables and order drinks.

From the road comes a growing clatter like a stampeding herd of cattle. The Navarros, I think and there they are like a forest of walking sticks, laughing, screaming with surprise and joy when they see the pool. We greet them, embracing their perspiring bodies with our cool arms as the people look on, probably wondering what kind of reunion is being celebrated in front of their eyes between three swimmers and a motley crew in straw hats, boots and tennis shoes, bearing lances like an invading army.

Within a few minutes the Navarrese are in the water, the quiet pool of this little town suddenly transformed into churning froth as they swim, splash, climb out and dive in over and over again, the surface as choppy as the tank of an aquarium full of frolicking porpoises. They've conquered and occupied the pool with their elan and energy, just as they do every other place they go.

The crowd at the pool has begun to thin out as the midday meal approaches; the Navarrese decamp as quickly as they arrived in order to meet their van for lunch.

Sagrario, Josemi and I sit at a wobbly table in the bar to eat a lunch of fried veal-steak and potatoes prepared by the old man, washed down with red wine of course. A new group of pilgrims walks in: a thickset bearded man speaking English to a blond boy and a lanky, younger man also with a beard, who wears a kind of safari hat adorned with dry wildflowers. We introduce ourselves and another macaronic conversation gets under way, in English and Spanish this time as we invite each other to rounds of beer and wine.

The Englishman is named Mike, a philosophy professor at a school near London; he's making the pilgrimage for the second summer in a row with his son Kes. The tall man is Claudio, an astrologer from Valencia.

Remembering the signs written on the pilgrims' blackboard, I tell him "You must be the one who wrote the planetary symbols at the refuge in Nájera. Didn't you also sign with another name besides Claudio?"

He laughs and says "You have a good memory. The other name is Panorámix." He's probably in his thirties but when he smiles and narrows his eyes behind his metal-rimmed glasses, contracting the lines of his face, he looks like a mischievous child, an elf or gnome.

"What does that name mean?" I ask.

He laughs again: "Oh it comes from a character in a comic strip about the ancient Gauls."

Mike says "Panorámix is the wizard or sorcerer in a series called 'Asterix'—it's popular all over Europe. He has a long beard too and Claudio uses the name as a pseudonym."

"It's a way of not taking yourself too seriously" adds the thin one.

He speaks better English than any Spaniard I can remember, with a slight British accent. I'm surprised because most of his countrymen are poor students of foreign tongues—a remnant of imperial times when their subjects were expected to learn Spanish, I think. Same as the British, along with Americans the worst speakers of other peoples' languages. In fact Josemi, Sagrario, Mike and Kes are having a hard time with their conversation; they feel so frustrated that they decide to go swimming. Claudio sits down at the table with me.

"Your English is superb" I tell him.

"It should be" he answers blushing like a little boy. "I have made many trips to Ireland, Scotland, Wales and Cornwall—the Celtic parts of the British Isles. I must have been a Celt in a former life."

"How many times have you made the pilgrimage?" I ask.

"This is my fourth. I accompanied Mike and Kes last year on their first. We walk at very different paces—the little one's legs are so short—but we always meet at an agreed place to spend the night. Is this your first pilgrimage?"

"Yes" I tell him.

"It's important to find your own pace and to follow it. Trying to keep up with someone else is no good. When you find your own rhythm in walking and breathing, you tire less, you calm the restlessness of the mind, your senses become more receptive to the scenery and you begin to see, not only to look at things, you are a part of nature."

He pauses then asks "What brings an American to make a pilgrimage in Europe?"

"That's a question I've often asked myself without finding a clear answer. I teach Spanish language and literature at a university in

Kentucky, have spent a lot of time in Spain and have been intrigued by the history of the Camino for years. I'm from a state with a large Hispanic population—California. Did you know that there are places in California and Texas named after Santiago?"

"No but it doesn't surprise me" answers Claudio. "After all, the Spaniards named rivers, mountains, cities and provinces after him in South America and the Caribbean, so they must have done the same when they explored North America."

"It's more than just place-names. Some churches in the American Southwest still have images of Santiago, and he is one of the Hopi gods and ancestors—a katchina."

I notice Claudio hasn't touched his glass of red wine. "Is there something else I can order for you?" I ask.

"Thank you, I'll have an orange soda. I don't drink alcohol but I did not want to mention it when others preferred wine and beer."

I order him a soda from the old bartender. Claudio lights a cigarette with a wax-tipped match. By this time I shouldn't be surprised to see any Spaniard smoking but for some reason the cigarette looks out of place in the long fingers of his hand. Christ with a pistol, I think, remembering Josemi's words. With his olive complexion, light green eyes, thick beard, angular frame and leather sandals on dusty, sockless feet, Claudio in fact resembles the traditional image of Jesus.

We finish our drinks, pay and go outside in the sun. Claudio leaves his backpack on the ground while he goes to change into his swimsuit.

I notice two scallop shells sewn to the rear of the pack, pierced with tiny holes at each end for the thread. One is the concave half, the other the flat side of the same calico scallop. I've never seen both valves of a shell on a pilgrim's pack. I ask Claudio about it when he returns.

"Most pilgrims use only the concave half of the shell" he says, "the one that can be used as a receptacle for drinking water. I have both halves on my pack because I found that scallop live on a rock at the beach in Finisterre after my first pilgrimage. In those days I was not a vegetarian; I ate the flesh of the mollusk raw and kept both parts of the shell. There is an old medieval tradition that says the two halves symbolize the two rules of charity with which a pilgrim should surround himself, as the shellfish protects itself with double armor—love of God and love of neighbor."

I look carefully at the shell, soft purple, pink and white. Symmetrical flutes radiate from the straight-edged base like rays of light or fire, I think as they reflect the bright sun.

Claudio realizes that I'm admiring this perfect specimen: "For me it is the most universal emblem of pilgrimage" he says, "more than the palm frond of Jerusalem or the crossed keys of Rome. Look at the flutes closely: they resemble the bones of human fingers for example, joints and all. Others say the flutes converging at the base of the shell are the paths of the world coming together in Compostela. For me all roads lead there." Looking at the shell's flat valve, I can easily imagine fingers or roads.

"The Romans used it as an amulet" he goes on, "to ward off the evil eye. It was made of every material you can imagine—silver, gold, azabache . . . how do you say it in English?"

"Jet" I answer.

"Jet" he repeats as if to engrave the word in his memory. "Jet, lead, tin, clay, ceramic. At the height of the pilgrimage the trade in Jacobean shells was so lucrative that a special guild of concheiros, or shell makers and vendors was formed in Compostela. They sensed that the cockleshell was the most appropriate symbol of the pilgrimage to Santiago because the city is so close to the sea."

"Not that much closer than Rome or Jerusalem, right?"

"The difference is that pilgrims to those places do not necessarily cross a land mass," he replies, "moving constantly toward the sea as we do on the road to Compostela. After walking for weeks, perhaps months on earth it is only fitting that a pilgrim to Santiago should continue another few days to Finisterre, Land's End, the water, the sea."

"I don't know if my feet will hold out that long."

"I urge you not to stop in Compostela" he says. "Continue all the way to Finisterre, Eduardo. It was a sacred place for the Celts a long time before St. James. You don't have to look any farther than this shell to realize how the pilgrimage to Santiago has absorbed pre-Christian elements. Of course you know that the ancients believed Venus was born in a scallop from the sea foam. Baptismal fonts in the shape of a cockleshell also suggest this idea of birth, new life from the sea. The Greeks and Romans considered the shell to be a symbol of woman's sexual organs."

"So do your compatriots" I say smiling, recalling all the erotic puns on shellfish I've heard in Spain and Latin America. As Claudio takes out another cigarette, it occurs to me that he doesn't seem like the sort of man who would make such jokes. Unlike most Spaniards he doesn't sprinkle his speech with interjections like joder, cojones, coño. There's a sort of moderation and chastity in his demeanor that is unusual in

10   Claudio. (Photo Keller Dunn)

Spain. His speech is so mellow, so friendly that I enjoy hearing him, listening to his choice of words and the inflections of his voice.

Claudio gets up asking "Do you feel like going for . . . " His last words are drowned by a blare of rock and roll from a loudspeaker next to the bar. He laughs, comes over to me and says directly in my ear, "Let's go for a swim and get away from that speaker."

He takes off his hat and places it on the grass. For the first time I see his head—covered with a short fuzz of dark hair like a Buddhist monk's. He has high temples and is prematurely bald.

We jump in the shallow end. I swim a few laps then dive to the colder water at the bottom, come to the surface and float on my back, looking up at the afternoon sky—the same deep-blue color as the pool. Meanwhile Claudio stays near the side, looking awkward and out of place.

"The water reminds me of the scallop shell again" he says. "I was just thinking that if I were an astronaut I would carry it with me to remind me of my planet, my home. And if I had to show one object to an extraterrestial as a memento of our world, so blue with its seas as it turns through space, it would be this shell."

Getting out of the pool, I notice the people on the grass, the music still blasting from the loudspeaker. "You know" I tell Claudio, "I've almost been oblivious to everything around us, talking about a simple seashell with you as if it were the most important thing in the world."

"Perhaps it is" he says solemnly, then breaks out in his impish laugh from the bottom of his belly.

The music on the loudspeaker must be waking the town from its siesta: more people are coming through the gate. Some of the Navarrese return and quickly become the center of attention by forming a human tower in the pool, standing on each other's shoulders, then collapsing with screams and belly-flops in the water.

Two more pilgrims come through the gate, loaded with their packs, looking at the water with disbelief. They're young, not more than twenty, an intense-looking boy and a girl so beautiful that almost everyone around the pool is staring at her, men and women alike. She's tall and lithe, her skin the tawny brown of the earth in this part of Spain, her auburn hair catching light from the sun reflecting off the pool. Although she wears the typical T-shirt, short hiking pants and boots, her carriage, a yellow scarf around her long neck and a single gold earring make her look as nonchalantly graceful as a mannequin. She's one of those young women in southern Europe whose ripening bodies seem to be made of dark, sweet-smelling honey.

Spotting Claudio, they smile and come over to greet him. He introduces me to Marta and her companion Gorka, both from Bilbao. They remain only long enough to drink in the water with their eyes; I notice that hers are green. As they leave, Marta draws more stares with her slow, syrupy walk.

"These chicos hardly have a peseta to their name" Claudio says. "That's probably why they didn't go swimming; if they bought tickets for the pool they would have to go without food tonight. Mike and I have walked a couple of days with them and we have never seen them eat more than a little bread and cheese. And they're too proud to accept handouts."

"There's something I've been wanting to ask you" I tell Claudio. "But I'm too thirsty. Can I get us some drinks first?"

"A tonic please."

I return from the bar with the tonic water and a beer. Claudio is sitting on the grass now. I tell him "You know, seeing that lovely girl reminds me of something I've been wondering for a long time. This is the third time I've been in a pool since I began walking—the others were in Pamplona and Nájera. In both places I felt attracted by the women. Even before Pamplona, between Roncesvalles and Zubiri I came upon a beautiful shepherd woman in the woods; I couldn't get her out of my mind for days. Here of course I was taken by Marta yet she didn't affect me like the shepherdess or the women at the other swimming pools. It was more like a sort of detached wonder that I felt. Do you know what I mean?"

"I think so" says Claudio drinking his tonic from the bottle. "The walking, the sore feet, the blisters, the tired muscles are all part of a discipline and purgation, a wearing down and wearing away of these bodies of ours, a dying to our old selves that we must seek and suffer on the road. For this reason the monastics punished their bodies in order to kill desire, to transcend sexuality and reach a higher level of consciousness."

"What about lovers and couples?" I ask him, thinking about Josemi and Sagrario, who are out of earshot.

"Even they can walk for weeks to Compostela without the need for sexual intercourse. When you walk the Camino with a woman, she soon becomes a companion, a friend, simply another pilgrim."

"It's strange" I tell him. "I never would have believed it if I didn't feel it myself. I wonder how long it will last after the pilgrimage."

"Some couples have told me they did not make love until several days afterwards, maybe a week later. It's as if the body is floating and needs time to land, to come to the ground before returning to a normal life."

"What happens after that—weeks, months later—that's what interests me."

Claudio finishes his drink. "It's not easy. People like you always struggle between the power of passion and the spirit."

I'm taken aback by his words, spoken as if he's known me for years. "What makes you say so?" I ask him.

"As an astrologer I cannot help guessing under what sign people are born. Almost everything about you—your love of the water, your taste for beer and wine, the way your eyes almost came out of their sockets [he pronounces it "soak-ets"] when you saw Marta, your sense of humor, your high forehead and thick eyebrows, the way you open yourself to a new friendship, the kind of questions you ask—for me it's very clear that you must have been born in late October."

"Jesus Christ!" I say unable to hold it in, "how could you have guessed that? October 29 in fact."

"I have just told you, hombre" says Claudio with his leprechaun's laugh, showing the spaces where he's missing some of his front teeth. "For a while I was going to guess earlier in October—you have some Libra in you but not as much as Scorpio."

I find it hard to believe that Claudio has almost guessed my birthday. I feel a little uncomfortable as if I were all at once exposed, transparent.

Taking a small notebook and a pencil from his pack, he looks at me like a man getting down to work: "Can you give me your place of birth, the year and time of day?"

"What's wrong, can't you guess them too?" I ask him. He laughs. "All right I'll tell you: Colorado Springs, Colora—"

I haven't finished the sentence when a new record blares on the loudspeaker—Bruce Springsteen's "Born in the U.S.A." Claudio and I look at each other, he throws his notebook and pencil in the air and we both begin to laugh so hard that the people around us are staring, Mike hears us and comes ambling over, we tell him about it and now we all have tears in our eyes, Josemi and Sagrario arrive but it is too much, the freshness gone out of it, my chest and ribs aching now. I have the feeling that my stolid Basque friends think we're a little crazy.

The Navarrese see our new group and don't want to miss anything: they join us too. I introduce them to Claudio and Mike. As we sit, talk and laugh together, the sun lower in the sky, Springsteen rasping "born in the U.S.A.!" time after time, I feel as if I've known these friends all my life, as much at home here as I would be at a swimming pool in California or Kentucky. I recall other moments of plenitude on the road: the pilgrim's blessing in Roncesvalles, the shepherdess, Eunate, the field of sunflowers, the vineyards in La Rioja. Here, now I also feel the lightness in my head, a surge of well-being as I wonder why, what have I done to deserve this human warmth, this brotherhood, this overflow of life?

The Navarrese invite us to their encampment on a poplar-shaded threshing floor close to the pool, covered with mounds of wheat. We sit on folding chairs from the old yellow van, talking as the sun drops. Our hosts take out a pair of homemade stilts; we laugh trying to walk on them with our blister-sore feet, falling onto the hills of threshed, golden grain. We're all happy.

Claudio, Mike and Kes are preparing to leave. "We want to reach the refuge in the next town, Castrogeriz before dark" Claudio says. Lowering his voice he tells me "By the way, don't forget to ask the monjas clarisas, the nuns of St. Clare for an interview when you go through Castrogeriz."

We give them hugs and wish them good luck on the road. The pilgrims from Estella invite Sagrario, Josemi and me to spend the night with them in an abandoned schoolhouse nearby. We pick up our gear at the pool and walk back to town. It's the time of afternoon when pilgrims start to think about getting sleep for the next day's journey.

The mayor of Hontanas and his wife are there to greet us at the old school. As we're talking a farmer parks his giant combine in front of the building; the mayor reprimands him and they engage in an argument that brings all the town's dirty clothes out in the open. The mayor's wife apologizes for them, telling us the men are so fatigued from the harvest this time of year that the least provocation makes them explode like gunpowder. While middle-class, more or less educated Spaniards can afford to leave home and go on a pilgrimage during the summer, many others, less fortunate, must stay behind to harvest the crops, thresh the wheat and produce the goods that keep the country running.

In a few minutes we convert the crumbling, dusty schoolroom into a home. The Navarrese serve us a light Spanish supper. There's no bathroom so we have to use a weed-grown field next to the building. (It reminds me of old Ramón's backyard.) I relieve myself looking up at the Milky Way, like a string of jewels across the sky.

13 Exhibits of Life and Death

O I see now that life cannot exhibit all to me, as
the day cannot,
I see that I am to wait for what will be exhibited
by death.

—Whitman

We depart before dawn. We're walking on a road lined with poplars and elms in a narrow, green valley. It must be a part of Hontanas' water system, an oasis that extends beyond the town in the cool of morning with birds singing in the wind-rustled trees.

Following Claudio's advice and my own experience by this time, I don't alter my step to keep up with my companions. I move at my own pace and fall into a natural rhythm of walking and breathing. When the sun begins to appear, the others are already out of sight ahead.

Coming around a curve I see a strange vision: ruins of a Gothic church spanning the road. I hardly believe it as I approach the worn stone that looks pink with the rising sun; I go under the arch as if I'm passing from one world, one era to another. I can make out what used to be a towering nave, a graceful apse, the north façade with the outlines of worn shapes—men and women, animals, trees?—sharing the space with grass, weeds and wildflowers growing from cracks in the stone.

"CONVENTO DE SAN ANTÓN" says a sign. Here the old order of monks attended pilgrims on the Camino, especially those afflicted with the enigmatic St. Anthony's fire, a toxic disease that ravaged Europe in the tenth and eleventh centuries. How much has changed since that time when many pilgrims were not healthy citizens on vacation but the sick and desperate in search of a cure for their ailments, pardon for their sins. St. James supposedly restored sight to the blind, hearing to the deaf, speech to the mute; he was also famous for healing dozens of other infirmities. Right now I'd settle for having my blisters healed: the skin of my feet has softened from being in the pool yesterday.

I stop to rest, feeling a kind of uneasiness among these ruins surrounded by nothing but fields. No wonder people say that unusual things still occur in this area; not too many years ago two dogs guarding a flock killed almost three hundred sheep. Some believe a treasure is buried under the ruins. Of course the esotericos attribute the aura of the place to some undivulged mystery guarded by the monks of St. Anthony, who were said to keep alive the ancient initiatory wisdom on the Camino de Santiago, like the Knights Templar. All I know is that these lonely ruins, this broken arch of time create an atmosphere, an ambiente as the Spaniards say, unlike any other I've felt until now. You don't have to stretch your imagination to hear the bells worn by lepers to warn of their approach; the moaning of pilgrims inflicted with dropsy, gout and sores, dragging themselves to these portals for shelter and food; the cries of pardoners selling papal bulls, seals and indulgences; hawkers peddling scallop shells, amulets, talismans, relics. I hear them, I see them, they swarm around me, the lame and blind, epileptics, imbeciles, syphilitics, maniacs: all of them walking, riding century after century in a never-ending dance of life and death, the living always walking in their ancestors' footsteps on this road where hundreds of thousands, millions of shoes have been worn out, countless feet have been blistered like mine.

It takes me a while to bring my mind back to the present. At the first fork in the road I see a cruceiro—a stone pillar surmounted by a crucifix, the right arm of Christ and the cross pointing the way to Santiago. Beyond a clump of poplars I can make out the bare, conical mountain of Castrogeriz topped by a ruined castle, one of those strategic fortresses that must have changed hands many times during the wars between Arabs and Christians. Seeing the town on the flank of the mountain reminds me of Claudio: he advised me to stop here at the convent of St. Clare. His words surprised me because he doesn't remind me of an orthodox Catholic, not even a Christian for that matter.

A lone figure is approaching on the road. As we draw closer I make out the figure of a peasant worn down and stunted by years of hard work, his skin dried, tanned like leather from the extremes of the Castilian climate—nine months of winter and three of hell, as the saying goes. He's pushing a cart overloaded with grass and weeds.

"Muy buenos días tenga usted" he greets me, removing his soiled boina. He has no teeth and his face looks as if someone had squashed his features together, his nose, cheeks and jaws sucked, almost swallowed into his mouth.

"Muy buenos" I answer. "Can you direct me to the convent of the Poor Clares?"

"With pleasure, Señor. Bear to your left when you enter town. You cannot miss it." He pauses looking at my staff and pack. "Peregrino?" he asks in a voice as dry and cracked as his appearance.

"Yes."

"The sisters will receive you. They welcome pilgrims but are wary of strangers nowadays with all the crazy things that occur. Of course the Señor knows they are cloistered nuns."

"No."

"Very strict. Most still go barefoot all year long. Inside those walls it's so cold in winter that some of the sisters have chilblains on their hands and feet."

"How can they receive me if they're cloistered?" I ask.

"The lady abbess will probably speak to you through the torno." I don't recognize the word.

He wipes his brow with his shirtsleeve. Like many Spanish peasants he's wearing black corduroy pants and vest, a uniform for all seasons.

"The Poor Clares have undergone hard times" he says. "They cannot even afford the upkeep of the building so they depend on help from volunteers in town. I clear the weeds from the patio every fall. Be so kind as to tell them Pedro the muleteer guided you to the convent."

"I will. Where are your mules?"

"You're looking at one" he says smiling and pointing to himself. His are hands that have known the earth: black fingernails, dirt embedded in the whorls of skin. "Once a muleteer always a muleteer" he goes on. "Around here a name sticks like a burr, people forget nothing."

"Thank you for your help."

"A sus órdenes, Señor, at your service" he says tipping his boina again. "May all go well for you on the road and may nothing bad befall you." He's an apparition out of the past, I think as he walks away slowly, his cart creaking and groaning.

I follow the good man's directions and come to a large, dilapidated building with a cross on the roof. A bell rings inside when I pull a cord. The door opens; an old woman greets me. She's not wearing a habit.

The woman seems to know what I want: without asking questions she leads me to a chair in front of a varnished wooden cylinder with a built-in tray, framed in the wall between this room and another. It's much cooler here than outside.

"Write your message for the lady abbess here" she says, pointing to a sheet of white paper and a sharpened pencil placed neatly on the tray—a still-life painting, I think. The woman pads out of the room.

I don't know what to write so I decide simply to state the truth: "I'm a pilgrim to Santiago de Compostela."

I put down the pencil and wait a few minutes. The cylinder rotates, the tray disappears in the wall. This must be the torno, I think, a kind of revolving dumbwaiter. I notice that the side facing me has a peephole in it. I resist the temptation to look.

"Welcome, you are the sixth pilgrim this year" a voice utters with the clear, vigorous accent and hissing s's of Old Castile. "How goes your pilgrimage, hijo?"

The maternal words make me feel more relaxed: "Well" I answer.

"Are you far from home?"

"Very far."

"The Clarisses sisters would like you to feel at home in this humble house, as much as possible under our rule of confinement."

"Thank you."

"Were you overwhelmed by feelings and doubts before you began the pilgrimage?"

"Yes."

"It is true of many, son. Pilgrimage is a penitence and a progress toward death, salvation and a new life."

"I don't feel worthy of salvation. Often I can't believe in it." I'm surprised by the frankness of my own words; she makes me feel so welcome that I speak without inhibition. "It's often hard for me to believe" I go on. "Especially when I'm discouraged by what I see in the churches on the Road." ·

"The Church is more than its properties, its temples and priests" she says, now pausing. "Look at the plaster peeling off the walls around you, and think that in this crumbling edifice the sacrament of communion has been offered for eight hundred years. Through the centuries, in the midst of wars and revolutions, famine and plagues that holy mystery has been celebrated without interruption, without missing a single day. That mystery is the Church, not the building or the people in it."

I remember José Ignacio, the priest from the town in La Rioja, probably because I confessed to him too. It's much easier for me to accept this woman's words; the fact that she's invisible adds a resonance they wouldn't have if I were sitting face to face with an old nun.

Suddenly I have a feeling that I shouldn't prolong this encounter. I want to keep it intact.

"Can you give me some advice for the road, Sister?"

"I am glad to sense that you are anxious to return to the journey" she answers, "like a good team of horses. That is how things should be, as God commands: nuns in the convent, priests in the parish, pilgrims on the road."

"By the way, Pedro the muleteer asked me to tell you that he gave me directions for coming here."

"You were well directed. He is one of God's poor souls. A great soul, in fact." She pauses. "Go on walking, my son, continue on the road, always go forward. Don't linger on the way, don't give up, never turn back. Keep yourself a stranger and a pilgrim on earth."

"May I have your blessing?" I don't even know if nuns have the same privilege as priests.

"Of course" she answers blessing me in the name of God, Mary, Christ, St. Francis and St. Clare.

I stand, so moved that I barely manage to mumble "Gracias."

I've been touched by the feminine, I think, by something I haven't found in the cult of Santiago nor in other places on the Road. I remember Claudio and I understand why he advised me to visit the convent of the Poor Clares. I feel grateful to him. As I go out the door, I place a donation in a straw basket hanging on the jamb.

Still elated from the meeting with the abbess, I walk through Castrogeriz. It's a town traversed by a single, mile-long road, the Camino de Santiago, along the southern slope of the tawny mountain: like an old, mangy lion whose heart has been pierced by an arrow. At least half a dozen churches line the road on both sides. Some of them are abandoned. Along one narrow section, massive walls flank the Camino, so tall they don't allow the sun to pass. A skull and crossbones is carved in the stone on each side, one with the inscription "O Mors," the other "O Aeternitas": a message for pilgrims on their way to Santiago and on their journey through life. I remember the abbess' words about the pilgrimage as a progress toward death and salvation. Everything seems to be carrying me back to another age: the Gothic ruins, the cruceiro, Pedro the muleteer, the Poor Clares, this memento mori—"O Death," "O Eternity." Hontanas with its sweet waters in the middle of the plain was a kind of cleansing, a baptism before the arid, solitary meseta.

Beyond the town I see little piles of rocks placed along the way, especially at the crossroads where a traveler might doubt which way to go. Pilgrims in the Middle Ages, who didn't have maps, used these "mountjoys" to guide them. The small pyramids of stones, ancestors of today's yellow arrows, are a welcome sight to me, more reminders of all those pilgrims in whose footsteps I walk, little hills of joy prefiguring the final promontory above Santiago de Compostela.

On the old bridge over the fast-flowing Río Pisuerga, I cross the boundary between the provinces of Burgos and Palencia, between the ancient kingdoms of Castile and León. The day is still fresh, the sky pure blue, the river banks waving with green rushes and yellow grain, a grove of tall poplars bending in the wind on the far shore.

After another dry stretch, the road follows the rushing waters of the Castilian Canal. Somebody is calling and waving to me from the tall grass on the opposite side. Little by little I recognize the figures of Sagrario and Josemi. I cross the canal at a lock thundering with water and join them near a small Gothic hermitage on a rise overlooking the town of Frómista.

"Wait till you see what's waiting for us on the other side of the church" says Josemi with a mischievous smile.

As we approach the solitary building, I hear raucous voices. The Navarros, I think and when we turn the corner of the church I see their encampment in the shade: the battered yellow van, a huge table covered with dishes of food, bread and bottles of wine.

"Welcome to the fiesta, Eduardo!" they shout taking off my pack, showing me where to wash my face and hands at a spigot with a trough by the church wall.

As they pour us glasses of wine, they explain that this is the last day of the fiesta in their hometown of Estella, always celebrated with an abadejada, or codfish stew. Before setting to, they sing the most rousing grace I've ever heard, clapping their hands on their knees and on the table; it trembles from the impact and from the weight of food upon it. These are the new Catholics, I think, remembering the old ones like the abbess at the convent.

After lunch we share in clearing the table and washing dishes. We lie down for a siesta in the shade of the church, which turns out to be the hermitage of Santiago and the Virgen del Otero, Mary of the Knoll.

Before walking to Frómista we thank the priest and the driver, an eighteen-year-old boy, for preparing this banquet in the middle of the Camino. Our celebration ends like a real fiesta—in a bar where we drink coffee and cognac, some of the men smoking cigars. Frómista seems to have prospered since Georgiana King described it as a "forlorn little town, situated between a small river and the Canal of Castile . . . with a handful of noble desolate churches, and a plentiful lack of cafés."

The group has commandeered a modern building for the night; the local government owns it and the church runs it for pilgrims. When we arrive the building is empty, without electricity or hot water but within a few minutes the ingenious Navarrese have scavenged light bulbs from who knows where, screwed them in the sockets by standing on each other's shoulders, switched on the current and hooked a big orange butane tank to the shower. Traveling for a few days with these healthy, intelligent, energetic pilgrims has made me understand how Spaniards could find, explore and conquer the New World.

After showering we sit in a little plaza and wash one another's feet as Sagrario and Josemi taught me. A bracing, scirocco-like wind is blowing when Claudio appears, fresh from the road. It's good to see him and I realize how much friendship we've developed in just one afternoon together. He tells us Mike and Kes are staying in the old post office, another refuge for pilgrims.

As Claudio washes his face, arms and feet in the little fountain of the plaza, I tell him and the others about my visit to the convent of the Poor Clares.

"The first time I stopped there" says Claudio, "they changed my attitude to monastic life. I used to believe it was only an escape from the world."

"Qué va, what do you mean 'escape'?" scoffs one of the Navarrese women. "My boyfriend has an aunt who's a cloistered nun in Estella; she's suffered more than all of us put together. Nuns and monks suffer and pray for the rest of us, for everyone, all over. How can we be sure that prayer doesn't do more than action to change the world?"

"Peace can only be born in our own hearts" says Claudio. "That is how monks and nuns can touch the whole world." After a pause he asks us "Are you going to visit the church of St. Martin?"

"We're waiting for the others" answers the woman.

"Come on, Eduardo, you should not miss it" says Claudio, "the best thing in Frómista."

We walk a few blocks in the warm, dry wind and see the church standing alone, elevated above the street. From the outside it's the most immaculate Romanesque temple I've seen, looking as if it had been constructed in the twentieth century instead of the twelfth, as compact as a scale model. The simple nave, cylindrical towers, transept and octagonal cupola are built of a light-colored stone almost the color of wheat. It seems to glow in the late afternoon light.

"This church looks too perfect to be true" I tell Claudio.

"Maybe too perfect" he answers. "About a hundred years ago they saved it from decay but they over-restored it by changing many details, like those little carvings you see beneath the roof. They changed some figures that must have been a joy to see: men and women urinating, defecating, masturbating and making love. Spain also suffered a Victorian period."

We enter the church through a round-arched door on the south side. An official seems to recognize Claudio, greeting him. He sells us tickets.

The interior is pure and sparse, giving an impression of stability, proportion, well-being. This church was built to the measure of man and woman.

We walk down the nave in silence. Nobody else is in the church. We face the simple altar and crucifixion.

"When I walked the Camino for the first time" says Claudio, "I stopped here to rest. I was seated in a lotus position, meditating when a busload of middle-aged women stormed in, how do you say it . . . dressed to murder?"

"Dressed to kill" I tell him, smiling.

"Well they wanted to murder me, judging from the way they stared. They began to recite the rosary but it was more like shouting than praying. It seemed like a profanation of the peace and silence that reigned here before their invasion. As they walked out the door, I could hear them complaining to the ticketman that 'Hindus' should not be allowed in Spanish churches. When I left, the man told me 'Son del Opus, they're from the Opus. Don't worry, I knew you were Spanish all along.'" Claudio laughs. "That's why he recognized me just now."

I think of telling him the story of José Ignacio, the priest from the Opus Dei in La Rioja. But I'm too relaxed and fatigued to make the effort.

We leave the church and Claudio heads for the old post office where he plans to spend the night with the English. I'm sorry to see him leave yet I have confidence we'll meet again.

Back at the refuge the Navarrese introduce me to a new pilgrim, a sixty-one-year-old teacher from Bilbao. He has asked them if he can tag along and be the abuelo, the grandfather of the group.

The old man and I hit it off at once, I guess because he feels a little out of place with the younger pilgrims. He's a live wire with a sonorous voice, an alert sense of humor and a vocabulary that would make even many Spaniards blush. Hearing him string together one obscene expression after another, I realize how clean-spoken the others are, in a country where profanity is an art form.

More pilgrims continue to arrive until dark. Five of us end up like sardines in our sleeping bags on the floor of a small room—Sagrario, Josemi, one of the Navarrese women, the newcomer and I.

When the lights are turned out the woman says to the old man: "Abuelo, could you promise not to swear tomorrow when we walk together?"

"I promise you por la puta madre que me parió" he answers, "by the whore who gave birth to me."

Sagrario, a peacemaker tries to head off a confrontation: "Did you know that in my language, in Basque there is no profanity?"

"So that's why nobody speaks the puñetera lengua, the fucking thing except the Basques" retorts the newcomer, a fighting cock spoiling for battle.

"How can you be on a pilgrimage to the tomb of an apostle and talk like that?" asks the Navarrese woman. Josemi and I are enjoying the conflict.

"If Santiago was worth his salt he would have sworn his head off like any good soldier fighting the Moors," the man replies. "How can the patron saint of Spain be anything but foul-mouthed, joder!" His last word stabs in the dark like a flashing knife.

"Haven't you ever heard the proverb" asks the woman, " 'En la casa del que jura, no falta desventura, in the house of the man who swears, misfortune is always there'?"

"Don't tell me about misfortune, young lady—me, the father of ten kids" he answers in his stentorian voice. "If Spaniards couldn't blow off steam by cursing we'd really be up shit creek."

"Do you consider yourself religious?" she asks. Each of her questions is an opening for the old man to parry with his rapier.

"You're goddamned right I do. What in hell do you think I'm doing on the Road to Santiago at my age?"

"How can you be religious if you cuss every time you open your mouth?" Her voice sounds exasperated.

"You know what I tell my students?" he asks. "That only a people as close to the divine as we Spaniards could shit on God. Not to mention those who shit in the bloody drawers of the Virgin—a curse that challenges the greatest doctors of the Church as to whether the Immaculate Conception prevented the Mother of God from having her period."

Josemi and I are elbowing each other in our sleeping bags, losing the struggle to contain our laughs in spite of the well-intentioned woman from Navarre. She has no reply: the old man has turned theology, the queen of sciences, against her own argument.

We say good night to each other. Every few minutes Josemi and I have to fight back another convulsion of laughter. We fall asleep hearing the scirocco rustle through the trees.

14 Desert of the Lions

Life is a journey, the universe an inn.
— Attributed to Buddha

Again I set out with the group before dawn. Today makes two weeks on the road for me; it seems I've been walking forever. I bring up the rear, watching the sunlight on Josemi's pack and on Sagrario's golden legs. The new light, a softer breeze, something seems to be impelling us forward, always forward. (I remember the abbess' words.)

Soon I'm alone in a landscape of tawny stubble, straw and threshing floors. This is the Tierra de Campos, the breadbasket of Roman and Visigothic Spain. The endless wheatfields give their name to the towns—Población de Campos, Revenga de Campos, Villarmentero de Campos.

In Villalcázar de Sirga I see the oversize church above a pile of adobe houses. I walk up the steps of St. Mary the White, named after an image of the Virgin who is missing both her right arm and the head of the Christ-child in her lap. She was supposed to have worked so many miracles here that she became a rival of St. James in the thirteenth century. But old Santiago had more staying power than his competitors; the cult of the White Mary fell into provincial oblivion while the apostle continued to be worshiped all over Spain and the New World. He had more battalions on his side.

I return to the road feeling tired, already sapped by the hot sun, almost blinded by the light. The huge, white grain elevators of Carrión de los Condes appear ahead of me like a mirage in the desert. For a thousand years or more, church towers marked the skyline and were the first buildings spotted by pilgrims when they approached a town. Now we see monuments to the stomach—our time.

My faithful Basques are waiting for me at the edge of Carrión. We stop at a bar where we eat bocadillos and a salad, shared from the same bowl, Spanish style. For the first time on the trip, I don't feel like touching wine or beer.

Sagrario and Josemi are anxious to catch up with the speedy Navarros. I tell them to go ahead without me; I prefer to rest for the long, dry stage between here and León—few villages, bad water and the most forbidding desert on the way. We walk to the bridge over the

Carrión River, give abrazos to one another and say goodbye. Although I feel certain that Claudio and I will meet before Compostela, somehow I don't believe the Basques and I will see each other again. I'll miss them.

After finding a shady spot on the shore of the Río Carrión, I fall asleep, exhausted. All afternoon and evening I'm attacked by giant mosquitoes, the plague of Egypt on the Road to Santiago.

With the new day I walk some thirty-six kilometers to Sahagún de Campos, crossing into the province of León. I succumb to the temptation of silence, not talking to a soul all day or night, sleeping alone in a field.

The next morning I poke around Sahagún before leaving. The streets look evacuated. This town was once the seat of the mighty Cluniac Order in Spain, from which it controlled more than fifty monasteries and priorships with their lands and dependencies; located in the middle of the Camino, it was an obligatory stop for most pilgrims. Now the place looks like a dust-red Mexican village in a bad cowboy movie.

Crossing the main square, I see the ubiquitous French pilgrims loaded with their packs. Another walker has joined them: they introduce me to Michèle, a friend of Bernadette's who also lives in Logroño. She's in her mid-thirties with dark brown hair and smooth, olive skin.

Generous as always, they invite me to walk with them. The long-necked, awkward René takes the lead, striding ahead of us with his loping gait, his boots turned oddly inwards. His feet must be killing him.

Walking next to me, Michèle guesses my thoughts: "René is an ingénieur du bois—I don't know how to translate it. He suffered an accident on the job that injured his feet."

"Probably means a forestry engineer" I guess. "Isn't walking painful for him?"

"Yes. That's one reason he's here, I think. He wants to overcome his weakness. He's a man of great faith."

After walking a few hundred yards more, Michèle asks "Did you know that Sahagún is exactly halfway between Roncevaux and Compostela?"

"Yes."

"Are you familiar with the idea of the axis mundi, the axis of the world?"

"I don't think so."

"In the Middle Ages the Camino de Santiago and the Milky Way were seen as the axis mundi" she says. "It's interesting that you've begun walking with us at the very center of the Road, in the middle of the world so to speak."

"Seems more like chance to me. Anyway we carry the center of our worlds around with us wherever we go."

"That kind of attitude can negate the whole purpose of pilgrimage" she says. "Sounds very Protestant, the God within and all."

"Actually I'm a bad Catholic."

"Me too" she says smiling. We've fallen behind the others. Probably because we talk so much, I think.

"You know, Edouard" says Michèle, "Berna and I have a woman friend in Logroño who is a vidente, a seer. She predicted that we would begin traveling with a man, a foreigner in the province of León midway to Compostela."

"So many strange things have happened to me on the Camino that I'm not surprised." I tell her how Claudio practically guessed my birthdate.

"Is this Claudio an astrologer from Valencia?" she asks.

"Yes. Have you met him on the Road?"

"No, he's the one who was featured on a television program about the Camino de Santiago last winter. When Berna and I saw it we decided to make the pilgrimage. We weren't the only ones."

So that's why Claudio seems to know and be known by so many people on the Road, I realize. Of course he's too humble to have told me. I cannot think of a more unlikely person to be on television.

René, Guillemette and Berna have stopped by a clump of trees, the only shade in sight.

As we approach them, Michèle whispers "If we reach Compostela together I may tell you what else the seer said."

The women take off their boots while René peels oranges and passes them around. "We walk for fifty minutes, then rest for ten" he says.

After the break he shouts in a mock military voice "Chaussures! Allez, en route! Shoes! Get moving, on the road!" René is the gentle leader of this French expeditionary force.

We walk for miles across the bleak land without seeing a village or a soul. This is the dreaded paramera leonesa, the Desert of the Lions where many travelers have perished. I think how fortunate I've been to run into the French pilgrims; I'd hate to be alone in this wasteland.

The town of El Burgo Ranero has a Sunday feeling: a few stores are open, people are taking the paseo, or leisurely stroll after church. None of us wants to walk further in the heat today.

We find lodgings with a woman who rents rooms. She serves us an abundant, home-cooked meal. The heat and fatigue have taken away my appetite. Feeling nauseous I go upstairs to my little room. There's no sink and the bathroom is too far to reach in time. Luckily for me the place is old-fashioned enough to have a chamber pot beneath the bed.

I feel better afterwards but I begin to shake with chills. Feeling lonely and depressed, I get in the old metal-frame bed. What a place to get sick—this village of adobe and dust in the middle of nowhere. Falling asleep I imagine myself languishing in this bed for days while my friends continue on their way.

A knock on the door awakens me. It's Michèle asking if I would like to join the others for coffee.

I tell her to enter, remembering too late that the chamber pot has not been emptied. She comes in, feels my forehead, picks up the pot and leaves. Soon she returns with Guillemette; I remember gladly that René's wife is a nurse. She takes my temperature, tells me I have a fever of 38.1 degrees centigrade, places a damp washcloth on my forehead and gives me a solution of lemon juice and mineral water for my stomach. She and Michèle are bustling about the room, talking to each other softly in French, telling me they've sent Berna and René to the pharmacy for medicine. I fall asleep feeling safe in the hands of these friends, these women who barely know me yet are taking care of me as if I were one of their family.

The light has almost gone when I wake from my nap. Touching the wet sheets, I realize that I've sweated off the fever. I get out of bed, put on a dry shirt, walk downstairs to the bathroom. The French must hear me; they're waiting at my door when I return.

Berna tells me she couldn't find the medicine because the only pharmacist in town has gone to a discotheque in Sahagún for the evening. She and René have brought me several plastic bottles of mineral water, bicarbonate of soda and two little cartons of lemon yogurt—good for the stomach, says Guillemette.

I get back under the sheets while the four of them sit around me on the bed.

René speaks and Berna translates for me: "Edouard, you are not the first pilgrim to have problems on this part of the Road. Did you know that in the old days a Frenchman was devoured by wolves just before Burgó Raneró?" (René accents the last syllable of all words in Spanish.)

"I guess the heroic times have passed" I tell him. "Nowadays we only get stomachaches."

Guillemette speaks, Michèle translating: "Another Frenchman also got sick somewhere before León. I remember reading about it because his Spanish nurse used a bizarre remedy for the fever. She got a handful of nettles, took off his shirt, made him turn facedown on the bed and rubbed his kidneys with the nettles, which of course must have been rather unpleasant. Then she covered him with heavy blankets and made him sweat something like eight or nine changes of shirts. By the following day his fever was gone."

"But of course his kidneys ached for the next month" adds René smiling.

"I've sweated one shirt and my fever has also gone away" I tell Guillemette—"just in case you plan to use the nettle remedy on me." Berna translates for the older woman, who laughs with her little eyes glowing.

Michèle says "I think those Frenchmen and Edouard have something in common—a fatigue that accumulates in this desert halfway between the Pyrenees and the Atlantic Ocean. I believe the exhaustion and illness are also mental. In your case, Edouard, your doubts and fears may have had something to do with it. I haven't seen you fully relaxed until now, when you're in bed."

Guillemette smiles and says something that makes the others laugh. Berna translates: "She says you're getting the double French treatment today: first we nurse you back to health then we submit you to psychoanalysis."

In good spirits they say "Bon soir," retiring to their rooms. I fall asleep thinking that the Way of St. James is still a Camino francés, a French Road, luckily for me.

In the morning I wake to the sound of rolling thunder. Through the window I see my first rain in eighteen days on the Road to Santiago.

Downstairs in the kitchen, Guillemette gives me a cup of hot tea. It feels good on my empty stomach. Traveling with the French is civilized, even on a pilgrimage.

Amid whispers and swishing of our nylon rain gear, we leave the house quietly to avoid waking the owner. The thunder is more distant now and the rain has turned to a light drizzle. Outside the town we have an astonishing sight before us: the plain is sheeted with ice. White pellets fill the furrows of the ploughed fields; it must have just finished hailing. The contact of the ice with the warmer earth has caused a low mist to rise. Feeling a sudden drop in temperature, we pull sweater from our packs. I look at my little zipper thermometer—8 degrees centigrade, about 47 Fahrenheit—very cold for this part of Spain in August.

René and Michèle take out their cameras and shoot pictures of us in our rain pants, jackets and hoods against the bleak white background. "Edouard, explorateur polaire" René titles his shot of me; for once I don't need a translator. Michèle says I look more like a monk. My illness has broken down the formality between us.

Back on the road we meet a shepherd with a big flock of merinos. Holding a curved staff, he wears a kind of rough sash across his chest; a heavy blanket is folded neatly on his left shoulder.

"Qué tipo, what a type" Michèle whispers to me.

The man tells us that the rain is the first since April—too late to help the wheat crop. Talking to him I remember we're on one of the ancient cañadas, or causeways of the Mesta, the powerful corporation of sheep and cattle owners that dominated the Spanish economy for centuries. Its network of paths was as intricate and extensive as the highway system of a modern nation. Nowadays trucks and trains carry many of the animals, the shepherd tells us; few herds still migrate north to the Montes de León for summer pasture, south to Castile and Extremadura in winter. Stock owners are finding it harder to recruit shepherds willing to lead flocks for several weeks a year, to sleep outdoors and put up with the heat and cold.

We wish each other good luck. Saying goodbye to a shepherd in Spain is like bidding farewell to a way of life forever.

After crossing the steppe we enter the modern world again, spending the night at a truckstop on the highway.

Early in the morning we see León, its profile of walls, towers and spires destroyed by derricks, cranes and high-rise buildings. When we reach the church of Santiago, Mass is being celebrated. We remove our gear, loosen our boots and sit on the pews while Guillemette and René take communion.

The French find a hotel downtown; I go to the pilgrims' refuge in the basilica of San Isidoro. We have a farewell lunch for René and Guillemette who will be taking the train to Compostela tomorrow. They've walked the pilgrimage in two stages: from León to Santiago last summer, from St. Jean-Pied-de-Port to León this year. Berna, Michèle and I will miss them very much. The couple has been with Berna ever since the Pyrenees, with Michèle since Logroño. How can we forget their unflagging good spirits, their constant smiles and kindness, René's calls of "Chaussures! Allez, en route!"? Traveling without them will be a little like losing your mother and father.

15 Through León

"Grandmother, where is the Road?
Grandmother, I don't see it."

"Look and you'll see a ribbon
of thick white floury dust,
a blur that looks like silver
or mother-of-pearl. See?"

"Yes.

Grandmother, where's Santiago?"
"He's up there with his cortège,
his head decked out with feathers,
his limbs with tiny pearls,
the moon lying at his feet,
the sun hidden in his breast."
—Federico García Lorca,
"Santiago (Innocent Ballad)"

With Burgos and Compostela itself, León is one of the three great cities on the Jacobean road and a traditional stopping place. We decide to regale ourselves by resting, exploring the town and writing letters for the remainder of today and tomorrow. Although the people are used to pilgrims walking through their streets, I feel uncomfortable here. Cities and pilgrimage don't go together.

Everyone who ever wrote about the Road to Santiago has described León. I could tell you about the powerful Romanesque church of St. Isidore, the male rival of St. James who was also mobilized as a Moorslayer in the war against Islam. I could tell you about the Renaissance Hostal de San Marcos, former seat of the Knights of Santiago, now one of the finest hotels in the world. But tourism seems less important with every step I take toward Compostela. All I want to remember now is the cathedral, blond beauty of Spanish churches, the fairest of all.

The authorities are more lenient than in Burgos; they allow us to enter with our short pants and T-shirt. Standing in this church is like being in the heart of a jewel, said Georgiana King. It seems to have more stained glass than stone, less glass than light. How it must have awed pilgrims in the Middle Ages: could they have thought they'd already been granted a heavenly vision? After walking across the steppe, the pulchra leonina reminds me of an arrow shot toward the sky, a forest of white pillars, vaults and columns, fireworks of color and light.

Coming out of this church, you feel lighter on your feet and in your head. On the west façade I touch the column supporting a statue of Santiago; the creamy stone has been rubbed smooth by the lips and hands of numberless pilgrims.

A giant scaffolding covers one of the belltowers and spires. Like most cathedrals in Spain, this one is being restored, "en obras." But the technique and its vast scale make this restoration unique: instead of replacing the old stones at enormous expense, chemists clean and treat the surface with an acrylic varnish that rejuvenates the color while protecting against further corrosion. One of the workers tells me that the master masons of the Middle Ages probably used some kind of whitewash to protect the stone too, but they didn't have to worry about pollution. The dirty air of the twentieth century has done more damage to this church than the previous seven hundred years.

Next morning at the Lista de Correos I pick up the only mail I'll receive on the Road to Santiago. It makes me happy to hear from María and my parents. Reading their letters, I realize how far I am from home, how different my daily life is from theirs.

Michèle, Berna and I leave León in the afternoon, walking into the sun. None of us speaks; we feel the absence of René and Guillemette. After our first rest I try saying "Boots! Get moving, on the road!" in my bad French. Berna and Michèle smile politely; it's not the same. The French couple have left their mark on us. The people you meet along the Camino can change you, give you a part of themselves. Knowing Guillemette and René, walking with them for three days has deepened my idea of what it means to be a pilgrim.

This will be our shortest stage; night overtakes us in La Virgen del Camino, the only modern church on the entire Way. Built in 1961, its vertical thrust, stained glass and filtered light are smaller, contemporary reminders of the cathedral in León. The Dominican friars let us sleep in a schoolroom across the street. There a black cat crawls through a broken window and goes all night from one sleeping bag to another—the little tramp—looking for warmth.

After a few miles this morning Berna takes over René's job as point of our reduced Franco-American expeditionary force. Unlike Michèle she doesn't enjoy talking on the road: she advances briskly without looking to either side.

Slower walkers, Michèle and I converse to make the time pass. I tell her about my life in America while she talks to me about herself

11 Cathedral of León , detail. (Photo José Luis Herrera)

and Berna. Both have lived in Logroño for several years. Berna teaches French at a private school; with her gold-rimmed glasses and serious manner, she looks just like a teacher in fact. Michèle works in the foreign department of the Banco Hispanoamericano, one of the largest in Spain.

I tell her: "I can't imagine an officer of an American bank making a pilgrimage during her summer vacation."

"Oh they think I'm crazy alright, especially with my interest in the occult. But they have to respect me because I'm a hard worker and I know the business."

We go on talking and she tells me that she separated recently from her husband, a Spaniard from Navarre. Divorce in Spain is relatively new and the process slow; the paperwork is still dragging on.

"The Camino de Santiago has allowed me to get away from it all" she says, "to clean the cobwebs from my mind and come to terms with my life alone, to search for a new peace inside myself."

Soon we're crossing a river on the long, many-arched bridge in Hospital de Orbigo, famous in Jacobean lore. On this same bridge for thirty days before the Jubilee of St. James in 1434, a gentleman named Suero de Quiñones challenged all mounted passersby to knightly combat. No fewer than 78 combatants appeared, 177 lances were broken, 1 rider was killed, 11 wounded. For what great cause such commotion and bloodshed? For a whim: in order for Quiñones to be honorably released from his vow to wear an iron chain around his neck each Thursday in token of his captivity to an unknown lady. And did he win her? The books tell everything but the upshot, the part that excites the curiosity of a modern reader accustomed to having his love stories end sadly or happily, but at least end. I can find out nothing about the mysterious lady who was the cause of the whole thing. All I know is that Suero went to Compostela after the Paso honroso, his gentle Pass of Honor and made an offering of gratitude to Santiago.

Michèle, Berna and I talk about the jousting on the bridge as we cross it and see a small hotel on the left bank, the Paso Honroso. Hospital de Orbigo has no other claims to renown.

"What amazes me" says Michèle, "is that Suero de Quiñones is remembered as a hero. In any other European country I think he'd be considered a crackpot."

"In France they would have called him a lunatic, un fou" says Berna, always commonsensical. Suero's exploit would not have won *her* love, I think to myself.

"It's the old obsession with honor" adds Michèle. "I know something about it because I was married to a Spaniard and suffered for his honor's sake, not mine of course. Every Spaniard thinks his country is the finest in the world, his patria chica or region the best in the country, his village the best in the province and guess who's the top man in the village? Him, naturally."

"Which also makes him the best man in the whole world" laughs Berna. "Suero de Quiñones must have thought so to challenge every passerby to such a crazy feat."

On the other side of the bridge an overpowering aroma of fresh-baked bread reaches us. We follow it to an old doorway, enter and find ourselves in a patio whose walls are covered with vines, giant sacks of flour on the ground. Some elderly women are sitting on chairs in the shade; they wave us inside to a large kitchen. We feel the heat of the oven and touch the fresh loaves of bread, still warm on a table in the middle of the room. We buy more baguettes than will fit in our packs or stomachs.

On our way out Michèle says "It's for things like this that Berna and I put up with Spaniards and their honor, their machismo and all the rest."

"In what other European country could you walk into the baker's house and buy a loaf of bread?" asks Berna.

Munching our crusty treasure, we walk through the streets of Hospital de Orbigo looking for a place to spend the night. The Paso Honroso Hotel looks too expensive; we leave the famous bridge behind.

We find rooms at an inn by the road. Our waiter at dinner tells us he'd like to walk to Compostela himself some day.

"The pilgrimage is still not dead" says Berna as we go back to our rooms.

The waiter who served us last night unlocks the doors for us to leave before dawn. Bleary-eyed he wishes us "Buen viaje".

It's pitch-black outside. Berna has a powerful flashlight to guide us. She must have been a Girl Scout, I say to myself. A few trucks come roaring past us in the opposite direction, almost blowing us over. Berna says nothing, unruffled, bearing the charge of those monsters in the dark.

When dawn begins to break, Michèle and I fall back as usual, letting our leader move ahead with her clockwork march, her flashlight casting its intrepid beam in the half-dark.

"Our Joan of Arc" I say to Michèle.

She laughs. Between us an unspoken irony has developed about Berna's fortitude and righteousness.

We walk hard to a ridge over the city of Astorga, its plain and the Montes de León: the end of the steppe. We cross the plain and climb the steep old streets to the main square. Although Astorga was an important Roman and medieval city, we're not in the mood for sightseeing, with many hot hours ahead of us on the road. We even forego visiting the Museo de los Caminos, Museum of the Ways in the neo-Gothic, fairytale Bishop's Palace designed by the great Catalan architect Gaudí.

The sun is beginning to bear down. We plod through Murias de Rechivaldo and Santa Catalina de Somoza, decrepit towns far less beautiful than their names. On their semi-abandoned, rock-strewn streets we have the sensation of being watched as we pass emaciated dogs who scavenge among the ruins, crumbling houses with empty doorways and window frames. Instead of the adobe and rubble-work we saw in the Leonese desert, these dwellings are made of square-hewn stones. Some buildings have whimsical, multi-tiered chimneys perched on their roofs, worthy of Gaudí's imagination. After the slate roofs of Navarre and the classic red tile of Castile, we begin to see houses covered with straw.

An old man seated on a doorstep greets us, saying "Hoy hace un calor del alma, today it's hot enough to melt the soul."

We're in the country of the Maragatos, an enigmatic people about whom everyone has a theory. Some believe they descend from the Visigoths, others from the Moors, others from the Berbers, still others from the Mozarabics—Christians who lived among the Muslims in southern Spain. The most likely, least exotic theory is that they're descendants of an ancient Asturian tribe in northern Spain. For a pilgrim passing through their region, what stands out is the misery of the towns and their inhabitants. In the shimmering heat, the dust, the silence of midday and time, everything seems unreal, a dream of what happened long ago.

We stop to eat lunch under some scraggly encinas or evergreen oaks beyond Santa Catalina. Berna warns that they have the reputation of being the worst shade tree; compared to chopos, or poplars for example, they're supposed to offer little relief from the sun.

"One shade is the same as another" I say removing my pack and sitting down against the gnarled trunk.

We eat more bread from the bakery in Hospital de Orbigo, accompanied by cheese, chorizo and chocolate that has melted in the heat. My thermometer reads 91 degrees in the shade. Ants and flies are attacking the food.

"You know, Berna" I confess, "I think you're right about the evergreen oak. It not only seems to generate heat—also insects."

We try to take a siesta but the heat and bugs make it impossible. We go back to the road; it's unrelieved by vegetation or curves. At least we can see the Montes de León ahead. Tomorrow we'll have to cross them.

Berna is far in the lead as usual. When we see the sign for the town of El Ganso, The Goose, Michèle asks "Do you know about the legends of the goose and the Road to Santiago?"

"Not very much."

"The name crops up in quite a few places along the Road, in both its Spanish and its French root—oca from our oie, you know, as in Mère l'Oie, Mother Goose and all. There's this town, then the beautiful Montes de Oca, La Rioja—from Río Oja."

"Come on Michèle, it's too hot for lessons in etymology."

"Also, the markings in the stone of certain churches on the Way, like Eunate, have been interpreted as stylized goose's feet. I'll show you."

Taking a stick from the road-shoulder, she traces a figure in the dirt:

Y

"The goose is an animal that lives in three elements" she goes on, "land, water and air, and it can be related to the fourth, fire in the myth of the phoenix, the bird reborn from its own ashes."

"What's that got to do with the Camino de Santiago?"

"Some of the esoterics believe the goose was related to the secret meaning of the Road to Santiago as an initiation, a rite of passage, a spiritual death and rebirth—just as the goose/phoenix was consumed and reborn from its ashes. Also, there's an ancient board game, the juego de la oca, whose stages recall death and resurrection."

"Do you think we'll ever be able to prove the relation between the goose legends and the Camino de Santiago?"

"Probably not" answers Michèle, "but it's fun trying."

Berna is waiting for us at the entrance to El Ganso. Just as we join her, a dusty car stops next to us on the road. A middle-aged man at the wheel, ignoring me in favor of the two women, tells us he's the owner of the town bar and would like to invite us for a drink.

We follow him along an unpaved street to a stone structure that looks like a farm building. He gets out of the car, fumbling with his keys.

"Joder I can't find it" he says. "Don't go away." He walks to a house down the street while we refill our canteens at a neighbor's well.

The man returns shaking a large key on a ring: "Anda como las putas, de mano en mano, it's like a whore, it goes from one hand to another."

He opens and we enter a large room. It looks like a combination of a warehouse and general store. The man serves soft drinks to Berna and Michèle, a beer to me, also giving us homegrown pears and apples for the road. Within a few minutes the townspeople have gathered to buy drinks and observe us, the foreign oddities. Meanwhile swallows are swooping back and forth above our heads, building a nest of mud high up on the far wall. Any bar with birds flying around it must be a special place, I think.

We say goodbye and walk back to the road feeling refreshed, cooler and a little happier.

Berna is already oblivious to us, picking up her pace, staring straight ahead at the horizon. I wonder what drives her. She leads us to Rabanal del Camino, once an important town with its church, two hermitages and a hostal for pilgrims. Only a handful of permanent dwellers remain. But today is the Ascension of the Virgin, the village holiday, an irresistible attraction for the former residents who've returned in their small cars bearing license plates of Bilbao, Barcelona and Madrid—the industrial centers where they've been forced to migrate in search of jobs.

We walk up the steep road that forms the axis of the town, past ruined houses, stables, walls, corrals. Down the middle of the street runs a stone channel into which a rivulet flows from each building or corral. It's nice to see and hear running water again after the dry, barren steppe. Less nice to smell: our noses soon tell us that the channel serves as the town's sewer, the same it must have had in the Middle Ages.

In the village square, musicians are playing as people dance. We enter the abandoned school that is the town's only refuge, full of pilgrims with their sleeping bags on the floor, eating or resting. I hear them talking in English and Spanish. An elderly, ruddy-faced Englishman tells us they belong to Pilgrims International, a group run by an Australian named Kosti Simons. We've heard him mentioned several times on the Road. The Englishman makes it clear that there's no room for us. With the odor of ruins and sweat here, we're not overly saddened by the news.

After topping up our canteens at the village fountain, we begin walking out of town. Darkness is falling; we'll have to find a place to sleep soon. Beyond the last houses we come to the town washing-place just off the road: a rectangular stone basin overlooking a wide valley. A large bearded man is washing his feet in the basin.

"I'm Kosti Simon" he says in English. It's the first time I remember a pilgrim introducing himself by his first and last names. With his accent and full beard, whitening at the edges, he reminds me of an Australian Hemingway.

We introduce ourselves. I discover that Michèle can speak a little English.

"Is this your first pilgrimage to Santiago?" he asks.

"Yes, for all of us" answers Michèle. "And you?"

"Oh I've almost lost track by now. The first time I walked barefoot all the way from Paris." He points to a rucksack leaning against the stone basin, with large letters stenciled across the back: "PARIS-SANTIAGO".

"Well if you'll excuse me" he adds, "I'm going to bed down for the night. Buen viaje."

As we take off our boots and immerse our feet in the cool water, we watch the man walk down the hill to a flat spot where he unrolls his sleeping bag.

"Obviously wants to be alone" says Berna.

"His group sleeps like sardines in a stinking, ruined school-house" says Michèle, "while he spends the night à la belle étoile, under the stars."

"We're going to do the same" says Berna. "I've always wanted to sleep in the open at least one night on the Road. I kept telling René and Guillemette but they're a little too old-fashioned for that kind of thing."

After drying our feet, we walk to a pasture above the washbasin. The ground is uneven and strewn with piles of cow-dung. I remember the names we had for them as boys: meadow muffins, cow patties, barnyard biscuits and so on. Repeating those words in my mind for the first time in years, in my own language, makes me feel suddenly homesick.

Michèle doesn't have a pad for her sleeping bag. I give her my self-inflating mattress, saying "It's the least Suero de Quiñones would have done for his lady."

"Too bad I don't have an iron chain for you to put around your neck" she laughs. "You're a gringo knight-in-arms, Edouard" she adds concealing her gratitude with humor.

I'm not very comfortable on the bumpy ground but who cares: the night has fallen, a gibbous moon is setting to the west, we're sleeping à la belle étoile. The nearest city is miles away and we're far enough beyond the last lights of Rabanal to see the sky in its glory.

"On a night like this the Virgin ascended to heaven" says Berna. She must be more devout than Michèle or me to believe that, I think. Our Joan of Arc.

I haven't seen so many stars since I was a boy: in fact I feel like a child again, as if I could reach up and touch them. A shooting star falls to the horizon. I remember José Mari and Míkel on the bridge in Puente la Reina: "A child has been born or a soul has begun its long journey." When the moon sets, we see the Milky Way as men and women saw it in the great days of the pilgrimage. To my wonder it's not a uniform stripe across the heavens but an organic thing with arms, branches, tributaries, inlets, lakes, peninsulas—luminous, complex, alive. El Camino de las Estrellas, the Road of Stars.

16 The Pass

Drunk on stars, I've hardly slept. Yet I don't feel tired. Watching the sky has calmed my mind and given me a cold new kind of energy.

After a breakfast of dry granola, we begin the steep climb to Monte Irago, higher than the Pyrenees before Roncesvalles. We walk through a bleak, burnt-out landscape where trees are dwarfed and bent, probably from winter storms. Higher up we see tall red and green stakes for marking the way in snow. In the old days this part of the Camino was impassable in bad weather.

Near the top of the mountain we enter Foncebadón, an abandoned village according to our pilgrim's guidebook: "The only remaining inhabitants of this solitude are the widow María and her son Angel, who devote themselves to tending flocks." Unfortunately the spot is less bucolic than its description in the book. The widow and her son are nowhere to be seen amid the crumbling houses with uneven roofs of slate or straw, with grass and weeds growing out of the stone. American ghost towns look like resorts compared to grey Foncebadón, gloomy as its name, with ghosts at least a thousand years old.

At the pass beyond the village we see the famous Cruz de Ferro, a lopsided iron cross on a twenty-foot wooden pole rising from a pyramid of rocks and shards deposited by travelers over the centuries. A small hermitage has been built next to the man-made hill. Some of the English and Spanish pilgrims are taking photos of each other next to the cross.

We climb the pyramid. Like everyone else, we touch the wooden pole. Picking up stones, we read the inscribed names, hometowns and dates of pilgrims. At an elevation of about five thousand feet, we have an unobstructed panorama of the great peak of Mount Teleno and the desolate Valley of Silence, unchanged since the Middle Ages; the fertile basin of El Bierzo and beyond it the mountains of Galicia. We're exhilarated: the land of Santiago!

"We've walked more than five hundred kilometers, all the way from France to see this view" says Berna, the wind of the pass blowing through her short blond hair.

12 "The supernatural emptiness of Foncebadón." (Photo and caption by José Luis Herrera)

"Speaking of France" I say, "did you follow the custom of bringing a stone from the place where you started the pilgrimage?"

"We're carrying enough weight already" answers Michèle with a frown.

"I guess that makes me the only one" I say, taking off my pack to look for the small stone at the bottom.

"Don't tell me you've carried a rock all this way!" cries Michèle.

"That's right. I found it on a hike in the Daniel Boone National Forest before coming to Spain."

I finally retrieve it at the bottom of my pack, next to the scallop shell and Ramón's cross. My talismans. As I hold the stone in my palm, it scintillates in the clear mountain light.

Michèle bursts out laughing: "That little pebble? How heroic of you, Edouard! I thought you meant a real rock!"

"It's the idea that counts" I tell her. "For thousands of years men and women have been throwing stones onto this pile." Michèle cannot stop laughing as she takes out her camera and tries to focus it.

Berna feels sorry for me, I think: "I like the custom, Edouard. Michèle and I are jealous because we didn't bring stones ourselves. Did you know that the Romans called these piles 'mountains of Mercury'?—their god of the roads. The Celts had a similar divinity. Travelers left stones as an offering in exchange for the god's protection on the difficult way ahead. Then the custom was Christianized, of course."

"Do you know what I find most moving of all?" asks Michèle finally holding back her laughter. "Besides the scenery, I mean? That this humble pile of stones and this flimsy cross are standing after so many centuries, while so many grander monuments have collapsed in ruin."

I'm glad when Kosti's group continues on the road and Michèle finishes her pictures: I want to stand on this promontory and feel the wind in my face, undisturbed by human voices or the clicking of cameras. I haven't felt so close to the sky anywhere on the Camino, not even last night under the stars or in the Pyrenees. There the mountains are wooded and scenic; here they're so stark that your sight is undistracted, drawn to the bald peaks, the clouds and sky.

When Michèle is not looking, I drop the tiny stone at my feet. I'm leaving something here but I also take something with me.

My rapture doesn't last long: going down the mountainside we see a factory belching smoke on the western horizon.

"The blast furnace of Ponferrada" says Berna, always well informed. "We'll be there the day after tomorrow si Dios quiere, God willing."

We border the Valley of Silence, a great gorge with a few rocky, inaccessible towns clinging to the sides where they blend with the stony earth. Then we're in Manjarín, also abandoned except for some former residents who return for a few days in the summer. Unlike Americans, most Spaniards are incapable of leaving their hometowns for good—their pueblo, their patria chica. You know these people have lived in cities from the way they turn away to avoid conversation, also from their big, aggressive dogs—Dobermans and German shepherds. The indigenous dogs of Foncebadón and Manjarín belong to a different species, mangy, rib-caged mongrels who slink away instead of challenging us.

13   Cruz de Ferro, the Cross of Iron. (Photo Emilio Peláez)

Going down the hill we see a pilgrim ahead of us, limping so badly that he looks almost crippled. In addition to a pack, he carries a staff and two handbags.

"No wonder he's limping" says Michèle as we draw closer, "with all that luggage."

When we have nearly caught up, he turns around with a smile, holding out his hand: "Valentín de Valencia, at your service."

"Is that your last name or where you're from?" asks Michèle as we shake his big, heavy paw.

He lets out a burst of hoarse laughter: "Where I'm from, silly. You know, 'Va-len-cia'" he sings to the well-known marching tune, "ta-túm-ta-túm-ta-túm-ta-túm-ta-túm-ta-TUM-TUM."

He's about my age and height with a beard, round head, high forehead, bulbous nose and a mischievous smile that makes him look like some sort of gnome. If you painted his face with white greasepaint and a red nose, he'd be a perfect clown.

We introduce ourselves and continue walking. We move at a slower pace so that he can keep up.

"My feet look like a battlefield" he tells us, laughing.

"It would help if you got rid of those extra bags" says Michèle, always willing to give advice.

"This one with my books is killing me" he says holding up the bag with his left arm: it's bulging with sharp angles at the zipper and seams. "By the way, I saw the three of you last night in Rabanal del Camino" he goes on. "I was in the old schoolhouse when you stopped there."

"Were you traveling with Kosti's group?" Michèle asks him as we see a village with slate roofs and chimneys below us.

"No I just happened to stop at the same place. Do you know what my first impression was when I saw the three of you?"

"What?" asks Michèle with unfeigned curiosity.

"That you were a priest and two nuns" he answers smiling like Puck. We laugh.

"You're a little off the mark" says Michèle.

"That's a new one" I tell him. "Quién sabe, who knows maybe the Camino is making us holier."

In the village I ask an old woman if there is a fountain to fill our canteens. She points up a little hill.

"Would you mind filling this?" Valentín asks me, holding out a red canteen. "Every step is torture on my feet. I'll wait for you."

The three of us climb around the hill and top up the canteens with the cold water trickling from the slope. We return to the spot where we left Valentín: empty.

"He's disappeared like a ghost" says Berna looking around.

"In fact he reminded me of a duende, a kind of demon or genie" adds Michèle.

"He must be waiting for us at a shady spot in the town" I say.

As we walk down the single, unpaved street looking for Valentín, a carload of young Spaniards pulls up.

Putting his head out the window, the driver asks me "Are you the American named Eduardo?"

"Yes" I answer looking with amazement at Berna and Michèle. I've never seen him or the passengers.

"We're friends of José Ignacio, the priest from Hervías" the driver says. Then they all chime in, men and women: "We walked the pilgrimage with him a few years ago" says one, "He asked us to watch for you" says another, "Now we're doing the Camino by car," "He told us you'd be somewhere in this area by now," "Is there anything we can do for you?", "Good luck we'll pray for you in Compostela" and the little car is bumping down the potholed street, arms waving from the windows.

I feel moved by this encounter out of the blue; I can still sense the energy of those young Spaniards. No matter what happened, Opus Dei and all, José Ignacio is redeemed in my eyes. I tell the two women about my meeting with him.

As Berna strides ahead, Michèle says "You know, Edouard, you're an unusual pilgrim. Almost everyone else on the Camino either wants to walk alone or to be with friends, like Berna and me with René and Guillemette. From what I've seen and what you've told me, you seem to walk long stretches of the Road by yourself yet you manage to make plenty of acquaintances along the way—the priest and us, for example. You don't seem to fit into any category, you're both a loner and a bon enfant, a good fellow as we say in French. I can't figure you out."

"Why should you?"

"I have a passionate interest in people" she answers, "much more than Berna. It's what keeps me going at work. It's also what keeps me from reaching the top in my career because I'm more concerned with individuals than with finance, profits or success."

We enter another town with ancient houses whose balconies overhang the street. Berna is waiting for us beneath the eaves of a bar in the main square.

"Guess who's in there?" she asks us, pointing to the bar. "Listen."

We stop. The gravel laughter of Valentín reaches us from inside.

"The Duende" says Michèle.

"I suppose he expected us to know where he was" says Berna smiling. "He sure puts a lot of trust in people whom he barely knows."

We enter the bar and smell the good aroma of old wine barrels, olive oil and time. Cured hams and strings of garlic hang from wooden rafters. Valentín is sitting at the center of a large table, surrounded by men who must be from the village. He's showing them a scrapbook of photographs.

"Here I am at a party during the Fallas in Valencia, St. Joseph's eve" he tells them. Seeing us he cries out "Where have you been peregrinos? I'm already on my second glass of wine."

He pulls up chairs for us and we ask a lady in an apron for three glasses of mineral water.

"Mineral water!" he shouts. "Didn't I say you were a priest and two nuns!"

"It's to restore the body salts" says Berna meekly.

"Wine has all the body salts I need" he replies turning the pages of the scrapbook for the villagers. "Here I am as the Medusa" he says. "It took me hours to do up that snake-hair."

I don't think the onlookers know what to make of this man with the infectious laugh and the smile of a clown. They hang on his words, silent, staring at the pictures of Valentín as Casanova, Don Quixote, King of the Carnival in Rio de Janeiro.

"How do you make all those disguises?" asks a toothless local.

"Aha, professional secrets, my good man. I'm the chief makeup artist for Radio Televisión Española in Valencia. When you go there ask anyone for Valentín." The man's chances of going to Valencia look about as likely as mine for going to Mars.

Berna, Michèle and I have finished our mineral water and look at each other, anxious to be on the road again. We have several more hours of walking today.

Valentín realizes and rolls his brown eyes, saying "Ready, peregrinos?" He has attached himself to our group whether we like it or not.

I return his canteen and offer to carry one of his bags. He gives me the one with the books; it weighs almost as much as my whole pack. We say goodbye to the villagers, or rather Valentín does it for us, inviting them all to visit him in Valencia. While we pay for our drinks he walks outside; either he has paid already or his wine was on the house.

"This is the first day of the rest of your life!" Valentín shouts for the whole population to hear as we cross the square. But nobody else apppears in this village whose name we haven't bothered to learn.

We descend a narrow valley full of huge chestnut trees, the largest I've seen since coming out of St. Jean-Pied-de-Port on the first day. That seems ages ago, I think. How could I have known then that I'd end up walking with two French women and a makeup man for Spanish television?

As we go down from Mount Irago, Valentín tells us the story of his life, as if he had known us for years: a childhood of poverty in the dark 1940s, his mother's death, his father's struggle to raise him and his two sisters, his escape to Paris where he studied at a fashion school, a long stay in Rome, his return to Barcelona where he took classes in design, finally his job at Spanish TV. Last month they tried to fire him, claiming he was only a part-time employee ineligible for medical and retirement benefits. He responded by initiating a lawsuit against RTE.

"I came on pilgrimage to Compostela in order to leave all that behind" he finishes.

"Each one of us has his own reasons for walking the Road" says Michèle.

Berna can't stand Valentín's talking and slow pace; she moves ahead. Michèle and I stay with him on the hard path down the valley and gorge. Carrying his books, I think how much my situation has changed since I was the cripple, depending on José Mari and Pili, Sagrario and Josemi, the Navarrese and finally the French when I was sick. Now I can take care of myself and Valentín needs help. I don't mind carrying his books no matter how much they seem out of place in this remote valley.

Finally we see the town of Molinaseca below us, looking like an oasis after the miserable villages near the pass. We stop to cool off on the shore of a fast stream lined with poplars. A vegetable garden with tomatoes, cabbage and green peppers comes right down to the bank. Changing into our bathing suits, we wash ourselves in the cold, shallow water; this is the first bath Berna, Michèle and I have taken since Hospital de Orbigo. While the women soap themselves and frolic in the rocky stream bed, Valentín and I towel off, put on dry clothes and sit at the table of a shady merendero—a spot for taking the traditional afternoon snack. We don't have food but leaning back on our chairs, putting our feet on the tabletop and hearing the laughter of Michèle and Berna in the rushing water, we feel like two ancient river-gods.

"Get your feet off the table!" whispers Valentín urgently. "Somebody's coming."

We settle into a less godlike posture as two men and two women come through the garden, picking tomatoes. They're as shocked as we are to see somebody else.

"Good afternoon, Señores" says Valentín in his resonant voice, smiling without a hint of shame for trespassing on land that probably belongs to these middle-aged couples. "We are pilgrims on our way to Santiago de Compostela. We trust you don't mind if we have stopped to refresh ourselves at this bucolic place after fifty kilometers of strenuous walking today." We couldn't have covered more than twenty k's from Rabanal del Camino, I think.

"Fifty kilometers in a single day?" asks one of the men. He wears a boina and looks like a prosperous peasant.

"Sí señor, and I have these blisters to prove it" answers Valentín, holding up his bare feet. He was right: they look like a battlefield.

"Won't you have a vinito, a little wine we've produced?" asks the other man. The women remain silent, standing plumply behind their husbands.

"We would be honored" answers Valentín.

The man pulls a large wicker-covered bottle from the tomato plants, two topless Coca-Cola cans strung to its neck. He pours red wine from the bottle while the man with the boina holds the cans. Then they put everything on the table so we can drink.

"Are you gentlemen and ladies going to join us?" asks Valentín.

"We only have two cans" says one of the men. "We know how the wine tastes and we haven't walked fifty kilometers today."

Valentín rings out his husky laugh and drinks the wine. I do the same, feeling a little awkward for accepting their generosity. The wine is not bad if you make allowance for the aluminum cans.

"Nectar for our dry throats after such an arduous hike" says Valentín smacking his lips.

They conceal the bottle among the tomatoes and wish us "Buen viaje," saying we can spend as much time as we like in their garden.

Berna and Michèle have heard everything from the stream. They come out of the water, chiding Valentín for his fib as they dry off and change into new clothes behind the poplars.

We walk into Molinaseca. The town must be in fiesta: Latin American music is blaring from loudspeakers. We find refuge at a schoolhouse that has already been commandeered by Kosti and Co. Michèle, Berna and I decide to set up our sleeping bags in an orchard behind the school. Valentín prefers to stay indoors.

No belle étoile tonight: the lights of Molinaseca and fireworks from the fiesta make the stars almost invisible.

17 Paradise and Hell

When we awake at dawn the fiesta is still going strong. The young men of Molinaseca are throwing buckets of water at each other as we walk out of town, joined by Valentín.

"Remind me not to walk the Camino again in mid-August" says Berna. "All these fiestas are rough on a pilgrim."

"Not on me" says Valentín. "I had a great time in town last night while you were going to sleep. I even danced."

"You danced on those feet of yours?" asks Michèle. Valentín is limping more than yesterday.

"Nothing can stop me when there's a party" he answers. "Nobody can take away my festive sense of life. It's all I have" he says looking away.

"You're a strange one, Monsieur Valentín de Valencia" says Berna as she quickens her pace and moves ahead. Michèle and I lag behind with poor Valentín, the two of us carrying his extra bags.

Soon we enter Ponferrada, the grimmest city I've seen on the Road or anywhere in Spain: drab buildings, grey river, empty streets. Even the sky is grey. I feel a heaviness, a pall in the air.

We come to the immense castle of Ponferrada, set on the high ground. It must cover the equivalent of several city blocks.

"It's big and ugly like everything else in this place" says Berna.

"We're going to see it though, right?" asks Valentín sounding worried. "One of my books says it's the largest and most important castle of the Templars in Spain."

We decide to satisfy him, walking up a ramp to the main entrance, an arch framed by two turrets. A woman seated at a table gives us tickets for a few pesetas.

Valentín asks her "Señora, can you tell us where the famous treasure of the Knights Templar is buried?" She laughs but not as hard as he does, infected by his own humor.

As we explore the vast grounds, Valentín tells us the story of the castle. Founded in the 1100s to protect the Camino de Santiago at the crucial doorstep to Galicia, it stood until the Templars were abolished some two centuries later. "It was the greatest police roundup in history" says Valentín. "They were accused of being sodomites, worshipers of the devil, sorcerers, Christ-haters who spat on the cross. The kings of France and Spain envied their wealth and the Church saw them as rivals for men's souls. The Order had named itself after Solomon's Temple, symbol of perfection and ancient knowledge. When it was wiped out we lost one of our last ties to that wisdom. I remember a book that says the Knights' true edifice was the temple of the soul, built in silence without hammers or other tools."

"I like that" says Michèle. Berna looks skeptical.

Everyone except our new companion feels disappointed by the castle; we expected to find it better restored. To our amazement Valentín actually seems to believe the fabled treasure of the Templars may still be buried here. I remember Easter egg hunts when I was a child as he feels along the rubbled walls, climbs to the top of ruined battlements, searches dungeons with the smell of stale urine.

"It's got to be somewhere" huffs Valentín, "either here or in the coffers of some Swiss bank or multinational corporation."

Berna and Michèle are too fond of Valentín to say anything. They too must be asking themselves, Can he really believe this?

On the way out I cannot resist: "I'll bet you play the national lottery, right, Valentín?"

"Every week. How did you know, Eduardo?"

"Have you ever won?"

"Not yet" he answers looking at me with his sad round eyes. I regret my words. He realizes I'm poking fun at him.

Valentín becomes suddenly morose: "My feet are bothering me too much to continue" he says. "I'm going to the nearest Red Cross station."

We offer to accompany him but he insists that he doesn't want us to fall behind on his account. He'll hitchhike or take a bus to catch up later. He's so adamant that we give in, agreeing to wait for him at the Church of Santiago in Villafranca del Bierzo where we plan to spend the night.

Valentín mopes back to the town on the Sunday morning street, limping and loaded down with his bags.

"It's my fault" I tell the women. "I shouldn't have said anything."

"How could you have known he would react like this?" asks Berna.

"I knew" says Michèle.

With Valentín gone, about five people seem to be missing. I feel guilty because I suspect there was some kind of malice behind my words. Before we met him on Monte Irago, I was the only man with Berna and Michèle. I thought that I'd overcome sexual feelings for them or any other women on the Road, yet perhaps some deeply buried residue of male possessiveness made me taunt Valentín.

"Pobre Valentín!" cries Michèle.

"He's not the only one who takes this business seriously" says Berna, less emotional than her friend. Turning to me she asks "Have you met the 'Templarios' anywhere on the road?"

"I saw a message signed 'Templars' at the refuge in Nájera."

"They call themselves after the ancient order" explains Michèle, "and they consider themselves its true descendants. It's a group of men—no women of course; we met them a few days ago. They told us they're walking the Camino as representatives of many other 'ultras' or extremists on the right, in order to 'transform decadent Spain.' Those were their words. Guillemette and René thought they were crazy."

"So did I" adds Berna. "I didn't like the way they looked at us, the women." She and Michèle are enjoying the expression of incredulity on my face.

"They don't wear uniforms but they do have boots and they march instead of walking" Berna adds.

"Come on you're both pulling my leg" I tell them. "That's about as likely as Valentín's treasure."

"I wish we were joking" says Michèle. "They march carrying a banner with a symbolic chessboard on it. One of them told us they keep their swords in a truck with the rest of their paraphernalia. They never spend the night with other pilgrims because they don't want anyone to witness their secret rites. Yet they consider themselves Catholics, Holy, Roman and Apostolic with a special devotion to the Virgin Mary."

"They're weirdos" says Berna with a shudder. "Creepy!"

"I wonder if old Valentín knows about these Templarios" I say.

"Oh they wouldn't get along" says Berna. "I was afraid, really afraid of those characters. Valentín wouldn't hurt a fly."

"Only himself" adds Michèle, the oracle.

We cross the grey River Sil for the second time and reach the far side of Ponferrada. The road winds around a mountain of coal at the thermoelectrical plant, the same one we saw spewing smoke into the sky from the Cruz de Ferro, I think. The greyness of the city and the sky, the Sunday lifelessness, my guilt over Valentín's departure, now this eyesore on the Camino all make me anxious to get out of here.

I insist on stopping at the first bar beyond the city to have a beer and wash Ponferrada out of our systems. If I were John Bunyan, I think quaffing my beer, this place would be my Slough of Despond, my Valley of the Shadow of Death, my Giant Despair.

I feel much better after the beer. We walk through villages with vegetable gardens growing down to the edge of the road. The dry, sterile part of León province lies behind us now as we approach El Bierzo, the Spanish Switzerland. The terrain becomes hillier, the vegetation greener, big white cumulus clouds rolling across the sky.

When the clouds build up, we smell the approaching rain. We reach the town of Cacabelos just in time to take refuge under the portico around the main square. The storm hits with a clap of thunder and a downpour.

"Our first real rain on the Camino" says Berna. "We slept through the storm that night when you were sick, Edouard."

"Isn't it wonderful?" asks Michèle staring at the rain as if it were a miracle. "After all that heat and the desert."

We wait out the storm in the "Pub Edén," a café under the portico. When we return to the road, a light drizzle is still falling. I raise my head toward the sky to feel that gentle, wet caress on my face.

The clouds flee and the bright sun steams moisture from the earth. We can feel and smell the warmth rising from the ground. El Bierzo lies before us in the washed, transparent air: soft hills and green meadows covered with vineyards, fruit and nut orchards, patches of woods. The landscape is more human, less wild than Roncesvalles, the Montes de Oca or Mt. Irago. But it has duende too. No wonder monks, nuns and anchorites chose this secluded place to build convents, hermitages, cells and sanctuaries for centuries.

"Look what I've found!" cries Berna waiting for us in the middle of an orchard. Her hands are overflowing with plums: "They were so ripe that the wind and rain knocked them to the ground. These are Claudia plums and they're ready to eat." She bites into one, crying "This is paradise!"

Michèle and I drop our packs and rush to pick up the tender plums from the wet ground. They're green with tints of yellow, soft to the touch, juicy and sweet in our mouths. We lose track of how many we've eaten, stuffing the pockets of our backpacks for the road. I remember when my pack was bulging with apples that first day in the Pyrenees. It was a French man and his wife who gave them to me; here I am with two French women. Camino francés.

I feel so much energy from the rain and the plums that I go on without Berna and Michèle, who are still gathering fruit, laughing like two little girls. The Camino isn't well marked on this stretch. I have to follow the sun to come out on the edge of Villafranca del Bierzo, nestled in wooded hills and valleys.

The little chapel of Santiago sits above the road on the left, alone, its walls a golden color in the afternoon sun. The women are not in sight so I walk up to the church, a small, simple building of the twelfth century, condemned and locked for years. The most interesting part is the north portal with its carved capitals and arches in pure Romanesque style—the Puerta del Perdón, Door of Pardon. Since the Way beyond Villafranca passes over rugged mountains, any pilgrim who was unable to continue beyond this point had the right to the same indulgences he would have received in Compostela.

I sit on the grass facing the portal so that Berna and Michèle will be able to spot me. Now I have a chance to look carefully at the carvings—Calvary, the Magi following the star, the Adoration. The figures seem to be here for me only, standing out from the stone, speaking to me across eight hundred years.

The women finally arrive. They tell me the plums didn't agree with Michèle and her stomach has returned them to the earth they came from. She's recovered now and looks at me with a sheepish smile.

We agree to take turns waiting at the church until nightfall in case Valentín shows up. I feel so happy here that I volunteer to take the first shift. Meanwhile the French go into town to reconnoiter and find rooms at a pensión. Valentín doesn't appear. I return to the pensión at dark and tell the women that our friend must be spending the night in Ponferrada.

The next morning we're on the road before dawn, passing through a tunnel on the National VI where refrigerator trucks speed by in the opposite direction, engulfing us in their fumes as they rush seafood from the ports of Galicia to Madrid and points south. The intrepid Berna, our little Joan of Arc leads us with her flashlight through the dragon's mouth of the dark valley. Without seeing it, we hear the rushing water of the Valcarce River. When the day begins to lighten we see trout leaping in the clear water, chasing insects for breakfast.

Drizzle falls. For the first time on the trip, my waterproof jacket and pants are useful in the rain; until now I've used them only against the wind and cold. We pass through early-morning towns with the warm odors of cow-dung and hay. We're still in the province of León but this land once used to be considered a part of Galicia. Already it looks, smells and feels like that green, moist region, the Spanish Ireland. Our baptism of water from the sky has come on schedule here, at the doorstep to Galicia. We're already within the sphere of Santiago; we can feel it pulling us.

When we take our first rest at a village fountain, a black-dressed woman with a shawl over her head tells us: "You're going to have bad weather at the pass, pero será lo que Dios quiera, it will be as God wishes." We're in or near Galicia all right, about as close to the Third World as you can get in Western Europe.

Trudging up the Madrid-La Coruña highway, we pass more towns of timeworn grey stone, funneled in the hills above the river; green, ever-so-green meadows, fields and gardens with more varieties of cabbages than you've ever seen.

Somewhere in the fog and clouds we miss the turnoff for the old pilgrims' road, leaving it far away and inaccessible on the other side of the steep valley. I try to persuade the women to get off the highway and go back. Berna pays no attention, refusing to miss a beat of her mechanical rhythm, impelled forward by some invisible motor, Onward Christian Soldiers, Jeanne d'Arc, Vive la France. She's too obsessed with arriving, Michèle too passive to care if we're missing what's supposed to be a spectacular stretch of the ancient Camino de Santiago. In favor of what? This asphalt highway where we're buffeted by the wind of passing trucks, trailers, cars, splashed with water, mud and grease, swallowing gas and diesel fumes. Of course I know it's hard to turn around and retrace your steps when your back, legs and feet are aching from miles of climbing uphill in the rain. I know it's my fault for not insisting, for wanting to reach the goal too much, after all what's keeping me from turning around, I'm a free person, a pilgrim, why not go back myself, meet them at the pass? But I do nothing, glued to the wet highway, plodding on with the wind and rain in my face, cursing them with all the insults accumulated by Anglo-Saxons in centuries of war and rivalry with the Gallic peoples, Frogs, Frenchies, Parleyvoos, a pox of the French disease on them, running out of epithets in English and turning to Spanish, afrancesadas, gabachas, burguesas . . . now getting angry at myself, bringing down insults on my own wet head, gringo, Yank, foreigner go home . . .

Suddenly Michèle is talking to me: "If the plum orchard was paradise, this is hell." I've forgotten that she's right behind me, almost at the top of the pass now, Berna standing ahead of us on the shoulder, jumping up and down and laughing, pointing to the roadmarker for the province of Lugo, we're hugging each other in the rain, I forgive them for everything, forgive myself, we're in Galicia.

PART
THREE

18 Galicia

> There, far in the west, the most ancient people, the most ancient faiths, retreating slowly, lingered: and thither came, carried by the pilgrims, all that the rest of the world had come to think and feel.
>
> —Georgiana King

After spending the night in the town of Piedrafita, we get lost in the morning fog, so thick that our heads and shoes are soaked. I feel colder even than the day of the hailstorm. Michèle, Berna and I don't speak to each other. Somehow words would be useless in this place where sounds seem to be swallowed in the mist.

Out of the fog appear low, grey walls, a stable, now strange, circular hovels with thatched, conical roofs—pallozas. The three of us look at each other: to confirm that we are awake? This village out of the past, not a soul in sight, shrouded in mist is like a dream or vision. It must be Cebreiro, the town where they use these peaked huts as pilgrims' refuges.

Clouds blow around the sloping, wigwam roofs of the pallozas. We approach one of them. Close up we can see that the thatch is intertwined and held fast by plaited cords of broom. Berna and Michèle stand in front of the low entrance. They expect me to make the next move—not from fear or dependency, simply from female custom bred in their European bones.

I knock on the wooden door. Through the rough stone walls a muffled voice reaches us: "Pasad."

We push on the the heavy, creaking door and enter. Our feet step on a spongy layer of straw. It feels much warmer in here than outside. In the half-darkness we can make out the low, blackened walls and a solitary figure squatting in the middle of the oval room. When my eyes get used to the light, a shudder of recognition passes through me: it's Claudio. I'm happy to see him but I also feel that we're intruders who have violated his solitude.

"Hombre" he says rising to his feet to embrace me. "Qué alegría verte, it's a joy to see you."

"I knew we'd meet again." I introduce him to Berna and Michèle, speaking to him in Spanish so the women won't feel left out.

Claudio tells us he has spent the night in the hut with some pilgrims who've already set out this morning. "It's a marvelous place to sleep" he says. "The straw is clean and sweet and there's plenty of

14 Palloza, or thatched hovel, Cebreiro (Lugo), Galicia. (Photo José Luis Herrera)

room. These pallozas have been restored but they have probably not changed much since Celtic times, maybe since the Stone Age."

"Is there any heat?" asks Michèle.

"The straw keeps out the cold and damp of the earthen floor and the room seems to trap the body heat of the people in it. The gallegos used to live side by side with their animals who also gave off heat. And in the center of the room a lar or hearth was kept burning day and night, all year long."

"How did the smoke from the fire get out?" asks Berna, always practical.

"It didn't" answers Claudio pointing to the walls. "That's why the interior is so charred. No chimney or windows."

When I think that we paid for a humdrum pensión instead of spending the night in this once-in-a-lifetime place where pilgrims may have slept for centuries, my anger from yesterday flares up.

To let it out I say "We got lost and ended up in a town on the highway, Piedrafita."

"I stayed there on my first pilgrimage too" says Claudio. "Actually it's on the pre-Christian route to Compostela, just north of the present road."

"The 'Camino de las Estrellas'?" asks Michèle.

"Right. The one followed by the master stonemasons and alchemists."

Berna and Michèle are staring at Claudio, entranced by his words and gestures: it's as if he tries to capture the air with the spacious movements of his hands and arms.

"Would you like an infusion?" he asks us.

"Where will you heat the water?" inquires Berna.

"On my portable stove."

"A cup of tea would be wonderful after the cold out there" says Michèle.

Taking off our soaked rain gear and packs, we sit on the floor around the little flame of Claudio's camp stove.

"Four ancient Celts around the hearth" I say.

"You're probably the only one of us who doesn't have Celtic ancestors" says Michèle smiling at me.

"For your information I'm one-fourth Irish" I tell her smiling back. "My great-grandmother was born in Ireland, last name of Rooney."

Claudio laughs: "You can't get much more Irish than that." He pours water from a canteen into a worn pot over the flame. "You might not believe me" he says, "but I made three trips to Ireland before ever coming to Galicia, the most Celtic part of my own country. When I finally got here I realized it was the same as Ireland except for the language."

"Didn't they say something like that on the TV program?" asks Michèle. "The one on the Camino de Santiago?"

Claudio looks embarrassed; one minute he resembles an old sage, the next a little boy. "Don't believe everything they said" he tells the women, smiling uncomfortably. "Some of the crew was high during the shooting. By the way I have only two teacups" he says.

"We have two more" says Berna who has been quiet as usual with a new person. She removes the cups from her pack; I remember drinking from them the morning after I was sick.

Claudio takes out a small leather pouch and pours some dried leaves in the palm of his hand. "Herbs I've picked along the way" he says sprinkling them in the boiling water. "Don't worry, they're all beneficial, good for infusions." The leaves—green, brown, yellow and orange—swirl in the pot and give off a pungent steam in the windowless room.

"Did you pick those on the Camino too?" I ask him pointing to the safari hat he was wearing when I met him at the pool in Hontanas. It rests on the straw floor with its plume of dried flowers.

"Yes, I've picked them all this year. I'm trying to pay more attention to the vegetation on the road. It's strange, the first time I made the pilgrimage I followed the stars and ignored almost everything else. This time I've learned more about herbs, flowers, trees, bushes, fruits and berries. Birds too. The Camino is inexhaustible. You could spend a lifetime on it and never stop learning."

Claudio removes the pot from the flame, letting the herbs steep before filling the four cups with the infusion. His long-limbed movements are slightly awkward but full of concentration and an instinct for ceremony. I feel better than I have for days—since we slept under the stars and saw the Milky Way, I think.

"Why do you leave the flame burning?" Michèle asks Claudio, unbashful as always.

"I don't know exactly. It looks so nice and warm here in the semidark. Some Galicians still believe in keeping the lar burning constantly; they light the morning fire with the coals of the previous night. To let the fire go out is supposed to bring bad luck on the house and family. The gallegos consider the lar and flame to be alive. They also celebrate the noche de San Juan, Midsummer Eve with the best bonfires I've seen anywhere. Then there's the queimada; do you know about it?"

"I'm not sure" answers Berna, "but I've heard the expression."

"What is it?" asks Michèle.

"An alcoholic drink flambéed with a ritual incantation over the fire" answers Claudio. "Very powerful stuff in all senses of the word."

We sit drinking the infusion, watching the gas flame in the penumbra. When we move, giant shadows imitate us on the walls and lofty ceiling.

"This place has duende" says Berna in a hushed voice.

"Why are you whispering?" asks Michèle, speaking no louder than her friend.

"For the same reason you are" returns Berna.

"No wonder you were meditating here" I say softly to Claudio, infected by the women's murmurs.

"There's a lot of energy here" he says. "Most of the high places, the mountain passes on the Camino have it. But something new begins here, or something very old."

As we drink the bittersweet tea, the flame of the stove begins to sputter; it makes three final pops and dies. Claudio puts the stove in his pack while Berna and Michèle wash out the cups.

"Are you going to continue walking?" he asks us.

"Yes" responds Berna, "but I'd like to take a look at Cebreiro first. Maybe the fog has lifted by now."

"Don't get your hopes up" warns Claudio. "Listen."

We stop moving our feet on the straw floor . . . the muffled patter of rain on the thatched roof.

"The other sacred element in Galicia" Claudio says. "Water."

"Here we go again" Michèle sighs as she puts on her rain gear. "Ever since we entered Galicia it's been raining or misting so much that it might as well be rain."

"The bane of pilgrims" says Claudio, "here and everywhere else in the world."

"I don't mind it here, for example" Michèle says. "But yesterday on the Madrid-La Coruña highway it was unbearable with the cars and trucks splashing us."

"I know what you mean" says Claudio, "but putting up with traffic is part of the price we pay for being pilgrims in the twentieth century."

"Those cars and trucks are the evil of our time" says Berna.

"Like the bandits, plagues and famine of the Middle Ages" adds Claudio. "Or the dragons and monsters in peoples' minds in those days."

"You're sounding like a druid" I tell him, remembering his nickname Panorámix. "The traffic is the one aspect of the Camino I don't like at all, the only thing that might keep me from walking the Way again. Did you hear about the Belgian pilgrim who was struck by a car in Navarrete?"

"Yes" he answers.

"Life is cheap in Spain" says Berna staring at the high-pitched ceiling. "Even on the Road to Santiago."

Claudio looks at us and asks shyly "Do you mind if I walk with you?"

"Hombre, of course not" I tell him. "I assumed you were coming with us." He puts on his coat and pack. Sometimes he's as timid as a child among adults, I think.

We go out in the rain. The fast-moving clouds and the fog look ever so white after the darkness in the hut.

"Hold your noses" says Claudio pointing to a kind of stable ahead. "The regional government of Galicia has seen fit to approve the construction of a manure deposit right there, less than ten meters from the pilgrims' refuge, which also happens to be an archeological monument."

We walk through the wet, grey streets. Nothing else is moving in this village of slate walls, hovels and a dozen or so houses of unfinished stone, all of them invisible in the fog until you are a few yards away. Cebreiro seems empty as Foncebadón and the other ghost towns of Mount Irago yet it does not look abandoned; there is a kind of sheltering intimacy in its streets and dwellings as if they were all connected, part of the same courtyard or plaza.

"Can you believe it" asks Claudio, "that on a clear day in Cebreiro you can see all the way to the Cantabrian Sea?"

"We're lucky if we see the end of our noses today" answers Michèle.

Out of the fog appears a church with its squat belltower, probably a thousand years old. We step through the round stone arch of the portico and find the doors locked.

"Me cachis" says Berna, "darn it"—the closest she'll ever come to profanity, I think. "I wanted to see the place where the famous miracle is supposed to have taken place."

"What miracle?" asks Michèle.

"A peasant arrived here to attend Mass on a cold stormy night a long time ago," Berna begins. "The parish priest thought the man was stupid to be out in such weather; when he consecrated the host and wine they became the flesh and blood of Christ, right in front of their eyes."

"The miracle was associated with the legend of the Holy Grail" adds Claudio. "Some held that Joseph of Arimathea, who was supposed to have collected Christ's blood in the chalice at the Crucifixion, was one of those who carried St. James' body to Galicia. If people believed the Grail ended up somewhere on the Camino, either here or in Compostela, it would have been another motive for pilgrims to come to Galicia."

We walk out from the portico into the fog and rain. Claudio leads us with his loping, slightly bow-legged stride—the walk of a sailor, I say to myself. Berna follows him closely while Michèle and I come last, closer than usual because of the poor visibility.

In the cold air our breath makes mist, soon lost in the drizzle and swirling fog. I feel more uneasy here than anywhere else on the Camino so far, except for the beech forest of Roncevaux where I was alone. I'm grateful for company now. At least Claudio has been here before. Between him—half Christ, half Merlin—and Berna, our Joan of

Arc, we're well protected from the innumerable ghosts, witches and goblins of Galician folklore. As we walk through the fog I remember the story about the man who asked a gallego if there really are meigas, the fabled witches in his homeland. "I've never seen one" the Galician answered. "But as to whether they exist, you're damned right they do."

Claudio stops for a few seconds to let us catch up. With his impish smile he says "In weather like this I wouldn't be surprised to see the Santa Compaña."

"What's that?" asks Michèle.

"Do you mean that you're walking across Galicia and you don't know what the Compaña is?" he asks her, still smiling. Raindrops are caught in his thick, wiry beard. "Almas en pena, processions of souls from purgatory who walk on the fog with lights in their hands. I've never met a single gallego who didn't believe in them at heart."

Berna scoffs "Come on, Claudio, you know that's a bunch of superstition. Anyway souls from purgatory are only supposed to appear at night."

"It might as well be night—it's dark enough" says Michéle with a high-pitched laugh.

Even St. Joan is lacking her usual pluck: instead of striding ahead, she allows Claudio to take the lead once more. We seem to be alone in the world. Without seeing a sign of life, we pass through a wet, shabby village. Huddling inside the hood of my rain jacket I feel colder than when we set out this morning. I'd hate to think what it's like in winter here.

Suddenly Claudio jumps back and Berna stops. We hear a resonant clop on the stone road and the disembodied head of a cow, now another comes out of the fog toward us, passing so close that we feel their warm breath and now see the pink, swaying teats of their swollen udders, the freckles on the face of the young girl, not more than thirteen who carries a switch in her hand and greets us "Santos y buenos días, a good and holy day," singing as much as saying it.

"Santos y buenos" replies Claudio turning around to watch her fade with her animals in the fog.

"I can't believe there are still people who talk like that" says Michèle.

"This has been one of the ordinary miracles of everyday life here" says Claudio. "The ordinariness of the miraculous in Galicia—that's what fascinates me."

We go on, falling into our new order on a path of earth, grass and furze worn down by hooves of cattle whose prints overlap those of

Claudio's sandals and Berna's boots. With the muck and cow manure sticking to our feet, we must look like four moon-walkers. Anything above the ground is concealed in the fog. In Galicia the sky is covered so often that your eyes are drawn to the earth. In Castile and León with their flat, monotonous landscape, your gaze rises to the cloudless sky. Castile, land of mystics, the God of St. Teresa and John of the Cross. Galicia, land of local spirits of the earth, fire, water.

The fog blurs the outlines and colors of things; the rain, mud and grass muffle sounds. Only the sense of smell is not deadened: the aroma of herbs and grass crushed under our feet breathes from the humid earth. Galicians must have dreams of places with dim, fuzzy outlines, I think, a world where nothing is clear-cut.

As suddenly as the cows appeared, the massive head of an ox comes out of the gloom, horns swinging from side to side, muscle-quivering, muddy-flanked, now a second animal, a third followed by a man wrapped in a cloak, all of them created out of the mist before our eyes.

"Did you notice he didn't greet us?" asks Claudio. We're walking abreast on a wider path now. "The men in Galicia rarely initiate a conversation. On the other hand the women tend to be talkative and friendly."

"I suppose you mean that women are gossips and busybodies?" asks Michèle.

"I don't think so" Claudio answers, slightly embarrassed. "You wait and tell me if you don't find it to be true. Maybe it has to do with the fact that the women in Galicia are more visible than the men, who are often absent for one reason or another. For centuries they've been famous as fishermen, migrant workers during the harvest season in other parts of the country, emigrants to the cities of Spain and Latin America. The women are often left behind. That's why they call them 'widows of the living and the dead.'"

"That's also why they do the work of men in the fields" says Berna, "as well as the normal housework of course."

Enjoying this male-female repartee, I ask Claudio "Why are Galician women also known for having light morals?"

Before he can respond, Michèle puts in "Because their men are gone, silly."

"I'm the wrong person to answer your question" Claudio tells me.

We pass through villages where life is beginning to stir, some humans and animals moving in the muddy streets. The people are elderly peasants, most of them dressed in black, their heads and faces muffled against the rain. Hunched beneath his black umbrella, a priest scurries across the road trailing his cassock in the mire.

We can walk no farther: a huge ox, double-yoked to a wagon, blocks the way. He stands in the middle of the narrow street, motionless, staring into a puddle through sheets of rain. Once, only a day or two days ago it would have bothered me to stop, to lose time on the road. Now I enjoy the pause, taking in the sight, smelling the comforting odors of manure and smoke coming from nearby. I guess my companions feel the same; we wait without speaking. So serene is the ox's vision of rain and mud that I'm content to watch him. An ordinary miracle of Galicia, I suppose.

"I wonder what he sees in the mud" I say.

"If only we could see it too" answers Claudio. "A Galician nirvana."

"It's funny you should say that" comments Michèle staring into the mud too. "So far Galicia reminds me of the Middle East or India, where the animals are so long-suffering."

A man emerges from a doorway to our left and grunts at the animal, hitting him across the back of the head with a switch. Without ceasing to stare into the puddle, the beast begins to turn its haunches slowly, heavily. I look through the crooked doorway where the man came out: beyond an earthen floor I see a blackened, bell-shaped chimney and the reddish glow of a fire. Slabs of jerked beef hang over the hearth on dried, knotty vine-shoots.

Claudio is also looking through the doorway: "The lar" he says. "Judging from the smell, they must be burning jara or rock-rose. They burn anything in Galicia."

"How I'd love to be in there" says Michèle. "My feet are cold and they weigh a ton with all this mud caked on them." Turning to Claudio she asks, "Aren't your feet cold without socks?"

"Yes" he replies, "but I like the feel of the earth on them now and the fresh air when it's not raining. The ventilation keeps me from getting blisters."

The ox has finally abandoned his revery, pulling the creaky wagon to the side of the road. We walk forward through the mud, out of this town and into others, all of them with early-morning smells and cattle in the streets. After a quick, steep ascent we come out on a paved road at the Alto do Poio, the highest point on the Way of St. James. The rain and clouds prevent us from seeing more than a hundred yards in any direction.

"This is the one mountain pass on the Camino without duende" says Claudio. "It's the watershed between the Cantabrian Sea and the

Atlantic Ocean, about 1,350 meters high but it can't match Ronces-valles, Montes de Oca, Irago or Cebreiro, which all feel higher."

"The good part is that it's all downhill from here to Compostela" says Berna, always optimistic.

Joan of Arc never lies: we descend in the rain through places with sonorous names like Fonfría, Filloval, As Pasantes, Ramil, the poorest villages I've seen on the Camino. After the euphoria of Alto do Poio, the last major obstacle before Santiago, my heart contracts in these muddy hamlets: men and women living cheek by jowl with their animals, old, tired, sullen people with low foreheads and toothless mouths. The eternal Galicia of damp and dirt, the Spain of the Third World. A guilty silence descends upon us like a heavy bird as we huddle closer together.

"I don't like Galicia at all" says Michèle.

"Just wait" says Claudio.

After passing through a grove of ancient chestnut trees, we come out in the town of Triacastela. Claudio suggests we have lunch in a second-floor restaurant where he's eaten before.

As we sit down at a table, somebody comes up behind me, puts two large paws over my eyes and says in a loud, scratchy voice "Quién es?" Of course I know it's Valentín, the women and I give him a big hug, lots of slaps on the back, I'm glad to see that he's no longer morose, we introduce him to Claudio, joking about his reappearance true to form—a duende who comes out of nowhere.

Valentín is in fine feather. He tells us he spent that day in Ponferrada to cure his blisters, then "cheated" by hitching rides. "But don't worry about my soul" he laughs, "el Santo me perdona, the Saint forgives me."

Valentín is traveling with a middle-aged man named Emilio, an olive-skinned lawyer from León who started walking two days ago in Villafranca del Bierzo. They've already eaten and say goodbye to us: "We'll probably see you again."

After lunch the fog and rain have lifted, revealing the first sun and sky we've seen in Galicia. The Camino de Santiago leaves the paved streets of Triacastela and climbs to the right through a green, narrow valley between fast-running streams. Linnets and sparrows flit in and out of the high bushes on either side of the path, chirping, shaking drops of water from the leaves still soaked from the morning's rain. We walk by hamlets with stone houses and barns, small fields marked by hewn stones or low fences, smoke curling from the crooked chimneys.

We come upon an old woman sitting in a courtyard of moss-covered stones, rubbing grain from ears of corn. Her black skirt is gathered

15   Corredoira, Galica. (Photo José Luis Herrera)

around her waist and it is full of dry, yellow kernels. As we pass she tosses a few grains to the scrawny chickens at her feet.

"Alabado sea Dios, God be praised" she says looking up at us.

"Alabado sea" answers Claudio.

We have to press against the side of the path as a herd of sheep comes our way, crowding together with timid bleats. A shepherdess with staff follows, one of those ageless Galician women dressed in black who might be anywhere from thirty to sixty years old. Of course I remember the other shepherdess, coming out of Roncesvalles: she seems almost to be from another life, so far away. The miles of walking, the heat and cold, the fatigue, the rain and fog of Galicia have worn, dulled, consumed my sexual being. Could it really be the first time since adolescence that my body does not feel racked with desire? I would not have believed it unless I'd felt it myself on the Camino de Santiago, deep in my flesh.

The path goes through woods of chestnuts, oaks and birch, the sun-dappled ground covered with ferns and mushrooms. We've entered the world of the corredoiras, the narrow rutted paths that criss-cross Galicia like a maze, bordered by thatched walls or bramble hedges so thick that you cannot see beyond them, a canopy of treetops above, occasional glimpses of green meadows to the side and peaceful-grazing cattle.

From the path of mud, rocks and manure rises a cloud of butterflies, then another, hundreds of them. They fly around us with brown, orange-spotted wings. It's as if the earth were sprouting them.

The trees and bushes envelop us, drawing us into their recesses. I feel a closeness, an intimacy with this world where nothing is foreign to me. I'm pulled into the corredoira, absorbed, no longer an outsider but a part of it, inside, the landscape becoming me.

We walk for miles without speaking a word, following our own pace and thoughts, together but each of us alone. The night overtakes us in Samos: we see the massive monastery below us in a valley, sitting there like a fat monk in prayer, surrounded by chestnuts and cypresses, a hill on each side. A full moon is peeping over the far end of the valley.

"I knew there was something unique about today" says Claudio.

"I've changed my mind about Galicia" adds Michèle.

19 Samos, Sarria and a Cup of Milk

Camiño, camiño branco,
non sei para dónde vas,
mais cada vez que te vexo
quisiera poder t'andar . . .

Road, oh white road,
I don't know where you go,
but each time I see you
I want to follow you.
—Rosalía de Castro

A monk in the black Benedictine habit leads us slowly up a wide stair-case to the pilgrims' dormitory, telling us there are only twelve broth-ers left in the abbey. The room is as huge as everything else here: endless rows of bare bunks, a sort of Baroque army barracks, the dif-ference being that each bed is enclosed by a screen to form a semi-private cubicle, our pilgrims' cells for the night.

Before going to bed, I sit down at a table next to the bathroom where I leaf through the pilgrims' guest book. Nearly everyone else is asleep. I read a note in English dated yesterday: "How can such a loss be repaired? Please pray for me my friends. Michael Shearer." This must be Claudio's English friend, I think, whom we met with his young son at the pool in Hontanas. Turning the pages backwards I come to a message from Claudio dated August of last year, signed "Panorámix": "Two times I died, seeking myself in the ashes. To die truly is to forget everything, to remember everyone and to abandon the world. I love all of you. We will meet at the sunset, in the West."

The Spanish words read so well that I decide to copy them in my little notebook. I've hardly begun when Claudio walks by the table on the way to his bunk.

"I'm writing down your message from last year" I tell him. "Hope you don't mind."

"Hombre, don't waste your ink" he says with his self-deprecating smile. "Can't even remember what I wrote." He peers over my shoul-der: "Oh that."

"In what way is the pilgrimage a death?" I ask him feeling a little intrusive. I recall that José Ignacio, the priest from Hervías used sim-ilar words.

"It's not as mysterious as it sounds" he answers sitting in one of the chairs. "You see I've had two heart attacks." Claudio is the last person I would have expected to suffer from a weak heart. "But of course there is the other kind of death too" he says, "or perhaps it is really the same." He pauses for a few seconds, staring at the floor; I remember the ox in the rain. "Anyone's journey to Santiago must contain many small deaths and rebirths. The flat, bare plain of Castile is a kind of death to the senses and the world. But Hontanas where we met each other, with its miraculous waters is like a baptism, a rebirth before we go back to the dry plain. Of course a larger kind of death must take place at the end of the way. After all we are moving west toward a tomb in Compostela, toward the setting sun, no?"

He pauses again, taking off his tinted glasses. Looking at me with his olive, Mediterranean eyes, suddenly those of an older man he says "Eduardo, I urge you not to stop walking in Santiago."

"Why?"

"In order to follow the sun until you can go no further, to the place where it sets over the sea beyond Finisterre, Land's End. The Celts used to call those dark waters the sea of the dead, because the sun died there in the west each afternoon and nobody dared to go beyond that point, the end of the known world at the time. But each morning the same sun rose in the east behind the cliffs of Finisterre, as it rises today. We must die to our old selves if we want to be reborn into a better life. Land's End is exactly a three days' walk from Santiago, time enough for a death and resurrection."

He pauses, looking away. "I won't be walking with you tomorrow" he says softly. "I need to be alone for a while. Please tell Berna and Michèle. Perhaps we will meet on the road again."

I stand when he gets up from his chair to give me a Spanish embrace. He walks into the dormitory while I sit at the table again.

I was sure that Claudio and I would meet after our first farewell; now I feel less certain. His company has been unlike anyone else's: friendship, security, knowledge of the road, vision.

While I'm copying Claudio's words in my notebook, a pilgrim comes out of the bathroom with a towel around his neck, greeting me "Buenas noches." Short, stout, with a dark stubbled beard and black hair shaved to the skull, he has intense-staring green eyes.

"Do you mind if I sit down for a minute?" he asks.

"Of course not" I answer, continuing to write.

"How many kilometers did you walk today?" he asks in the formal, third-person usted rather than the familiar form used by other

pilgrims. Still saddened by Claudio's farewell, trying to finish the en-
try in my notebook and get to bed, I don't feel like engaging in a
conversation.

"I didn't count the kilometers" I tell him without looking up.

"I only walked twenty-seven today but I've done as many as fifty"
he says with a burst of energy, as if he could do that many again
tonight. "I have less than a month's vacation so I can't afford to waste
time" he adds. "What about you?"

I finish writing without raising my eyes or bothering to answer his
question. I can sense that he's anxious to talk but I feel too tired, my
eyes are bleary and the lids are shutting by themselves. I get up from
the table and say goodnight to him.

"Buenas noches, may you rest well" he answers. The same words
Father Javier said to me in Roncesvalles, my first night on the road.

In the morning fog we feel as lonely without Claudio as we did when
René and Guillemette stayed behind in León. How different they are:
the pale, middle-aged professional couple from Paris, staunch
Catholics compared to the younger, olive-skinned, bearded astrologer
from Valencia! Yet both have been matchless companions on the road;
both have left a hole in our lives. Only the Camino brings together
such diverse people, I say to myself, knowing they have nearly everything in common except appearances: a gentleness, humility, fellow
feeling, a thirst that drives them to the end of this old continent, one
of the men with a deformed foot, the other with a fragile heart.

Walking through green, misty valleys, thinking of yesterday with
Claudio, I also remember the dark-haired pilgrim who sat at the table
last night. There was a thirst, a hunger in his eyes too. I hope we run
into him on the Way.

We see the town of Sarria before us. This is fair-day and our road
goes by the central marketplace. We're jostled by sturdy Galician men
and women carrying boxes, bags, squawking chickens, rabbits; pulling
cows, sheep, pigs, goats, horses and mules to makeshift corrals and
pens. We pass stalls with wooden crates of fruits and vegetables, hanging loops of garlic, braids of salami, chorizo and morcilla, bleeding
quarters of veal, pork chops, lamb chops, hams, pigs' ears—a Galician
specialty; jars of marinated olives, barrels of anchovies in brine, wheels
of dry cheeses, the moist queso de tetilla in the shape of a woman's
breast, straw-colored flagons of wine, iced baskets of tangled octopus
and cuttlefish, pink langostinos, scallops, clams, hairy mussels,
breem, hake, flounder, silvery sardines. With our gear and backpacks

we feel cumbersome and out of place, aliens, pilgrims and strangers on our way to another land.

In the early stages of our journey I would have been tempted to buy something, unable to resist this feast of the senses. My repasts with José Mari and Pili in Pamplona come to mind, then with Josemi, Sagrario and the Navarrese. In the second half of the pilgrimage I seem to have eaten and drunk less. Walking continues to stimulate my appetite but food and drink do not attract me as before. Could the road be dulling my hunger as it has dulled my sexual drive? Food and sex, gluttony and lust: the two great Christian sins. Passing the convent of the Fathers of Mercy in the outskirts of Sarria now, I understand more than ever that monastic life is a way of suppressing those instincts in order to purify the body. The Camino de Santiago is slowly doing the same for me.

We're glad to leave the town behind and to be in the country again, walking on a sun-patched corredoira. All at once we see the shape of two human bodies on the forest floor ahead. As we approach I recognize Mike, Claudio's English friend and his son Kes. The boy is sound asleep on his stomach while his father, lying on his back, stares straight up at the treetops. Mike hears us and props himself on his elbows.

"Do you remember me?" I ask him, feeling strange to be speaking English.

"Yes, the pool at Hontanas. Ed, the Yank isn't it?" He looks bad, pale and distressed as if he had just awakened from a nightmare.

"Right. These are my friends Michèle and Bernadette. They don't speak much English."

"I'm used to that" he says. "Afraid I'm not in very good shape. Got sick yesterday in Sarria and have just collapsed here. I've lost two stones in weight since we started walking a month ago. Kes is fine but I'm feeling pretty rotten."

I translate for Berna and Michèle and soon they have me asking him questions about his illness, getting his complete medical history. The French women take charge the way they did with Guillemette when I was sick in Burgo Ranero: diagnosing the problem as a lack of sodium, they give Mike a small bottle of salt pills with instructions to take them every two hours.

Kes wakes up rubbing his eyes and is quickly recruited by the nurses to heat water on his camp stove. They make a bouillon soup for Mike, who wolfs it down as if he hadn't eaten in days. He insists that he feels well enough to start walking again.

"Your arrival was more timely than the U.S. Cavalry" says the Englishman as we set off together.

The addition of the newcomers changes our little pilgrim group and the way we walk. The women become maternal with Kes, taking the lead with him. Mike and I, older, lag behind. He claims that he's feeling better but walks slowly and looks preoccupied. He says he had almost decided to call it quits when we popped up from nowhere. I think he's being too generous yet I'm beginning to suspect that we all tend to exaggerate the influence of other pilgrims on us, at the same time underestimating the effects we may have on them.

Mike seems to become more brooding and tense. Remembering his words in the pilgrims' book at Samos, I ask myself what terrible loss could he have suffered? Soon he tells me that he and Claudio separated in León because they were having trouble getting along with each other. The farther we walk, the more I realize that Mike is a man with a lethal mixture of gloom and anxiety who'd be better off alone, at least for the time being. Claudio must have known. I feel pity for the man and his son.

Gradually I pull ahead of Mike, stopping at intervals to look back and make sure he's following. In the meantime Kes has tired and fallen behind with Michèle while St. Joan is out of sight by now.

I enjoy walking with the English boy; his youth and optimism are like a tonic after being with his father. He reminds me of a younger Alberto—also blond and blue-eyed—and the day we walked out of Pamplona together.

Kes is still young enough to awaken the maternal affection in the Galician women along the way, who salute him with words of endearment in their singsong language: "Pobriño, está cansado . . . Pobre rapaciño . . . , poor little one, he must be tired . . . " When I translate for him, he tells us that in Castile the passersby urged him on instead of feeling sorry for him. "They cried out 'Valiente' and 'Adelante'" he says. Without knowing it the boy has put his finger on the great differences between the severe Castilians, forgers of modern Spain and the impoverished Gallegans with their permanent sympathy for the underdog.

We pass through villages whose names are like music, Peruscallo, Cortiñas, Lavandeira, Casal, Morgade, Couto, Moimentos. They have the odors of hay, cattle, smoke and fermenting grapes. Here we see the first hórreos, the small, elevated stone granaries typical of northwestern Spain. I feel happy and ask myself why the Galician landscape affects me more than any other. Could I have some obscure, ancestral memory of this place, this Spanish Ireland, the most Celtic region in Spain?

We reach the village of Moutrás in a fertile valley. Wiping the sweat off his brow with his shirtsleeve, Kes asks if we can stop for a rest. We sit on the stone steps of a farmhouse, stained with ageless, mustard-colored lichen. An old Galician woman comes out of an open doorway, followed by a ewe and two lambs nudging at their mother's teats. She is dressed in black like all her Galician sisters.

She begins the usual litany when she spots Kes: "Poor lad walking all the way to Santiago, how cute his blue eyes and all, may the Apostle bless him, poor thing, how about a cup of fresh milk to give you strength for the road?"

When Michèle translates for the boy he answers "No, I had an upset stomach yesterday."

Grasping the ewe by the thick fleece around its neck, the woman asks Michèle if she would like the milk.

When she declines I realize that the honor of all foreign pilgrims in Galicia now rests on my shoulders: "Yo la tomo, señora, I'll drink it" I tell the woman, regretting my words as soon as they come out.

She leads the animals through the doorway, caressing the ewe's snout and urging her gently "Sus! Quedo!"

"Ay, Eduardo, I hope the milk is good" says Michèle when the woman has left, probably feeling guilty for not accepting it herself. "I have to be careful after the incident of the plums the other day, you know."

The woman is taking her time to fetch the milk. "Everything is slower in Galicia" says Michèle sighing.

I decide to see what's wrong, walking through the doorway timidly, brushing against leather harnesses hung from the thick lintel. Before my eyes adapt to the light, I smell fresh clover and the warm breath of animals. Gradually I make out several cows chewing their cuds over the feeding troughs, looking at me indifferently, nodding their heads. On both knees, her back to me, the old woman is milking a black-and-white cow with her right hand, holding a cup in her left. The ewe lies next to her in the straw, giving suck to the lambs. From a glassless window high on one wall a beam of sunlight traverses the room, specks of dust dancing in it, making a little square of light on the floor. The only sounds are the chewing of the cows and the milk squirting into the cup. I don't know how long I stand still, forgetting myself, immersed in this moment now, here, always, at peace with myself and the world.

The woman must sense my presence: without turning around she says "Look what fat teats she has, señor." Patting the cow on the flanks, she gets to her feet. "Let's go see if the boy will drink some of it."

Outside is the other world: the bright sun brings me back to it. Kes refuses to drink of course, seeing the old cup made of cork with a few cow hairs floating in the milk. I quaff the warm, sweet, frothy liquid in one gulp, bottoms up. It tastes sweet, rich as butter.

The old woman has made us this gift and deserves the right of our company—all we have to offer her. After we satisfy her curiosity about ourselves, she tells us the story of her life and miracles: her great adventure occurred at the age of nine when an aunt and uncle migrated with her to Havana, where she worked for a few years in a hotel frequented by American tourists. "All right! Yes!" she exclaims with her almost toothless mouth, pronouncing the words with a Gallegan lilt so foreign to English that I have to repeat them in order for Kes to understand. More than half the village has emigrated to Madrid, Mexico or Cuba, she tells us; in fact Fidel Castro's family comes from nearby Sarria and Triacastela.

The good woman bids us farewell, urging us to take good care of "the poor little one."

As soon as we leave the town, Michèle makes funny faces, asking me "How could you drink that stuff? I hope you don't die of tuberculosis. If Guillemette were here she would tell you to head straight for the Pasteur Institute."

"That milk was the best I've ever tasted" I tell her.

The energy of the milk and those moments in the barn carry me all the way to Portomarín, a traditional stage on the Road to Santiago. The old pilgrims' village lies under the waters of the Miño River, flooded by the hydroelectric company in order to make a dam. The modern town, looking a little too clean and foursquare to be Spain, sits on a hill dominated by the church that has been moved stone by stone to the new site.

There are only two hotels in Portomarín; whichever one you stay in, you'll wish you'd chosen the other. Judging from the Mesón del Peregrino where we spend the night, they must have brought the bedbugs when they relocated the town. Ay de mi España.

20 On the Road

"Man, the road must eventually lead to the whole world. Ain't nowhere else it can go—right?"
—Jack Kerouac

Mike and Kes are still sleeping when we leave. Since their pace is so much slower than ours, we may not see them again. I worry about whether or not they will arrive in Compostela. Good luck, comrades!

Crossing the foggy Miño we catch up with Valentín and his friend, who tell us they also spent a sleepless night—in Portomarín's other hotel. Emilio, with his black beard, balding forehead and diabolic smile, suggests we follow the ancient custom of Japanese pilgrims upon leaving a bad town: "They would squat with their backs to it and mark the land in the oldest way a man knows how. Called it the dung monument."

"I think we should be content to shake the town's dust off our feet, like St. Teresa" Berna tells him curtly.

Emilio looks at us as if to say "Who's *she*?" With his blue T-shirt, cut-off jeans, striped socks and tennis shoes he reminds me of a middle-class man on vacation at a beach resort. He has none of our road-worn look. Only last weekend he decided to take to the Camino because his marriage was falling apart, he tells us; he wanted to have some time to himself for thinking it over.

Everyone has reasons for walking the Road: this man's marriage is on the rocks, Michèle is going through a divorce, Valentín has lost his job and is involved in a lawsuit, the Englishman is undergoing some kind of bereavement. In one way or another they all want to put their lives back together. Berna is an enigma but she seems to have the least selfish motives, perhaps closer to those of pilgrims in former times—a desire for penance, forgiveness, a renewed faith? And what about me? If I'm so good at analyzing their motives, why don't I understand my own? What makes me think theirs are any less complex than mine?

Emilio is trying to flirt with Michèle. I don't feel the old possessiveness as when Valentín joined us on Monte Irago but I'm bothered by the chatter and repartee. I envy Berna, far ahead of all this talk.

The fog lifts as we draw away from the Miño valley. It looks like this will be a crystal-clear day, rare for Galicia. With the joking and laughing from Michèle, Emilio and Valentín I'm unable to concentrate on walking or the landscape. One place looks like another and I have the impression that I'm moving in circles. Yesterday, immersed in the road, I felt as if I were returning to a place where I'd been long ago.

Berna is waiting for us on a rise with an extensive view, a beaming smile on her face as she points to the west. "Pico Sacro!" she shouts and we see the outline of a summit on the horizon, its shape as pure as Mt. Fuji's. The moon hangs over it, no longer quite full.

"That's the valley of the River Ulla ahead" says Berna. "According to legend, Santiago's disciples carried his body upstream on the river, all the way from the Atlantic Ocean to that peak."

"How did it get from there to Compostela, Mademoiselle le Professeur?" asks Valentín with his mocking voice.

Berna knows that he's teasing but doesn't pay attention: "I need water first" she says taking out her canteen and drinking. "The disciples went to the local ruler" she goes on, "a certain Queen Lupa who had resisted St. James' missionary work. They said the famous words to her: 'Accept in death the one whom you rejected in life.' She told them to yoke a cart to some oxen on the mountain and to take the saint's body wherever they wanted, knowing that the beasts were wild bulls. But they turned as meek as lambs when the disciples made the sign of the cross, yoked them to the cart and carried Santiago to the site of the present city. The rest is history."

"And more old wives' tales" sneers Emilio lighting a cigarette.

"Pico Sacro was worshiped long before the Christians, for your information" replies Berna undaunted. "Even today it's considered so sacred by Galicians that its slopes are not worked by the plow."

We stop for the night in Palas do Rei, the last staging place before Santiago in the old *Book of St. James*. The town's so full of pilgrims that we have to double up in the rooms of a friendly woman who runs a restaurant and bar. I end up sleeping on the floor. At least there are no bedbugs.

The dawn arrives with rain. Valentín, Emilio and I decide to explore the country of the Ulla valley and work our way back to the Camino by evening. We invite Michèle and Berna but they want nothing to do with detours; they will take the straightest route between here and Santiago, thank you. We agree to meet about eighteen miles to the west in Arzúa. I've become very fond of the French women but I feel liberated to get off the beaten path to Compostela.

We walk through heavy rain until we stop for breakfast at a village tavern. The old woman who serves us, dressed in black of course, speaks of meigas and local superstitions. When I ask her if

16 The author and Valentín (right, with Corte Inglés bag over pack).
[Photo Emilio Oviedo]

she thinks the weather will clear up, she looks at me as if I've insulted her, saying through her single tooth "Yo no soy de ésas, I'm not one of *those*." As we leave the tavern, rain begins to pour harder and we joke that the woman really is a meiga, punishing us for prying into nature's secrets.

To keep his backpack and sleeping bag dry, Valentín fashions a cover out of a huge plastic bag from the Corte Inglés, the largest chain of department stores in Spain. Emilio does not look much less outlandish in his cut-offs and beach hat. With my rain gear and hood, I must resemble Admiral Byrd again. Each of us has a beard; that alone is enough to make us stand out from the few local men.

Some urchins yell at us when we pass a farmhouse: "Gitanos! Gypsies!" The people aren't used to pilgrims here off the main road to Santiago.

We see abandoned pazos, Galician country estates that have been turned into barns or stables. Some have strange coats-of-arms carved on the mossy granite walls—suns, moons, lions, birds, unidentifiable creatures. A ruined castle looms ahead of us, overgrown with bushes on its lichen-stained walls and turrets. We salute peasants, mostly women who speak only gallego, a language closer to Portuguese than Spanish.

It begins to rain so hard that we have to take shelter under an hórreo topped by a stone crucifix. A young man runs by dressed in overalls and knee-high rubber boots. He sees us and ducks under the granary too.

"Hola" he says, his long black hair dripping rain. "Come over and get dried off with me." He speaks the most vigorous Spanish I've heard in several days, with a hardly a trace of the plaintive Galician lilt. "Let's make a run for it!" he cries dashing off and we follow him across a courtyard to a vine-covered porch.

"Wait here a moment" he says going inside. Puddles of rainwater form under our feet.

He returns holding four white, immaculate, fragrant towels and offers one to each of us. They're warm to the touch of our clammy hands. This is the most civilized gesture I've seen on the Road to Santiago or anywhere else for that matter. I never would have guessed that a simple towel could mean so much.

The young man introduces himself as Marcial and asks us to sit down at a circular, rustic table protected from the rain. He disappears again, returning this time with a tray on which there is a bottle of white wine, four glasses, a queso de tetilla—the soft Galician cheese—and a dark loaf of bread. He excuses himself for the cloudy, acid wine that he has made himself. In this climate the sun rarely shines enough to sweeten the grapes.

With the chill in our bones, we're not very demanding: we polish off the contents of the bottle, devour the creamy cheese and the warm bread, also homemade, as Marcial tells us the story of his life. After studying in Santiago de Compostela and teaching for several years, he returned here to run the family farm when all his male relatives had either died or emigrated. He has three cows, some chickens and several acres of bottom land on the shores of the Ulla where he cultivates wheat, rye, grapes and a vegetable garden. His dream is to introduce flax to the area but he's been unable to find good seeds. Valentín says he knows people who grow the fiber in the famous Valencian huerta, the great tracts of irrigated land and orchards between the mountains and the Mediterranean. He promises to mail seeds to Marcial, who copies his address in Valentín's notebook with an inscription in gallego:

O camiño é longo mais faise camiño ao andar!
Bon viaxe!
(The road is long but one makes the road by walking!
Have a good trip!)

The downpour has changed to a drizzle. Marcial leads us to the road for Arzúa by a shortcut, crossing his acreage by the emerald-green, woods-lined Ulla.

"Along that river they took Santiago's body to Compostela" he tells us. I sense that here in the heart of Galicia, the name of Santiago does not refer to a remote legend but to a man as close as these chestnuts, oaks and eucalyptus trees through which we spot the fast-running, swollen Ulla.

We say goodbye to Marcial, all of us giving him Spanish hugs. Thank you, compañeiro!

We follow the course of the river to the bridge that marks the border between Lugo and La Coruña—the last province on the way to Santiago. To celebrate the occasion, we enter a tavern where the owner serves us red Ribeiro wine in the traditional cuencas, white ceramic cups without handles. When we ask if he serves lunch, like many gallegos he refuses to give a straight answer, telling us to wait a minute while he goes to the kitchen.

He returns to inform us that yes we may have lunch, provided that it's veal steak and fried potatoes. We have more Ribeiro while we wait for the food. Locals begin to appear for their afternoon coffee and oruxo, Galician firewater fermented from pressed grapeskins. Dogs, cats and children come in and out the door as we eat, drink and know the happiness of men who are far from home, embarked on a common adventure.

The rest of the day is plodding in the rain through forests of fragrant pines and eucalyptus, walking up and down green hills, splashing in puddles like kids, stopping in taverns to dry off and drink coffee, oruxo or brandy. When dark begins to fall and we're still miles from Arzúa, we decide that the only way to keep our rendezvous with Berna and Michèle is to hitch a ride, waiting in the rain until we finally jump on the open bed of a farm truck, all of us soaking wet, speeding through the soft, drizzling, female air of Galicia, screaming for joy to find the old, mad freedom in our souls.

In Arzúa we don't take very long to find Michèle and Berna in one of the town's few pensiones. They're eating in the dining room where we join them with wet abrazos, What took you so long, You're dripping wet, We also got soaked, Sit down for a hot caldo gallego, Galician soup with vegetables. At first we don't tell them we've hitch-hiked the final miles, feeling a little ashamed until they confess that they took a country bus this afternoon in order to meet us on time.

We all feel better when the truth comes out. "El Santo nos perdona" cries Valentín laughing. "The Saint will forgive us even if we didn't walk all the way!"

Emilio, who's spent a lot of time in Galicia, says the occasion calls for a queimada. He asks the waitresses to bring a flat earthenware pan. They light a flame beneath it and fill it with oruxo, adding lemon peels, sugar and a few coffee beans. When it all comes to a boil, the Gallegas recite one of the traditional incantations for us:

Forzas do ar, terra, mar e lume . . . , Spirits of the air, earth, sea and fire, we call upon you, if it is true that you have more powers than human kind, to allow the souls of our distant friends to partake of this queimada with us, here and now.

Berna, Michèle and I look at each other; they also must be thinking of René and Guillemette, Claudio too, the one who first told us about the queimada.

"El Santo nos perdona" Valentín chants over the queimada, laughing each time, mixing it with his motto, "Today is the first day of the rest of your life!"

We tell the women about our adventures in the rain. When we get to the part about Marcial and the warm, white towels, Berna springs up in her chair: "St. Martial was supposedly the one who held the towel when Christ washed the disciples' feet. He also helped serve the Last Supper."

Even the cynical Emilio turns quiet for a few seconds. Valentín breaks the silence with his refrain "El Santo nos perdona," interspersing it with the story of our ride in the open truck through the rain.

"I don't blame you for not walking all the way" says Berna. "After all nobody in the Middle Ages would have refused a ride on a horse, donkey or cart, right? Why should we try to be purer than the original pilgrims?"

For myself I'm glad we "cheated" by hitching a ride for the last few miles. It was a way of recognizing that our pilgrimage has not been perfect, never could be; perhaps it will motivate us to walk the Road again, to make it better next time. I also feel a new affection for Berna, who used to appear so inflexible and righteous. She seems less rigid, less infallible now, more like the rest of us. Even Joan of Arc wouldn't have turned down a ride today.

21 Detours, Lavacolla, Mountjoy

These are the laurel wreaths, the rose petals and the hurrahs offered to pilgrims, students and walkers on the doorstep to Santiago: a solemn declaration and demonstration, by all the social sectors, that the Camino de Santiago is stupid and superfluous.

—José Luis Herrera

Its feels like a family reunion to walk again with Michèle and Berna. The five of us—two French, two Spaniards, one American—get along with each other and have a good esprit de corps. I'd prefer less banter on the road but it's hard to resist Valentín's high spirits and hoarse laughter. With his dark, penetrating eyes Emilio plays the straight man to Valentín's clown.

Another day meets us cloaked in mist, clouds and orballo, a drizzle so fine that you can hardly see it. The grey shroud of the weather and our anxiousness to reach Compostela make all the towns look the same, with a transient, by-the-way air about them. We're shocked to find that the Camino has been diverted from the original route beyond Arzúa, cut by the construction of a factory. We have to take other detours before the small town of Arca. Here the local government has had the impudence to build a soccer stadium right in the middle of the Road to Santiago, as if they were competing with Barcelona for the 1992 Olympics.

These detours are nothing compared to the massive chunk of the Camino swallowed up by the international airport of Lavacolla. An endless fence topped with barbed wire forces us to walk on the shoulder of a busy, multi-lane highway. When the ground trembles and a jet takes off to the north, I realize that it's the first airplane I've heard or seen in a month.

"You can take direct flights from Compostela to the major cities of Europe" says Emilio, "even to New York, Rio and Buenos Aires."

"I wish this airport were located anywhere on the Camino but here, so close to Santiago" says Berna. "It sort of spoils the end of the journey."

"Not even St. James is a prophet honored in his own country" adds Michèle. "The closer you come to Compostela the worse the Road gets. The province of La Coruña takes the cake—even worse than Navarre with that horrible magnesium factory."

We pass several "clubs"—gaudy-colored, windowless buildings with electric lights around the doors. Young women in scant dresses sit on the doorsteps, smoking cigarettes.

"The local hookers" says the worldly-wise Emilio.

"El Santo las perdona también" puts in Valentín, "the Saint pardons them too." He laughs so heartily that the young women turn our way with lean-faced stares.

"Things haven't changed all that much over the centuries" says Berna. "The prostitutes and innkeepers of Compostela used to come out on the road to recruit clients among the pilgrims."

"We're not in any danger of being hustled if that's what you're worried about" says Emilio making fun of Berna. "Nowadays their clients all drive cars."

After walking farther along the busy highway, by commercial signs, banks, stores and gas stations, we decide to stop in the town of Lavacolla. Pilgrims often spent their last night here before entering Compostela, only six miles away. In spite of the closeness to Santiago, we all feel depressed by the noise, traffic, cement and concrete, so different from the rural Galicia of Cebreiro, Samos and the corredoiras.

The rooms we find in a pensión have no baths or showers. The rain has been our only shower since entering Galicia. I go to bed feeling dirty and let down, hoping tomorrow will be a better day: not the way I expected to feel the night before reaching Santiago.

The next morning we awake even earlier than usual, impatient to get on the road. Life is the same as always for the two Gallegos, a dark young man and woman who serve us a breakfast of coffee and bread at a bar on the highway. They take their time, yawning, half asleep. We ask them how to find the famous stream of Lavacolla, where pilgrims used to wash away the dirt of the road in order to purify themselves before reaching their goal.

"You can't miss it" they tell us as if they've heard the question a thousand times.

They overcharge us for our simple breakfast. When he pays, Emilio mutters "Camino francés, gato por res," the old proverb about getting cheated on the Road to Santiago.

It's a clear morning with bright sunshine and puffy clouds, the air cleansed by the rain. On the edge of town we have to take another detour. It doesn't bother us because we feel the excitement of near-arrival. All of us are looking forward to a bath in the stream of Lavacolla.

"I'll only wash my face and neck" says Berna. "That's what the name means, 'Lava-cuello'."

"There's another theory that it comes from 'Lava-cojones' " says Emilio with his malicious smile, "since pilgrims also had the custom of washing their vergüenzas in the stream, their private parts. Maybe they were preparing for extracurricular activities in Santiago."

"Have you all seen *The Milky Way*?" asks Valentín. "In that movie Buñuel has a whore seduce the two pilgrim characters within sight of Compostela." I remember the shepherdess and my own thoughts on the movie.

"How could I forget it?" asks Emilio. "A masterpiece. And do you remember what the hooker tells the pilgrims? That the crypt of the cathedral has been excavated and they've found the body of Priscillian there instead of St. James. He was also beheaded—the greatest religious figure of all time in Galicia."

"That's your opinion" counters Berna. "The difference is that Santiago was a martyr killed by the Romans, while the Church condemned Priscillian as a heretic."

Always ready to needle her, Emilio retorts "That makes him an even greater martyr in my book. Priscillian was the only Spaniard who managed to join the ancient Celtic religions of our forefathers with Christianity. He should be our national patron, not a foreigner like St. James."

"I love it!" exclaims Valentín. "The battle of the myths! Go to it Berna, your turn!"

She can't resist: "If the story of Santiago is only a myth" she asks turning to Emilio, "how can you explain such a great influence on your own country, on mine and on all of Europe? How can you account for all the pilgrims across the centuries, all the churches, chapels and shrines dedicated to Santiago with their paintings, sculptures and stained-glass windows? And what about all the songs, hymns, prayers, poems, ballads, proverbs, manuscripts, books? Most of all how can you explain the faith I feel in my heart?"

Emilio is taken aback by Berna's passion. "I still don't believe that the bones in the cathedral can be proven to be Santiago's" he replies. "There's not a shred of evidence that he ever stepped on Spanish soil."

Always the peacemaker, Michèle intervenes: "Come on, guys, let's not get into a religious argument when we're about to arrive. The apostle's shoulders are wide enough to bear the weight of skeptics and believers. By the way what ever happened to the stream of Lavacolla? That sign says we're coming to the town of San Marcos."

"Mountjoy is just beyond here!" shouts Valentín with the enthusiasm of a boy, looking at his *Pilgrim's Guide.* "Let's forget about the stream and see who's the first to spot Compostela from the top of the hill!"

I regret that we haven't performed the ritual bath but our only thought is to go forward; it would be impossible to turn back now. The road goes off the highway for the first time since the town of Lavacolla. We see a simple chapel at the foot of a small hill to our left. Could this unassuming, solitary, unmarked place be Monjoie, Monxoi, Monte del Gozo, the famous Mount of Joy from which pilgrims first sighted the towers of Santiago? By instinct we begin to walk up the flank of the hill, going faster as we get higher, the view opening to the west as we approach a wooden cross at the top. Berna is already there of course, a jubilant smile on her face. We see the grey towers of Compostela over the treetops, nestled among white buildings and red roofs, surrounded by the greenest of hills. We feel too moved to speak, standing on the same spot where pilgrims have stood for at least a thousand years, seeing the goal of their journey after days, weeks, months of travel.

Michèle, Berna and I turn our moist eyes from Santiago to each other, feeling the bond between us after so much time together on the road. So many days when Compostela seemed hopelessly far away.

"Berna wins!" cries Valentín, never silent for long. "The first to reach Mountjoy used to be recognized as king of the group—in this case queen. Long live Queen Bernadette!"

Michèle bursts out with a laugh, wiping the tears from her eyes: "She's king anyway—her last name is Rey-Jouvin."

Even Berna laughs: "That's right, just as in Spanish. They say that Leroy, King and other family names derive from the same custom. All of us may have some ancestor who made the pilgrimage to Compostela."

I've been traveling with Berna all this time, I think, without even knowing or thinking about her last name! Yet I trust her and Michèle like friends I've known for years. I don't know Michèle's, Emilio's or Valentín's family names either, nor do they know mine. Last names and everything that goes with them—social status, family, the past—mean nothing on the Camino de Santiago.

"Many pilgrims used to walk the rest of the way barefoot" says Berna as we prepare to leave. I recall the farm boy, friend of the priest José Ignacio in Hervías, who ran all the way from here to the cathedral.

As we begin the final descent through a grove of pine trees, I take a final look at Santiago. A waning moon hangs palely over her in the western sky: the identical phase I saw coming out of Roncevaux after my first night on the road. Now I've spent my last night on the road before reaching Compostela; that moon has completed one revolution around the earth in the time it's taken me to walk the Camino, more or less. Is it possible that only thirty days have passed since I received the blessing in Roncesvalles? Less than that since I saw the shepherdess, the field of sunflowers, the Milky Way and shooting star on the bridge with José Mari and Míkel? How much have I changed in these thirty days? My feet are like leather instead of being soft and covered by blisters. I still have some small pains—in my left shin now—but I've overcome my ailments as José Mari told me I must. The heat, sweat, dust, mud, rain, fog have weathered this body, broken it down, made it supple and uncomplaining.

I've seen so much land, met so many people, had so many thoughts during this month that I feel overwhelmed by it all. Too much has happened in such a concentrated time. I may have to wait before understanding; perhaps I'll never grasp it fully. This much I know: most of my companions and I have been uprooted from our former lives. To make the pilgrimage has been a way of proving that we could free ourselves from our daily existence, from all those small routines and obligations that mean nothing by themselves but together can prevent us from doing the things that really matter to us, can prevent us in fact from being ourselves. If we hadn't been driven by a need to overcome the banality of our everyday lives, we wouldn't be here. If we hadn't looked into the world and seen the great wounds there, we never would have taken to the road. The world we saw was so rotten that we knew it must be ripe for a transformation. Now we know the change must begin inside ourselves because the Camino has calmed the war in our own hearts. We saw the haste, the greed and solitude in ourselves and others; on the Road we've exchanged them for a growing peace, unselfishness and the solidarity between pilgrims. Walking, eating, sleeping, suffering side by side we've forgotten the boundaries between ourselves, between sexes, countries, classes, ages. This is part of what we were seeking, the measure of our hopes.

At any rate this is what I'm thinking as we go down the hill, the last oasis on the Road to Santiago. When we cross the huge Autopista del Atlántico, the turnpike that joins Galicia to Portugal, nothing seems as clear as it did up there on the Mount of Joy.

22 In the Camel's Stomach

Buscas en Roma a Roma,¡oh peregrino!,
y en Roma misma no la hallas . . .
(Oh pilgrim, you are seeking Rome in Rome!
But Rome herself you will not find in Rome . . .)
—Francisco de Quevedo

 Presences like these cannot be analyzed; you
must hear them, touch them, accept them, live
them with an innocent spirit, an open heart and
the candid responsiveness of a child or a cat who
wakes up in the morning for the first time.
—Fernando Sánchez Dragó

We walk through the outskirts of the city like sleepwalkers, wide-eyed, unable to believe that we're in Santiago de Compostela. There's something almost unreal about the empty streets; I expect to wake from a dream. Finally we realize that it's Sunday. The few passersby hardly turn their heads our way, walking with the busy step of people who have things to do, indifferent to the sight of five sweaty men and women who are entering their town with backpacks and walking sticks.

There's more activity as we get closer to the center of the city, entering the Puerta del Camino, going up the narrow, arcaded streets by the Azabachería, the legendary market where jewellers, trinket-vendors and money-changers used to await pilgrims. In the shop windows you can still see the polished black jet carved in the shape of scallop shells, crosses and higas—the fists with one raised finger that have been used for thousands of years as erotic amulets and charms against the evil eye.

Now we're in the shadow of the Cathedral, close to the heart of Compostela surrounded by chapels, convents, cloisters, palaces, domes, towers, belfries. Something looks Oriental here. Walls, buildings and streets are all hewn from the same square blocks of stone. Nourished by the climate of sea fog, mountain mist and drizzle, moss and lichens cover walls, fountains and stairways like scabs or parasites. In spite of the sun today, Santiago is somber, a grey city of granite.

We come out of the shade through an arch in the Archbishop Gelmírez's Palace. Suddenly we're in the ample Plaza del Obradoiro, one of the greatest squares in the world and one of the few places in this city where you see more sky than stone: the classic lines of the Hostal de los Reyes Católicos to our right, once a royal pilgrims' hospice, now a luxury hotel; the columned City Hall directly in front; part of the University catercorner to us; the soaring Baroque towers of the Cathedral to our left.

"We've made it" sighs Berna.

We walk into the sun. The whole life of the city seems to be concentrated in the plaza. Men read the Sunday paper, women push baby carriages and lead children by the hand, tourists spill from shiny modern buses, clergymen stroll and gossip with hands clasped behind their backs. All the bells of the Cathedral and the surrounding churches are peeling: high noon.

Moving with the tide of human beings toward the temple, we ascend the stairs in silence, go through the main doors and feel the coolness inside. We're standing in the Pórtico de la Gloria, the Gate of Glory where hundreds of figures carved in colored stone look almost as alive as the people around us. Following the others who themselves are following those who went before them, we stand in line behind the central column where the seated, life-size statue of St. James looks beyond us to the west in open-eyed ecstasy, his pilgrim's staff held firmly in his right hand. We approach the column. With its intertwined leaves and branches it represents the Tree of Jesse, the tree of life. Each of us in turn places the fingers of his right hand in the five openings hollowed in the stone by the touch of countless men and women. The grooves fit my fingers like a smooth marble glove, still warm from the heat of other hands. I've never felt myself more a member of the human race.

We follow the line of people to the other side of the colonnade where a kneeling statue of Master Maeto, the sculpter of the Pórtico, faces the distant high alter. Like everyone else we repeat the local custom of knocking our brows against the figure's forehead to acquire some of his wisdom; a few women rub their bellies on the stone to make their wombs fertile. We're in the very center, the Mecca and Medina of Spanish religion where pagan and Christian beleifs have been swallowed, mixed and digested. We're in the camel's stomach.

As the Mass begins we get in line to give the traditional embrace to the gaudy, lacquered statue of Santiago behind the main altar. With no Christ or Virgin present, it looks more like a Buddhist shrine than a Christian monument. When I put my arms around the broad-shouldered figure located directly above the saint's tomb in the crypt below, I have the sensation that I'm embracing an old friend, a fellow pilgrim who carries a walking stick and a scallop shell on his back.

We return to the nave and stand elbow to elbow with the crowd for the service. Just as we put our fingers in the Tree of Jesse and bumped our heads on the statue of Master Mateo, following others we take communion. During the silence afterwards I pray for those who asked me to remember them in Santiago: the old woman who gave Alberto and me the earthen jug of water; José Ignacio, the priest in Hervías. I pray also for others who helped me along the road: the smiling French couple who offered me the apples on the first day; Father Javier in Roncesvalles ("May you preserve the pilgrim's spirit, Estanton"); the flour-covered baker who gave me the half-baguette of fresh bread; José Mari, Pili and Alberto; José Mari's friend in Estella (can't recall his name now) who wouldn't let me pay for a single drink; the fruit-vendor who regaled me with the peaches just before Torres del Río; old Ramón whose little wooden cross has kept me company all this time; Joaquín and Codés who fed me with food and wine in the same town; the Navarrese who took me under their wings when I was lonely and suffering from blisters; the talkative priest of San Juan de Ortega; Josemi and Sagrario who helped cure my feet and were such cheerful companions for the road; René and Guillemette; Claudio; the abbess of the Poor Clares ("Keep yourself a stranger and a pilgrim on earth"); the Galician woman and the magic cup of milk; Marcial with his white towels. Have I forgotten anyone? What about the pilgrims I met and lost track of along the way? Mike and Kes (I pray for their safe arrival), Vim and Vigor in search of the moon, the businessmen from Bilbao who turned back, the beautiful Marta and her companion, Kosti and his group, the pilgrim whom I denied in Samos, all the others whose faces I recall without their names. I pray for my family too. I ask forgiveness and pray to forgive myself, the most difficult thing of all.

After Mass they crank up the Botafumeiro, the silver censer as big as a car's engine, worked by a system of ropes and pulleys like a church bell. It gains momentum, going faster and faster until it swings from one end of the transept to the other like a flying trapeze, filling the air with smoke and the odor of incense as the people look up in wonder. They say it was used in the Middle Ages to purify the air of the temple, jammed with reeking pilgrims who cooked and slept on the floor with their horses, mules, donkeys and cows. Now the Botafumeiro, the Smoke-Thrower is supposed to be a mere relic of the past; from the smell of my own body I know it still serves a useful purpose.

We pour into the plaza with the crowd, running into pilgrims we saw days or weeks ago on the Road. We don't know each other's names but we're like long-lost companions, all of us feeling the elation of arrival in Compostela. The Obradoiro square is the place where everyone comes to meet. I spot Marta, yes she's still with her lean companion, they must have lost ten pounds apiece, we hug one another, smelling the good stench of comrades, laughing while I introduce them to Emilio and Valentín. They already know Berna and Michéle because they're kissing and embracing too.

Marta and her friend lead us to the Chapter House of the Cathedral to pick up the Compostelana, the official diploma recognizing completion of the pilgrimage. In the old days this document would have been proof that we'd carried out a penance or a judicial sentence, excusing us from certain tolls and taxes and ensuring a safe passage home. Today it has only a private meaning except that it allows free entrance to certain museums and the chance for a complimentary meal at the Hostal.

Dressed in a cassock, the Chapter secretary inspects our pilgrims' certificates and records our names, nationalities and date of arrival. Using the unreadable flourishes dear to Spaniards, he fills out and signs each diploma, a buff-colored sheet with an image of St. James on top, the seal of the Cathedral Chapter and a Latin text.

As he writes, Michéle says to me in a whisper: "Santiago's not in here, is he?"

"I guess not."

"I think he likes it more out there on the road. In fact do you know what that seer-friend of ours predicted?"

"What?"

"That the man whom Berna and I were supposed to meet on the Camino would walk for three days beyond Compostela."

As we emerge in the sun, we ask Marta and her companion where we should spend the night. Santiago is one of the only major cities on the Road that offers no free lodging to pilgrims, they tell us. They lead us to a dormitory run by the Franciscans where we take our first shower in days.

The rest is walking through the town, eating the city's fresh seafood and drinking Ribeiro wine, listening to the tunas, the groups of student musicians who play in the old quarter at night. In the giant square in front of the cathedral we all burn a soiled, sweaty garment worn on the pilgrimage—a shirt, a pair of pants, socks, underwear. We dance around the fire and make tearful farewells to the pilgrims who are leaving tomorrow.

23 The End of the World

Teach me to go to the country beyond words and beyond names.

—Thomas Merton

I left that city of stone to follow the path toward the sea and setting sun at the end of the world. I was happy to be on the road again, alone for the first time since Castrogeriz and the Poor Clares, then Sahagún, nearly two weeks ago. Once more I remembered the abbess' words: go on walking forever, always forward.

Now my body seemed to walk itself, the road walking my body. I realized that I could go on walking around the world if only the land did not end. This I have learned from the Camino, I thought as I left Compostela: the body can be surpassed, shed like a snake's molting skin. My old body has died; in many ways I have also died to my old self. Thirty days are enough for many deaths and resurrections, as are these final three days from Santiago to Finisterre. My life, my work, my family will never be quite the same.

Of course I have not been transformed as I dreamed. I should have foreseen that no pilgrimage, no single journey or act suffices. I know that the change has only begun: just as the moon has come full circle now, the end of my trip is also a beginning. All that has gone before has been a preparation, all that comes after will be its unfolding. The journey will continue through a thousand stops and starts, half-successes, doubts, failures and surprises. Though the future is uncertain, the present is not: this month, these days, this moment will always shine out among the ashes of my life, full of grace and freedom. Perhaps I've already taken the decisive step, spoken the crucial word.

It rained in the outskirts of the city on the first day, and in the green hills, in the woods of chestnuts, pines and eucalyptus. On the second day it rained on Mt. Pindo where Queen Lupa is supposed to be buried, and on the bridge over the Tambre where the disciples fled with Santiago's body. It poured in Brañas de Fonte Romeu on the third day when I saw the ocean through slanting sheets of rain, and it was drizzling in Cée and Corcubión with the stale smell of all ports, the wind in my face and the sun setting through clouds over the sea.

I walked across the final stretch of land where the coast juts into the Atlantic: Finisterre, end of the earth, known for centuries as the dark waters, mansion of the dead who await the resurrection of the body. I saw a scallop shell in the dark sand at my feet, picked it up and placed it in my backpack.

Peeling off my wet clothes, I ran into the surf. After the shock of the first cold, the sea felt warmer than the air. I dove under a wave and swam beyond the breakers, the water slipping along my arms, sides and legs, stinging my pores, soothing my limbs. I rolled over on my back, floating, the drizzle caressing my face, the swells rocking me back and forth as I looked up at the sky. I felt the pull of an approaching wave, swam in, waited for the crest, pushed off and was carried to shore in the foam. And I walked out of the water hearing the wind and crashing waves, the mighty rhythm of the world.

Other Readings

If you would like to travel the Road to Santiago on foot, bicycle or horseback, the indispensable guide is Elías Valiña Sampedro, *El Camino de Santiago. Guía del peregrino a Compostela* (Vigo: Editorial Galaxia, 1992), published simultaneously in Spanish, English, French, German and Galician. The contents are organized in four parts: 1) a brief historical summary and guidelines for planning the pilgrimage; 2) maps drawn to scale and a description of the route; 3) notes on places of historic and artistic importance; 4) up-to-date information on lodging, followed by bibliography, illustrations and photographs. Most of the other guidebooks are published in Spanish; this should not be an obstacle for English-speakers, since the most important part of these works is the maps, not the text. A recent guide is Fernando Imaz, *Camino de Santiago. Andando/bicicleta* (San Sebastián: Federación de Asociaciones Jacobeas, 1993), which the publisher hopes to keep current by printing a new version each year. The bi-monthly magazine *Peregrino* published a small *Guía práctica del Camino*, without maps, as a supplement to its June 1991 issue. To obtain this guide or to subscribe to the magazine (in Spanish), write *Peregrino*, Apartado de Correos 60, 26250 Santo Domingo de la Calzada (La Rioja), Spain. Each issue features reviews of new books. The February 1993 issue contains a supplement, *Catálogo de Bibliografía Jacobea*, with a list of books available at the magazine's library; many of them can be ordered directly.

If you plan to bicycle, there are two specialized guidebooks: Eloy Angulo and others, *El Camino de Santiago en bici* (Euzkadi: Editorial SUA, 1990), and Juanjo Alonso, *El Camino de Santiago en Mountain Bike* (Madrid: Tutor, 1993). Fernando Imaz's book, *Camino de Santiago. Andando/bicicleta*, mentioned above, contains information for bikers as well as walkers.

If you wish to drive along the Camino de Santiago, James Michener's account of his own pilgrimage by car is a good place to start your reading—*Iberia: Spanish Travels and Reflections* (New York: Random House, 1968). Michener journeyed to Compostela in order to fulfill a vow made to his patron saint after recovering from a heart attack. By writing the Spanish Tourist Office, you can obtain a brochure in English on driving the Camino: 665 Fifth Avenue, New York, NY 10022.

Among firsthand accounts of the pilgrimage to Santiago, I recommend Georgiana Goddard King's classic *The Way of St. James*, 3 vols. (New York, London: Putnam, 1920), discussed above in Chapter 11; Walter Starkie, *The*

Road to Santiago: Pilgrims of St. James (New York: E.P. Dutton, 1957); Edwin Mullins, *The Pilgrimage to Santiago* (New York: Taplinger Publishing, 1974); Laurie Dennett, *A Hug for the Apostle* (Toronto: Macmillan, 1987); Ellen O. Feinberg, *Following the Milky Way: A Pilgrimage across Spain* (Ames: Iowa State University Press, 1989). Marc Simmons, Donna Pierce and Joan Myers, *Santiago: Saint of Two Worlds* (Albuquerque: University of New Mexico Press, 1991) contains a firsthand account of the pilgrimage by Myers, plus her beautiful photos and the best available information on Santiago in the New World.

In Spanish there are many firsthand accounts; I recommend José Luis Herrera, *La hechura del Camino de Santiago* (Barcelona: Círculo de Lectores, 1986), and Alejandro Uli Vallaz, *¿Te vienes a Santiago?* (Zaragoza: Ediciones Octavio Pérez, 1990).

The most ambitious project on the Road is also in Spanish: Eusebio Goicoechea Arrondo's *Rutas jacobeas: Historia, arte, caminos* (Estella: Los Amigos del Camino de Santiago, 1971); it includes a 700-page volume with many photos, pilgrims' maps (now outdated in some parts), two long-play records and slides. Also in Spanish only are numerous books about the esoteric or initiatory aspects of the Camino: Fernando Sánchez Dragó, *Gárgoris y Habidis: Una historia mágica de España*, 4 vol. (Madrid: Hiperión, 1978), vol. II; Juan G. Atienza, *Segunda guía de la España mágica* (Barcelona: Fontana Fantástica, 1982); Jaime Cobreros and Juan Pedro Morín, *El camino iniciático de Santiago*, 2nd ed. (Barcelona: Ediciones 29, 1982); various authors, *Heterodoxos en el Camino de Santiago* (Pamplona: Ayuntamiento de Pamplona, 1991); Claudio J. Boquet, "El Camino de las Estrellas al fin del mundo: la astrología en el Camino de Santiago," in *La astrología como camino, 9º Congreso Ibérico de Astrología* (Valencia: Astrea Ediciones, C.B., 1992), 387-409.

You can subscribe to the only regular American publication on the Camino, the newsletter of the "Friends of the Road to Santiago," by writing Maryjane Dunn-Wood, Editor, 517 South Happy Holly Blvd., Omaha, NE 68106.

For a deeper study of the Camino de Santiago in its earlier stages, the indispensable starting point is Linda K. Davidson and Maryjane Dunn-Wood, *Pilgrimage in the Middle Ages. A Research Guide* (New York: Garland Publishing, 1993), and by the same authors and press, *The Pilgrimage to Santiago de Compostela: A Comprehensive Annotated Bibliography* (1994). You could read the famous twelfth–century guidebook, *Libro Sancti Jacobi* ("*Codex Calixtinus*"), which has two recent English translations: Paula Gerson, Jeanne Korchalis and Annie Shaver–Crandell, *Pilgrims' Guide to Santiago* (London: Harvey Miller, 1993), and William Melczer, *The Pilgrim's Guide to Santiago de Compostela* (New York: Italica Press, 1992). Other important works are Luis Vázquez de Parga, José María Lacarra and Juan Uría Ríu, *Las peregrinaciones a Santiago de Compostela*, 3 vols. (Madrid: Consejo Superior de Investigaciones Científicas, 1948–1949), reprinted in Pamplona by the Gobierno de Navarra in 1992, and Américo Castro, *The Structure of Spanish History* (Princeton: Princeton University Press, 1954), especially Chapter 6 ("Christianity Faces Islam"). On pilgrimage in general, see Victor and Edith Turner, *Image and Pilgrimage in Christian Culture: Anthropological Perspectives* (Oxford: Basil Blackwell, 1978), and Eleanor Munro, *On Glory Roads: A Pilgrim's Book about Piligrimages* (New York: Thames and Hudson, 1987). Oliver Statler's *Japanese Pilgrimage* (New York: William Morrow, 1983), a book of great dignity, shows suprising similarities between the Eastern and Western traditions.

Acknowledgments

I would like to thank José Luis Herrera, friend and pilgrim to Santiago, for the photographs which he has given me permission to use here with his credits. These photos were published in his book, *La hechura del Camino de Santiago* (cited in Other Readings, above).

I would also like to thank my friends Keller Dunn, Emilio Oviedo and Emilio Peláez for permission to use the photos reproduced here with their credits.

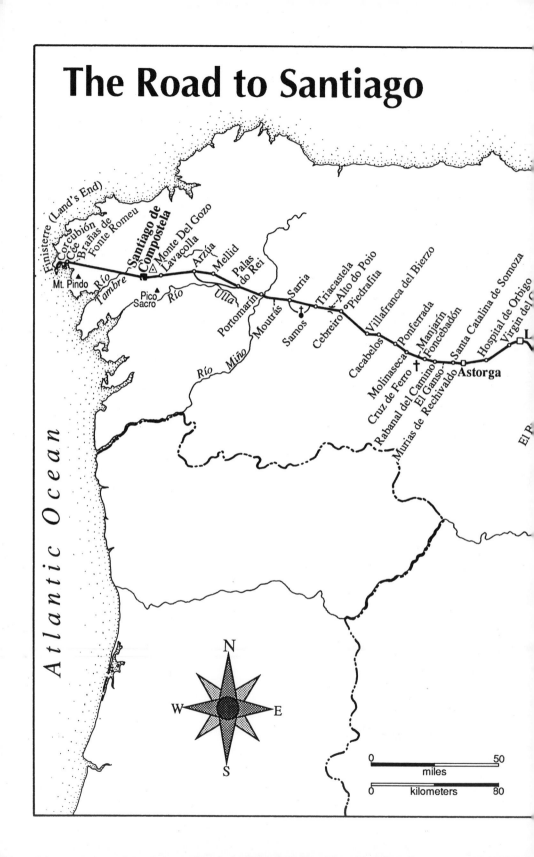

The Road to Santiago